INWARDNESS AND THEATER
IN THE
ENGLISH RENAISSANCE

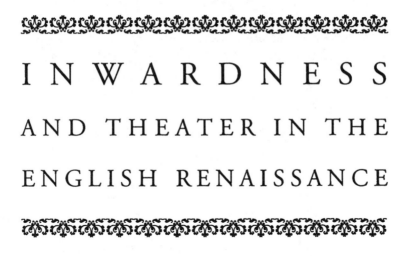

INWARDNESS

AND THEATER IN THE
ENGLISH RENAISSANCE

Katharine Eisaman Maus

THE UNIVERSITY OF CHICAGO PRESS

Chicago and London

KATHARINE EISAMAN MAUS is professor of English at the University of Virginia. She is a coeditor of *Soliciting Interpretation: Literary Theory and Seventeenth-Century English Poetry*, also published by the University of Chicago Press.

The University of Chicago Press, Chicago 60637
The University of Chicago Press, Ltd., London
© 1995 by The University of Chicago
All rights reserved. Published 1995
Printed in the United States of America
04 03 02 01 00 99 98 97 96 95 1 2 3 4 5
ISBN: 0-226-51123-5 (cloth)
0-226-51124-3 (paper)

An earlier version of chapter 4 ("Proof and Consequences: *Othello* and the Crime of Intention") appeared in *Representations*, no. 34, pp. 29–52, © 1991 by the Regents of the University of California; and an earlier version of chapter 6 ("A Womb of His Own: Male Renaissance Poets in the Female Body") appeared in James Turner, ed., *Sexuality and Gender in Early Modern Europe* (New York: Cambridge University Press, 1993).

Library of Congress Cataloging-in-Publication Data
Maus, Katharine Eisaman, 1955–
Inwardness and theater in the English Renaissance / Katharine Eisaman Maus.
p.   cm.
Includes bibliographical references and index.
1. English drama—Early modern, 1500–1700—History and criticism.
2. Shakespeare, William, 1564–1616—Philosophy.   3. Intentionality (Philosophy) in literature.   4. Theater—England—History—16th century.   5. Theater—England—History—17th century.   6. Appearance (Philosophy) in literature.
7. Mind and body in literature.   8. Reality in literature.   9. Renaissance—England.   10. Truth in literature.   I. Title.
PR658.P48M38   1995   94-43099
                                                                                            CIP

For my parents,

Lois Schneider Eisaman and Leo Coburn Eisaman,

with love and gratitude.

CONTENTS

⅏ ACKNOWLEDGMENTS ⅏

IN THE YEARS THIS BOOK HAS BEEN IN PROGRESS, I have incurred debts to friends, colleagues, and institutions. I have presented versions of my work as lectures or seminars at the University of Wisconsin, the University of Virginia, the University of Western Ontario, Cornell University, Ohio State University, Princeton University, the University of Florida, the Massachusetts Institute of Technology, SUNY Geneseo, and the University of California, Berkeley. I also read papers based upon my work in progress at conferences of the Modern Language Association, Renaissance Society of America, Shakespeare Association of America, International Shakespeare Association, and Sixteenth Century Studies Association. For their many helpful suggestions, I would like to thank the audiences at these events, as well as the following people: Fred Everett Maus, Sharon Achinstein, Jennifer Brady, Gordon Braden, Michael Cadden, Heather Dubrow, Mark Edmundson, James Ferguson, Richard Finkelstein, Patricia Gill, Jonathan Goldberg, Stephen Greenblatt, Elizabeth Harvey, Richard Helgerson, Victoria Kahn, Dan Kinney, Clare Kinney, Laura Levine, James Nohrnberg, Carol Neely, Leah Marcus, Stephen Orgel, Peter Stallybrass, Patricia Parker, Lisa Jardine, Steven Mullaney, Tom Roche, Alan Shepard, Michael Torrey, James Turner, Charles Spinosa, and Luke Wilson. An earlier version of chapter 4 was published in *Representations,* and an earlier version of chapter 6 in *Sexuality and Gender in Early Modern Europe: Institutions, Texts, Images.* I am grateful for research leaves from Princeton University and the University of Virginia, and for a fellowship from the National Endowment for the Humanities.

❧ 1 ❧

INTRODUCTION: INWARDNESS
AND SPECTATORSHIP

❧ I ❧

'Tis not alone my inky cloak, good mother,
Nor customary suits of solemn black,
Nor windy suspirations of forced breath,
No, nor the fruitful river in the eye,
Nor the dejected havior of the visage,
Together with all forms, moods, shapes of grief,
That can denote me truly. These indeed seem,
For they are actions that a man might play,
But I have that within which passes show,
These but the trappings and the suits of woe.
                    (*Hamlet* 1.2.77–86)

IN HIS REPLY TO HIS MOTHER, his first extended utterance in
the play, Hamlet distinguishes between the elaborate external rituals
of mourning and an inner, invisible anguish. His black attire, his sigh,
his tear fail to denote him truly not because they are false—Hamlet's
sorrow for his father is sincere—but because they *might* be false, because some other person might conceivably employ them deceitfully.
Even reliable indicators or symptoms of his distress become suspect,
simply because they are defined as indicators and symptoms. It is
hard to imagine what could possibly count as "true denotation" for
Hamlet. The mere, inevitable existence of a hiatus between signs
("trappings and suits") and what they signify ("that within") seems
to empty signs of their consequence. Substitutes for something imagined to be more real, more true, and more primary, the "trappings
and suits of woe" derive their power from that reality, but ought never
to be confused with it.

Hamlet's conviction that truth is unspeakable implicitly devalues
any attempts to express or communicate it. The exemplary instance
of this devaluation is the theater: "For they are actions that a man
might play." The frank fakeries of the playhouse, its disguisings and
impersonations, stand for the opacities that seem to characterize all

relations of human beings to one another. This book will examine the significance of the issues Hamlet touches upon in his speech to his mother, as they are reflected in the culture and especially in the drama of the English Renaissance. It will explore the afflictions and satisfactions that attend upon the difference between an unexpressed interior and a theatricalized exterior: the epistemological anxieties that gap generates, the social practices that are devised to manage it, and the sociopolitical purposes it serves.

I announce this program aware that it may seem, to some, regressive or misconceived. Many sophisticated critics in the past decade have seemed extremely chary of Hamlet's contrast between an authentic personal interior and derivative or secondary superficies. Some critics claim that a conception of personal inwardness hardly existed at all in Renaissance England. Francis Barker, for instance, argues that Hamlet's sense of inwardness is "anachronistic," a premature manifestation of what he calls "bourgeois subjectivity." Only in the later seventeenth century, according to Barker, does bourgeois subjectivity come into its own, "redolent with the metaphysics of interiority."[1] Catherine Belsey likewise complains about those who approach Renaissance plays in search of the "imaginary interiority" of the characters, an interiority that in her view is the imposition of the modern reader rather than a feature of the Renaissance text.[2] Jean Howard, too, associates the "interiority and self-presence of the individual" with a modern period she assumes begins in the eighteenth century.[3] Another group of critics, including Jonathan Goldberg, Patricia Fumerton, Kay Stockholder, Ann Jones, and Peter Stallybrass, acknowledge that the rhetoric of inwardness is highly developed in the English Renaissance, but maintain that these terms inevitably refer to outward, public, and political factors. Goldberg argues that "the individual derived a sense of self largely from external matrices"; Jones and Stallybrass that "the supposedly 'private' sphere . . . can be imagined only through its similarities and dissimilarities to the public world." Stockholder claims that in the English Renaissance "one's place in the world was identical to one's self-definition, and to 'know

1. Francis Barker, *The Tremulous Private Body* (New York: Methuen, 1984), pp. 31, 58.
2. Catherine Belsey, *The Subject of Tragedy: Identity and Difference in Renaissance Drama* (New York: Methuen, 1985), p. 48.
3. Jean Howard, "The New Historicism of Renaissance Studies," *English Literary Renaissance* 16 (1986): 15.

2l.

oneself' was . . . to know the duties entailed by one's membership in an order on the hierarchical ladder." Fumerton maintains that "the private could be sensed only through the public," and that "the 'self' was void."[4]

Later in this chapter I shall return to these critiques and the assumptions that lie behind them, and specify my own rather complex relationship to recent new-historicist and cultural-materialist attempts to "write the history of the subject." For the moment I want merely to insist that when one looks at a wide variety of printed materials produced in the reigns of Elizabeth and James, it becomes difficult to claim that Hamlet's boast of "that within" is anachronistic—that Shakespeare has mysteriously managed to jump forward in time and expropriate the conceptual equipment of a later era. For in fact, Hamlet deals eloquently but almost truistically in matters that would have been commonplace for his original audience. His distinction between interior and exterior is a very familiar rhetorical tactic in the sixteenth and early seventeenth centuries. Philip Sidney invokes it in *The Defense of Poetry*, for instance, when he discusses the way Virgil presents Aeneas: "how in his inward self, and how in his outward government."[5] Richard Hooker, the great apologist for the Church of England, begins his *Laws of Ecclesiastical Polity* by distinguishing between God's "internal operations" and His "external working."[6] In *A Brief Discourse of a Disease Called the Suffocation of the Mother*, the physician Edward Jorden differentiates between "internal" and "external" causes of disease, and likewise between the effects of the illness upon "internal senses," by which he means imagination, reason, and memory, and its effects upon "external senses,"

4. Jonathan Goldberg, *James I and the Politics of Literature* (Johns Hopkins University Press, 1983), p. 86; Ann Rosalind Jones and Peter Stallybrass, "The Politics of *Astrophil and Stella*," *Studies in English Literature* 24 (1984): 54; Kay Stockholder, "'Yet Can He Write': Reading the Silences in *The Spanish Tragedy*," *American Imago* 47 (1990): 3–124; Fumerton, *Cultural Aesthetics: Renaissance Literature and the Practice of Social Ornament* (Chicago: University of Chicago Press, 1991), pp. 109, 130. Fumerton's position has, however, recently become more tentative than her earlier confident dismissal of the private sphere (cf. "'Secret' Arts: Elizabethan Miniatures and Sonnets," *Representations* 15 (1986): 90).

5. Philip Sidney, *The Defense of Poetry*, in *The Prose Works of Sir Philip Sidney*, ed. Albert Feuillerat (Cambridge: Cambridge University Press, 1963), 3:25.

6. Richard Hooker, *Of the Laws of Ecclesiastical Polity*, ed. Georges Edelen, 2.2 and 2.4 in *The Folger Edition of the Works of Richard Hooker* (Cambridge, Mass.: Harvard University Press, 1977). All subsequent references to Hooker will be to this edition.

by which he means hearing, sight, touch, and so forth.[7] In his treatise on marriage, *A Bride-Bush,* William Whately separates the ways in which a wife ought to reverence her husband into two categories: "inward in heart" and "outward in . . . speeches . . . gestures, countenances, and whole behavior."[8] The Puritan ministers John Dod and Robert Cleaver divide the ways of violating the Ten Commandments into "inward" and "outward" transgressions: groundless, unspoken misgivings about one's neighbor constitute "inward" false witness, for instance, in contrast to the "outward" sin of perjury.[9] The Protestant casuist William Perkins distinguishes between inward and outward sorrow, inward and outward uncleanness, inward and outward repentance, inward and outward worship, and so forth.[10]

౸ THE POINT OF SUCH DISTINCTIONS is normally to privilege whatever is classified as interior. For Hamlet, the internal experience of his own grief "passes show" in two senses. It is beyond scrutiny, concealed where other people cannot perceive it. And it *surpasses* the visible—its validity is unimpeachable. The exterior, by contrast, is partial, misleading, falsifiable, unsubstantial. Walter Ralegh opens his *History of the World* by asserting that "it is not the visible fashion and shape of plants and of reasonable creatures that makes the difference of working in the one and of condition in the other, but the form internal."[11] The wise man, Ralegh implies, knows better than to trust what he sees. Instead he penetrates the veneer of appearances to grasp a hidden reality. Tudor and Stuart polemicists against the theater, like Philip Stubbes, John Northbrooke, William Rankin, Stephen Gosson, and William Prynne, acknowledge the separability of a privileged, "true" interior and a socially visible, falsifiable exterior even as they decry that separation, emphasizing the obligation of "all men at all

7. *A briefe discourse of a disease called the suffocation of the mother* (London, 1603), F2ᵛ, E1ʳ. For ease of reading, I have modernized the spelling of all quoted passages; old titles are cited in the Notes in their STC form.
8. William Whately, *A Bride-bush: or, a direction for married persons* (London, 1623), A4ᵛ.
9. John Dod and Robert Cleaver, *A plaine and familiar exposition of the Ten commandments* (London, 1604), p. 327 and *passim.* This work was reprinted at least nineteen times between 1603 and 1635.
10. William Perkins, *The whole treatise of the cases of conscience* (Cambridge, 1606). This was another extremely popular work, running to at least ten editions in the first half of the sixteenth century.
11. Walter Ralegh, *The history of the world* (London, 1614), A1ᵛ.

[4]

times . . . to seem that outwardly which they are inwardly."[12] Persons and things inwardly *are,* all these writers assume; persons and things outwardly only *seem.*

The alienation or potential alienation of surface from depth, of appearance from truth, means that a person's thoughts and passions, imagined as properties of the hidden interior, are not immediately accessible to other people. Hamlet is not original in maintaining that the sight of his downcast visage is not the same as the sight of his grief. "Every one may discover his fellow's natural inclinations," claims the English Jesuit Thomas Wright in *The Passions of the Mind,* "not by philosophical demonstration, but only by natural conjectures and probabilities. . . . For that we cannot enter into a man's heart, and view the passions or inclinations which there reside and lie hidden; therefore, as philosophers by effects find out causes, by proprieties essences, by rivers fountains, by boughs and flowers the core and roots; even so we must trace out passions and inclinations by some effects and external operations."[13] In *Basilicon Doron,* James I recommends a careful orchestration of the virtuous king's visible gestures and action on the grounds that "they serve as trunch-men, to interpret the inward disposition of the mind, to the eyes of them that cannot see farther within him, and therefore must only judge of him by the outward appearance."[14] Social life demands the constant practice of induction, or what the physician John Cotta calls "artificial conjecture":[15] reasoning from the superficial to the deep, from the effect to the cause, from seeming to being.

The inductive process is, however, always liable to error. At times we may, as Wright suggests, trace out the roots by the evidence of the boughs and flowers, but as William Vaughan reminds us, some thoughts and passions are "concealed in a man's heart, as like unto a tree, which in outward appearance seemeth to be most beautiful, and is full of fair blossoms, but inwardly is rotten, worm-eaten, and withered."[16] George Hakewill spends two pages listing ways to describe

12. William Prynne, *Histrio-mastix: The player's scourge* (London, 1633), X4ʳ.
13. Thomas Wright, *The Passions of the Minde in generall,* ed. Thomas O. Sloan (Urbana: University of Illinois Press, 1971), pp. 104–5.
14. James I and VI, *The Basilicon Doron of King James VI,* ed. James Craigie (Edinburgh: Scottish Text Society, 1944), p. 15.
15. John Cotta, *The triall of witch-craft, shewing the true methode of the discovery* (London, 1616), p. 4.
16. William Vaughan, *The golden-grove, moralized in three books* (London, 1600), L4ʳ.

hypocrites: wolves in sheep's clothing, richly decorated apothecary boxes with poisons inside, beautifully bound tragedies, snowy Mount Etnas with volcanic interiors, elaborate Egyptian temples "which without shine with gold, and jet, and marble, but have within some secret aisle, a crocodile or serpent for the god, unto which they are dedicated."[17] Court flatterers arouse the fear and contempt of sixteenth- and seventeenth-century political commentators because "outwardly they show themselves with the face of friendship, within they have more malice than the stings of scorpions."[18] Like MacDuff, who laments in *Macbeth* that "there is no art / To tell the mind's construction in the face," Hamlet knows that the forms, moods, and shapes of grief can as well be a calculated pretense as the symptoms of a genuine inner state.

Once the possibility of deception has been granted, the effect of truthfulness can be difficult to convey to a wary audience even when there is no intention to mislead. At his execution in 1609 Robert Logan, one of the Earl of Gowrie's co-conspirators, professed his repentance to the spectators around the scaffold, but evidently believed that they were unconvinced. So "he for the greater assurance of that his constant and true deposition, promised (by the assistance of God) to give them an open and evident token . . . which he accomplished thereafter; for before his last breath, when he had hung a pretty space; he lifted up his hands a good height, and clapped them together aloud three several times, to the great wonder and admiration of all the beholders."[19] Of course, even this astonishing demonstration has no logical force; perhaps Logan kept something in reserve after all, and remained a performer to the last gasp. At another final moment, immediately before he was publicly hanged, castrated, disemboweled, and quartered in 1581, the Jesuit Edmund Campion poignantly insisted upon his innocence of treason. "The outward protestations of this man," fumed Anthony Munday, "urged some there present to tears, not entering into conceit of his inward hypocrisy."[20] The possibility of some secret motive, some unexposed residue can never be

17. George Hakewill, *The vanity of the eye* (Oxford, 1615), pp. 81–82.
18. *A discourse against flattery* (London, 1611), p. 8.
19. *State Trials* 2:720. The same story is told of George Sprot, another Gowrie conspirator, in William Hart and George Abbott, *The examinations, arraignment, and conviction of George Sprot, notary of Ayremouth* (London, 1609), p. 29.
20. Anthony Munday, *A discoverie of Edmund Campion and his confederates, their most horrible and traiterous practices . . .* (London, 1582), G1ᵛ.

wholly discounted, even when the gesture of self-revelation seems most generous and complete.

⚡ GIVEN THE UBIQUITY of such conceptual categories in the English Renaissance, it is hardly surprising that the "problem of other minds" presents itself to thinkers and writers not so much as a question of whether those minds exist as a question of how to know what they are thinking.[21] The short treatise Skeptic, or Speculation, attributed to Walter Ralegh, argues against the authority of sense perceptions on the grounds that each individual, necessarily limited to the evidence of his own senses, cannot know whether the perceptions of others correlate with his own, or to what extent anyone's perceptions give an accurate idea of "outward objects." Different people manifestly vary in their tastes and interests, and the perceptions of beasts are likely to differ from human perceptions even more radically: "If a man rub his eye, the figure of that which he beholdeth seemeth long, or narrow; is it not then likely, that those creatures which have a long and slanting pupil of the eye, as goats, foxes, cats etc., do convey the fashion of that which they behold under another form to the imagination, than those that have round pupils do."[22]

The progress of this argument is interesting. Ralegh destabilizes convictions about direct access to things-in-themselves by insisting that the internal working of other minds, what he calls their "inward discourse," is remote and inaccessible. "I may tell what the outward object seemeth to me; but what it seemeth to other creatures, or whether it be indeed that which it seemeth to me, or any other of them, I know not."[23] But this perspectivism seems to strengthen, not weaken, the impulse to investigate those minds. Ralegh's treatise is remarkable not for its solipsism but for its attempt to reconstruct the "inward discourse" of the beast and the alien. Ralegh tries to duplicate in himself the different conditions of animal perception, rubbing his eye into the shape of a cat's eye in order to see as a cat sees. At the

---

21. Though he concentrates on French rather than English texts, and on skepticism about the phenomenal world rather than about other minds, Richard Popkin, in his History of Scepticism from Erasmus to Descartes, rev. ed. (New York: Harper Torchbooks, 1964), provides a helpful overview of the development of philosophical skepticism in the sixteenth century and its connection to doctrinal problems posed by the Reformation and Counter-Reformation.

22. Walter Ralegh, Skeptic, or Speculation (London, 1651), p. 4.

23. Ralegh, Skeptic, or Speculation, p. 20.

same time, the skeptical principles which generate this attempt doom his empathy to remain inevitably unsatisfying and incomplete.

Ralegh's skepticism links the imperviousness of the perceived other, whose mysterious interior can never fully be displayed, with a troubling corollary suggestion about the limitations of the perceiving subject. Each consciousness is constrained by its own particular limitations, by quirks of which it has no way of becoming aware, even while those peculiarities shelter it from the inquisitiveness of others. We are trapped, as it were, inside our own heads. In *The Vanity of the Eye*, George Hakewill illustrates his discussion of this problem with a cautionary anecdote about "a wise, and grave man": "Travelling in a summer's morning through the meadows, he saw (as him seemed) one of his neighbors committing bestiality with a mare, but knowing the good honest reports of the man, and thereby misdoubting his own eyes, he gets him presently to his house; where he finds him good man, in his bed, fast asleep."[24] The moral of the story, for Hakewill, is that our eyes are untrustworthy. For a thoroughgoing skeptic, of course, the sight of the man in bed, or the evidence of "good honest reports," would be no more conclusive than the spectacle in the meadows. But like Ralegh, Hakewill seems less interested in the abstract philosophical problem—the possibility that *all* sense impressions might be deceptive—than in the practical difficulties attendant upon the undoubted fact that *some* sense impressions are deceptive. Interrogating our standards of reliability eventuates, in both writers, not in epistemological despair but in an attempt to articulate a remedy, even though the remedy itself seems unavoidably inadequate.

The problems posed by the gap between internal truth and external manifestation are not the exclusive concern of skeptical philosophy. They emerge at least as vividly from a program of faith as from a program of doubt. Christianity suggests a variety of analogues to the difficult social tasks of intersubjective understanding. The hidden Christian God provides a prototype of the invisible object of knowledge comprehended but partially through visible works. "Our soundest knowledge," Richard Hooker writes, "is to know that we know him not as in deed he is, neither can know him."[25] Sixteenth- and seventeenth-century sermons, devotional literature, and religious propaganda rely heavily on "arguments by design," reasoning infer-

24. Hakewill, *The Vanity of the Eye*, p. 60.
25. Richard Hooker, *Of the Laws of Ecclesiastical Polity*, 1.2.2.

entially from God's works to His concealed essence, from everyday events to His mysterious providence. Biblical hermeneutics similarly conceive of the literal text as a husk or veil that simultaneously obscures and indicates the contours of the truth at the sacred core.

It is difficult to know whether the interpretation of persons constitutes a particular application of a more general interpretive practice, or whether the comprehension of other kinds of phenomena—sacred texts, religious mysteries, or wonders of nature—is modeled upon the familiar tasks of social comprehension. Certainly the connection between the two kinds of tasks is made long before the sixteenth century, by Augustine in *On the Faith in Things Unseen*. Why, he asks, should we flinch from acknowledging the veiled truths of Christianity, when our intercourse with even our most intimate acquaintances is premised upon invisibility?

> Tell me, I ask you, with what eyes do you see your friend's will toward you? For, no will can be seen with bodily eyes. Or, indeed, do you also see in your mind that which is taking place in the mind of another? . . . Perhaps you will say that you see the will of another through his deeds? Then you will see acts and hear words, but of your friend's will you will believe that which cannot be seen or heard. The will is not color or figure that may be impressed upon the eyes; nor is it a sound or formula that may strike upon the ears; nor, indeed, is it yours to be felt by the affection of your heart. It follows, therefore, that, although it is not seen or heard or grasped inwardly by you, it is believed. Otherwise your life would be left barren of any friendship, or love bestowed upon you would not be paid back by you in turn.[26]

The difficulty, obviously, is in specifying criteria which would distinguish between faith and gullibility. On the one hand the interpreter must begin with what is literal and apparent: the purpose of exegesis, as Frank Kermode writes, "is to penetrate the surface and reveal a secret sense; to show what is concealed in what is proclaimed."[27] At the same time, Christ's career as well as the content of much of his teaching dramatically point up the perils of using external manifestations as interpretive guides.

Set against these epistemological qualms—indeed, provoked by

26. Augustine, *On Faith in Things Unseen*, ed. Roy Joseph Deferrari and Mary Francis McDonald, *Writings of Saint Augustine* (New York: Cima Publishing, 1947), 2:452.

27. Frank Kermode, *The Genesis of Secrecy: On the Interpretation of Narrative* (Cambridge: Harvard University Press, 1979), x.

those qualms—is the desire for a reliable means for achieving certainty. Even as Renaissance theism generates misgivings about human access to truth, it provides a context for thinking about what certainty would mean and to whom it could be ascribed. The Christian God exemplifies not only mysterious inwardness, but an effortless transcendence of the boundaries that frustrate human knowledge. When Father Wright declares that "hearts . . . be inscrutable, and only open unto God,"[28] he is typical in defining inscrutability as a relative and not an absolute phenomenon. On this issue he shares the convictions of the Protestant martyrologist John Foxe: "For a man to pronounce assuredly upon the secret cogitation and intent of either man or woman, further than by utterance or by speech is to him signified, passeth his capacity, and is to be left only to Him, who is 'scrutans corda et renes Deus.'"[29] The Puritans John Dod and Robert Cleaver claim likewise that "God . . . doth as well discern the most secret things of the soul, as any man doth the outward actions of the body. . . . For men first look to the outward behavior, and hence descend to judge of the heart, but God first approves the heart, and then the outward action."[30] God's immediate, superhuman knowledge of the hidden interior of persons is one of the primary qualities for which he is admired and feared by many early modern Christians. Thus in *A Treatise of Angels* John Salkend rejects the notion that angels have access to human thoughts, because preserving that kind of knowledge to God alone constitutes for him one of the most powerful motives for the worship of the divinity.[31]

In fact, for some writers the presence of an omniscient spectator seems so fundamental to the structure of human subjectivity that the fact of that subjectivity becomes part of the proof of God's existence. In *The Whole Treatise of Cases of Conscience*, for instance, William Perkins writes:

> Let it be demanded of the atheist, whereof does conscience bear witness? he cannot deny, but of all his particular actions. . . . Furthermore, to whom is it a witness? Neither to man, nor to angels: for it is impossible that any man or angel should either hear the voice of conscience, or re-

28. Wright, *The Passions of the Minde*, p. 27.
29. Foxe, *Acts and Monuments of these latter and perilous days . . .* (New York: AMS Press, 1965), 8:238.
30. Dod and Cleaver, *A plaine and familiar exposition of the Ten commandments*, pp. 29–30.
31. John Salkend, *A treatise of angels* (London, 1613), pp. 165–67.

ceive the testimony thereof, or yet discern what is in the heart of man. Hereupon it follows, that there is a substance, most wise, most powerful, most holy, that sees and bears record, and that is God himself.[32]

The startling logical leap in this passage does not seem to trouble Perkins, despite his normally rigorous argumentative style; such dubiously teleological reasoning was so widespread in the period that custom may have obscured its irregularity.[33] Perkins conceives each individual as simultaneously the object of a double scrutiny: of a human vision that is fallible, partial, and superficial, and of a divine vision that is infallible, complete, and penetrating. Without a continued tension between divine and human observation, human inwardness—constituted as it is by a difference between those scrutinies—would seem for Perkins to collapse. In other words, the inwardness of persons is constituted by the *disparity* between what a limited, fallible human observer can see and what is available to the hypostasized divine observer, "unto whom all hearts be open, all desires known, and from whom no secrets are hid."[34] This disparity is subject to fluctuation, and to intentional manipulation both by the viewer and the viewed.

Renaissance religious culture thus nurtures habits of mind that encourage conceiving of human inwardness, like other truths, as at once privileged and elusive, an absent presence "interpreted" to observers by ambiguous inklings and tokens. Hermeneutic difficulties arise from the fact that while particular instances of human vision might prove untrustworthy, a visual model simultaneously structures

32. Perkins, *The whole treatise of the cases of conscience*, p. 211. Perkins's argument is conventional; cf., for instance, John Howesoun, *A short exposition of the 20. and 21. verses of the third chapter of the first e pistle of St. John* (Edinburgh, 1600), B1ʳᵛ and B8ᵛ–C1ʳ.

33. Stephen Greenblatt has suggested that atheism "seems to have been almost unthinkable to the most daring philosophical minds of late sixteenth-century England" (*Shakespearean Negotiations: The Circulation of Social Energy in Renaissance England* [Berkeley: University of California Press, 1988], p. 22). It is harder than Greenblatt acknowledges to assess the accuracy of this claim. Unlike heretics who could look forward to a transcendental reward for declaring their allegiances, atheists would hardly find it expedient to broadcast their scandalous opinions. But if Greenblatt is right, perhaps the conceptual difficulty of atheism for the period has something to do with the way the structure of internal experience is thought necessarily to imply observation by a divinity.

34. *The Prayer Book of Queen Elizabeth, 1559* (London: The Ancient and Modern Library of Theological Literature, 1914), p. 92.

the conception of what real understanding will involve. On the one hand, the theistic context in which the problem of human inwardness is posed provides a standard of what would constitute certainty. On the other hand, faith itself encourages a kind of mistrust: for what is most true about human beings in such a system is simultaneously least verifiable.

ᔑ II ᘒ

WHY SHOULD AUTHORS so various as the Puritan Perkins, the Anglican[35] Foxe, the Jesuit Wright, and the heterodox Ralegh all yearn for techniques of penetration, excavation, exposure, while at the same time proclaiming their mistrust of those techniques? Perhaps the question itself seems odd. These writers may seem less to be reflecting the idiosyncrasies of their particular culture than to be illuminating or capitalizing upon a universal insight into the irreducible mysteriousness of human beings to one another. The difference between knowing oneself "from the inside" and knowing other people "from the outside" may seem so fundamental to social life that it cannot be the property of a particular historical moment. Experiences of having been deceived or misled, of having misinterpreted someone's motives or of having been misunderstood oneself, of having consciously withheld a truth out of charity, jealousy, politeness, or cunning: these may seem the inescapable conditions of any human intercourse.

Indeed, distinctions between a socially visible exterior and an invisible personal interior, if not cultural universals, have at the very least a long history in the Western philosophical tradition. Ralegh's arguments in *Skeptic, or Speculation,* for instance, are not novel ones; he is closely adapting material from the first book of *Outlines of Pyrrhonism,* a late-classical work by Sextus Empiricus rediscovered by the West in the sixteenth century. Sextus, moreover, represents himself not as an original philosopher, but as the heir to a tradition of thinking about the relation between sense perceptions and reality that reaches back to the pre-Socratics.[36] Renaissance thinking on this issue

35. The term "Anglican" may seem anachronistic, since it only came into use in the nineteenth century; but I find it a helpful way of distinguishing Church of England Protestants like Hooker and Foxe from nonseparatists to the left of them, like Perkins or Cooper.

36. For an account of the influence of Sextus Empiricus in the sixteenth century, see C. B. Schmidt, "The Rediscovery of Ancient Skepticism," in *The Skeptical Tradition,* ed. Myles Burnyeat (Berkeley: University of California Press, 1983), pp. 225–51.

is also influenced by Aristotle and his scholastic followers, who distinguish between appearances and essences; Stoics and neo-Stoics, who separate true inward goods from inessential externals; and Christian patristic writers, who emphasize the importance of the inner over the outer man. Of course, the schemata of inwardness prevailing among these different traditions of thought are not simply interchangeable: they are designed to address disparate philosophical problems and are often lodged within incommensurable metaphysical systems. A scheme that contrasts an external phenomenal world with an inward nonmaterial realm, for instance, differs in its implications and emphases from a scheme grounded upon an internal hydraulics of competing fluid "humors." A number of important studies in the history of ideas have explored the exceedingly complicated tradition of psychological thinking inherited by Renaissance philosophy and medicine, a tradition that can be traced back to the Greeks and that undergoes innumerable readjustments, transformations, and syntheses in the hands of various gnostics, patristic writers, scholastics, neo-Platonists, neo-Stoics, and Ramists.[37] Surely it is important that several traditions furnish accounts of personal inwardness in an intellectually syncretic period like the Renaissance, which tends to respect those traditions even while shaking religious and philosophical ideas loose from their original moorings and recombining them in new arrangements. The lengthy, complex pedigree of general notions of personal inwardness helps sustain their ecumenical acceptability in an age that honors the authority of the past.

It is not, then, that the Renaissance invents a previously unarticulated or inarticulable possibility. Rather, in late sixteenth- and early seventeenth-century England the sense of discrepancy between "inward disposition" and "outward appearance" seems unusually urgent and consequential for a very large number of people, who occupy virtually every position on the ideological spectrum. Whatever philosophical lineage might be adduced for conceptions of personal inwardness, the shape of the ideas that shall concern me in this book are not the property of a particular sect or school. Nor are they exclu-

---

37. Some of the interactions of the Platonic, Stoic, and monastic traditions of self-knowledge are described by Michel Foucault, *Technologies of the Self*, ed. Luther H. Martin, Huck Gutmann, and Patrick H. Hutton (Amherst: University of Massachusetts Press, 1988), pp. 9–49. In *The Body and Society: Men, Women, and Sexual Renunciation in Early Christianity* (New York: Columbia University Press, 1988) Peter Brown brilliantly discusses related issues in the late classical and early Christian period.

sively or primarily the concern of Renaissance intellectuals. The mere existence of various philosophical or religious traditions—Stoic self-fortification, Augustinian introspective piety, skeptic solipsism—does not produce of its own accord the Renaissance fascination with interior truths. The causal chain is more likely to work in the other direction: some social and political crises in early modern Europe make it worth rehabilitating authorities and schools of thought that address that emergency in especially pertinent ways.

The question, then, might be phrased thus: why, although the distinction between interior and exterior may seem tediously common-sensical, should it so rarely seem to "go without saying" in sixteenth- and early seventeenth-century England? Why must that distinction be endlessly reiterated in prefaces, satires, sermons, advice literature, medical treatises, coney-catching pamphlets, doctrinal debates, anti-theatrical tracts, speeches from the gallows, published reports of foreign and domestic turmoil, essays on the passions and on the soul? What engenders this curious state of affairs, in which everyone seems to concur with everyone else, but still feels obliged to announce those unexceptionable convictions with the emphasis usually reserved for novel or tendentious claims?

The following chapters will explore various quite specific ways in which the difference between socially observable externals and "that within" (whatever it might be) is established, elaborated upon, exploited, exaggerated, pointedly ignored, or violently erased in early modern England. At the same time, a more general explanation for what is clearly a sweeping phenomenon seems called for. Yet a general explanation is also more difficult. Mutually interacting social and ideological factors massively overdetermine the kinds of beliefs I shall be investigating. It is hard to disentangle cause from effect, and to weigh the relative importance of a variety of different influences. Lacey Baldwin Smith ascribes what he calls the "paranoia" of Tudor courtiers to Renaissance child-rearing practices that encourage touchy defensiveness and mutual suspicion.[38] Frank Whigham maintains that the rapid enlargement of the elite class in the later sixteenth century causes a crisis in aristocratic values, one consequence of which is an acute self-consciousness about the tactical deployment of socially visible behaviors, combined with an uneasy awareness of

---

38. Lacey Baldwin Smith, *Treason in Tudor England: Politics and Paranoia* (Princeton: Princeton University Press, 1986).

their artificiality.[39] Devon Hodges relates the English Renaissance interest in rhetorical strategies of "anatomy"—the peeling off of surfaces to reveal the layers beneath—to a new medical emphasis upon the dissection of cadavers.[40] Wendy Wall sees the persistent emphasis on a dynamics of concealment and disclosure in late sixteenth-century poetry as a way of coming to terms with the newly enlarged audience that print technology makes possible.[41]

All of these suggestions, plausible enough in their own terms, do not wholly explain the very widespread circulation of what might be called the "inwardness *topos.*" Smith and Whigham explain why aristocrats are chronically suspicious of one another, but not why the same skepticism should seem apt to commoners who had no court connections and whose childhood experiences would have been entirely different. Wall's discussion of the relationship between manuscript and print culture applies to nondramatic poetry but not to the theater in which Hamlet lays claim to an interior that escapes theatrical representation. Hodge's analysis is likewise generically restricted to a particular kind of prose treatise.

I am inclined to seek an explanation in the far-reaching political, religious, and economic realignments that constitute the English Reformation, because these realignments draw attention to certain relevant doctrinal and practical issues. Sixteenth- and seventeenth-century Catholics and Protestants, Anglicans and sectarians endlessly debate whether priests ought to wear vestments, whether communicants should kneel when they receive communion, whether infant baptism is acceptable, whether prescribed prayers have merit. To hostile commentators, religious practices they do not share seem superficial, self-evidently fraudulent: thus Protestants typically describe themselves as cultivating internal truths while accusing Catholics of attending only to outward "shows." Sixteenth- and early seventeenth-century Catholics themselves, however, hardly perceive their devotional lives as empty formalities. It is Cardinal William Allen and Father Robert Persons, S. J., who maintain that in difficult moral dilemmas "whatever [one] does as the result of the internal prompting of

39. Frank Whigham, *Ambition and Privilege: The Social Tropes of Elizabethan Courtesy Theory* (Berkeley: University of California Press, 1984).
40. Devon Hodges, *Renaissance Fictions of Anatomy* (Amherst: University of Massachusetts Press, 1985).
41. Wendy Wall, "Disclosures in Print: The 'Violent Enlargement' of the Renaissance Voyeuristic Text," *SEL* 29 (1989): 35–59.

the Holy Ghost, after having commended the matter to God and having considered his eternal salvation, is to be considered better and more acceptable to God than any other course of action."[42] Neither the rhetoric of inwardness nor the antinomian implications of that rhetoric were exclusively Protestant property.

In fact, whatever their position on the role of ceremony in the church, religious controversialists never question the existence of a distinction between what Augustine calls *homo interior* and *homo exterior*.[43] Rather Catholics, Anglicans, and sectarians contend over the *significance* of a distinction all parties are willing to grant. They argue not over how human beings are structured, but over how, given that structure, they ought to comport themselves. It is important to recognize in such altercations not merely the issues overtly under discussion, issues often of literally life-and-death importance to the disputants, but also the shared assumptions upon which even the bitterest of controversies may be predicated.

Moreover, as a practical matter the awareness of a secret interior space of unexpressed thoughts and feelings does not require commitment to a particular theology. It is an almost inevitable result of religious oppression, so that the seventeenth-century Puritan Daniel Dyke lists "the public persecution of the church" as one of the usual

42. William Allen and Robert Persons, "Resolutiones quorundam cassum nationiis Anglicanae [The resolution of certain cases of the English nation]," in *Elizabethan Casuistry*, trans. and ed. P. J. Holmes (Thetford, Norfolk: The Catholic Record Society, 1981), p. 67. This manuscript, probably used in the instruction of English missionary priests, was composed between 1581 and 1585; Holmes dates it 1582. Persons and Allen's position in this passage is derivable from Aquinas's insistence, in the *Quaestiones disputatae de veritate* 16–17, that even the erring conscience is morally binding upon its possessor. For an English version of this text see *Truth: Translated from the Definitive Leonine Text*, trans. J. V. McGlynn (Chicago: H. Regnery, 1953), vol. 2.

43. For a representative tract in which both Protestant and Catholic positions use Augustine's formulations to draw different conclusions, see, for example, *A true report of the private colloquy between M. Smith, alias Norrice, and M. Walker* (London, 1624). The topic of this dialogue is the relationship between the "outward and extrinsical" and the "inward or secret." The debate recapitulates some very old divisions among the fathers of the Church. For instance, Jerome argues that the existence of an inward realm to which only God has immediate access justifies religious dissimulation under certain circumstances; Augustine, whose account of that interior realm was at least as influential, placed rigorous limitations upon the extent to which external manifestations were allowed to deviate from inner truth.

ways by which a person may come to know his "inward heart."[44] Between the early 1530s, when Henry defies the authority of Rome, and 1558, when Elizabeth ascends to the throne, England changes religious course four times. The nationalized but doctrinally catholic Henrician church takes an aggressively protestant turn under Edward; but its leaders and many lesser adherents are exiled or crushed in Mary's return to militant Roman Catholicism, which is in turn displaced by Elizabeth's qualified return to the reformed church. Each major alteration, and some of the minor ones, involves the sometimes violent but never wholly successful suppression of what was heretofore the approved doctrine. John Foxe's *Acts and Monuments*, better known as the "Book of Martyrs," records the Protestant resistance to the reimposition of Catholicism under Mary. In the late sixteenth century Foxe's volumes are installed beside the Bible in English churches, keeping the memory of the Marian persecution alive in the minds of Protestants. At the same time, Catholics begin sending their own martyrs to the scaffold, victims of the reassertion of a Protestant hegemony and the political hostilities between England and Catholic Spain. Meanwhile Puritans and radical sectarians seem increasingly aggressive and defiant to the Anglican establishment, which reacts by implementing measures designed to punish severely their departures from the *via media*.[45]

In later chapters I shall deal in more detail with some consequences of these suppressions and conversions, and of the resistance mounted to them. At this point I merely want to clarify some of the general issues involved. Those who take matters of faith seriously,

44. Daniel Dyke, *The mystery of self deceiving* (London, 1641), p. 316. The first edition of this popular work was published in 1614. In *Ways of Lying: Dissimulation, Persecution, and Conformity in Eary Modern Europe* (Cambridge: Harvard University Press, 1990), Perez Zagorin describes how Jews in Spain, Protestants in Counter-Reformation Italy, sectarians and Catholics in England, and "libertine" crypto-atheists throughout Europe develop a similar range of options for dealing with inquisition and persecution, ranging from outright pretense through devious forms of avoidance to blatant defiance of majority practices. The anthropologist E. P. Dozier shows how members of the Pueblo Indian tribe, under Spanish pressure to convert to Catholicism, employed false conformity, verbal equivocation, code languages, and secret rituals to preserve themselves and their religion: strategies identical, that is, to the tactics used by Europeans. ("Rio Grande Pueblos," pp. 94–186 in *Perspectives in American Indian Culture Change*, ed. Edward H. Spicer [Chicago: University of Chicago Press, 1961]).

45. For an account of some of the relevant legislation see J. E. Neale, *Elizabeth I and Her Parliaments 1584–1601* (New York: W. W. Norton, 1958), especially pp. 280–97.

whatever their confession, are likely to find themselves in an awkward or even dangerous position at some point in the sixteenth or early seventeenth century. Often, however, they have the option of virtual invisibility. They are not distinguished from their neighbors by language, skin color, ethnic background, or habits of dress. Tudor and Jacobean religious dissidents face self-definitional challenges similar to what Eve Sedgwick describes as the challenges of modern homosexual identity[46]—the expediency, even at times the apparent necessity, of concealment; the physical perils and psychic relief attendant upon open declaration; the uncertainty about who and what might betray half-secret allegiances; the context-dependent fluidity of what "counts" as a heretical orientation.

Throughout the sixteenth century the religious leaders of all confessions struggle with the question of whether conscientious dissidents ought to conceal their true allegiances from hostile authorities. Some argue that frankness about one's beliefs is morally obligatory. John Calvin acknowledges "how hard a thing it is to confess Christ in these days of trouble" but nonetheless insists upon an open announcement: "Two men in one, God loveth not. If the inward man know the truth, why doth the outward man confess a falsehood? . . . If the tongue speak otherwise than the heart thinketh, both be abominable before God."[47] The record of religious persecution in England and on the Continent is full of heretics who prefer death in torment to conforming outwardly to a doctrine at variance with their inner convictions. For these people, the relationship between what they believe and what they decide to make apparent is posed in life-shattering terms.

Although it is impossible to estimate accurately the severity of the crises of conscience that accompanied official changes of faith, or the numbers who underwent such crises, those willing to suffer the extreme penalties for their beliefs must have always been in a minority. In *The Discovery of Witchcraft* Reginald Scot, arguing that supposed witches often confess out of terror, compares their panic to that of the Protestants under Catholic oppression: "He that . . . remembreth

46. Eve Sedgwick, *The Epistemology of the Closet* (Berkeley: University of California Press, 1990). Likewise pertinent are the binary conceptual oppositions Sedgwick discusses—the simultaneous tension and collusion between cognition and paranoia, between secrecy and disclosure, between knowledge and ignorance.

47. John Calvin, *Whether Christian faith may be kept secret in the Heart, without confession to the world* (1553), A2ʳ–A3ʳ; A4ᵛ–A5ʳ.

the persecutions in Queen Mary's time, shall find, that many good men have fallen for fear of persecution, and returned unto the Lord again."[48] Although the silence of fearful, skeptical, temporizing, or merely apathetic individuals leaves no historical trace, religious upheavals affect those who do not resist as well as those who do. Attempts to enforce religious conformity can become lessons in the advisability of keeping one's opinions—or the fact that one has no opinion—to oneself. This experience, too, while less sensational than the experience of the declared heretic, calls attention to the strategic difference between thought and utterance, secret conviction and external manifestation.

It was not merely the pusillanimous or unprincipled who hid their beliefs. Members of a beleaguered religious minority had to consider whether a circumspection that preserved their numbers might be not only in their worldly interests, but best for the future of their faith as well. Thus Roman Catholic casuists declare dispensable the consecration of altars, auricular confession, even in some circumstances the mass itself. This leniency had its dangers: as Peter Holmes points out, the ritual differences between Catholics and Protestants were probably more important to most lay believers than any doctrinal divergence.[49] Without Latin prayers or sacraments performed by an anointed priest, how were Catholic laypersons to distinguish themselves from the Protestant majority? Without the discipline and supportive community of the conventicle, how were separatist Protestants to avoid the hypocrisy of which they accused Anglican accommodationalists? Still, since everybody acknowledged that religion was most importantly a matter of inward commitment, conscientious believers could argue that one might participate in rituals one did not credit, if they were insisted upon by the civil authorities.

The drawing of a difference between the "inward disposition" and the visible but less-real "outward appearance" created such tempting opportunities for religious minorities that elaborate attempts to justify concealment to the tender of conscience proliferated in sixteenth-century Europe. Holinshed reports that when one Friar Forrest was apprehended in 1537 and accused of secretly rejecting Henry VIII's authority over the English church, he was asked why he had not de-

48. Reginald Scot, *The Discovery of Witchcraft* (1584), 2.12 (London: John Rodker, 1930), p. 21.

49. Peter Holmes, *Resistance and Compromise: The Political Thought of Elizabethan Catholics* (Cambridge: Cambridge University Press, 1982), p. 125.

murred to take the Oath of Supremacy. "He answered that he took his oath with his outward man, but his inward man never consenteth thereto."[50] In the period before he finally admitted the recalcitrance of his "inward man" to the authorities, Forrest had been practicing "equivocation," a notorious Catholic technique of giving riddling, evasive, or even downright misleading answers to queries posed by investigating authorities.

The theory of equivocation predated the Reformation: Thomas More, who later developed his own form of noncooperation with the authorities, addresses the issue in *A Dialogue Concerning Heresies.* The interlocutor claims that no one need confess secret deeds in court, "because that of secret and unknown things no man can be his judge." More replies that judges who ask random and frivolous questions need not be propitiated, but that when the judge's suspicions are based upon clear evidence, "there is he plainly bounden upon pain of eternal damnation without covering or cautel to shew and disclose the plain truth and to have more respect to his soul than to his shame."[51] Later Catholics, under severe pressure from Elizabeth's and then James's Protestant regimes, emphasized less the evidence possessed by the accusers than the legitimacy of their interest in knowing the answer. The Jesuits Persons and Allen go so far as to claim that no Protestants possess genuine authority to question Catholics, "because a heretic queen is not legitimate queen."[52] In different ways, however, both More and later writers make allowance for a domain over which the judge's curiosity gives him no entitlement: a domain which is not only inaccessible to human vision as a practical matter, but which the individual has an authentic interest in protecting. This realm is defined as the inwardness of mind or conscience, which is subject to God alone.

Like Hamlet, equivocation theorists insist not only upon the separation of the interior realm from the outer world, but upon its absolute priority. The English Jesuit Henry Garnet explains that "the essence or whole truth of every proposition is in the mind" before it is

50. Raphael Holinshed et al., *Holinshed's Chronicles of England, Scotland, and Ireland* (1587; reprinted London, 1808), 3:803.

51. *The Complete Works of Thomas More,* vol. 6, part 1, ed. Thomas M. C. Lawler, Germain Marc'haudor, and Richard C. Marius (New Haven: Yale University Press, 1981), p. 282.

52. Allen and Persons, "Resolutiones," p. 65. Persons repeats the argument in *A Treatise Tending to Mitigation* (1607).

uttered or written; the means of expression are merely "instruments or signs to express that proposition which is in the mind." Hence "the altering of the signs which do express our mind . . . alter not the verity of the proposition," and the employment of ambiguous or deceptive language "doth not make before God the proposition of any other condition than before."[53] Persons and Allen show how this distinction operates when they address the question of whether a captured Catholic may do his best to flee after having promised heretic captors that he will cooperate with them. Whether or not the escape attempt is wrong, Persons and Allen declare, depends upon the state of mind in which the promise was made. If the Catholic made the promise wholeheartedly, then he "intended to oblige himself" and breaking his word would be mortal sin. But if he equivocated, "adding mentally" such phrases as "if I cannot" or "in your presence," then he promised "with the intention of deceiving and not of obliging himself," and he may escape if he has the opportunity.[54] What matters to the casuists in these cases is the quality of the intention, something visible to God alone. In comparison the external, social world in which promises are uttered is of slight importance, morally almost chimerical.

The difference between the casuists' position and the position of a modern speech-act theorist like J. L. Austin could not be more marked. For Austin, promises are by their nature social acts, and their form is tied up in the syntactical operations shared by all users of a language. People may, of course, break promises; but if they have uttered the appropriate words, they have made those promises nonetheless. The effect of Austin's speech-act theory, as he points out, is to render irrelevant a secret, ontologically prior realm of intention.[55] The casuists, on the other hand, imagine utterances matching up, well or badly, with authoritative internal propositions; and so the promise

53. Henry Garnet, *A Treatise of Equivocation*, ed. David Jardine (London: Longman, Brown, 1851), pp. 9–12. For an illuminating discussion of the uses of equivocation by Catholics and other religious minorities, see Lowell Gallagher, *Medusa's Gaze: Casuistry and Conscience in the Renaissance* (Stanford: Stanford University Press, 1991), esp. pp. 63–93.

54. Allen and Persons, "Resolutiones," pp. 125–26.

55. Austin argues against the notion that the "seriousness" of promises "consists in their being uttered as (merely) the outward and visible sign, for convenience or other record or for information, of an inward and spiritual act"; his own theory "exclude[s] such fictitious inward acts" (*How To Do Things with Words*, 2d ed., ed. J. O. Urmson and Marina Sbisà [Cambridge: Harvard University Press, 1975], pp. 9–10).

is only binding upon its maker if it properly expresses what Garnet calls its preexistent mental "essence." The casuists' position, curious as it may seem, follows reasonably enough from the hierarchized distinction between insides and outsides, and the founding of that distinction upon the notion of an omniscient divine supervisor, that we have seen elaborated in other Renaissance contexts.

What was true for speech, according to the casuists, was true for all other forms of social self-representation. As the persecution of Catholics became more severe, Catholic clerics vigorously debated the ethics of "Nicodemism" or secret religious commitment, often shifting their position in response to the practical difficulties of open resistance.[56] The usual position of the casuist texts of the 1580s is that the open acknowledgment of one's belief is never positively sinful, but that fear of death or mistreatment is an adequate reason to conceal one's commitments, and that discretion may in many instances be the better part of valor.

On the other end of the religious spectrum the Family of Love, a radical Protestant sect, similarly distinguished sharply between the secrets of the heart and public behavior. Familists taught that provided the heart was right, the true believer might engage in any religious practice prescribed by the authorities without compromising his or her standing with God.[57] Familists could also make false statements to hostile inquisitors about their religious convictions without compromising their consciences. Provided they felt themselves physically threatened they were no more guilty of lying, asserted their

56. Peter Holmes, in *Resistance and Compromise*, describes the battles among English Catholics over the proper course of action during the Elizabethan period; Perez Zagorin, in *Ways of Lying*, has a useful chapter on Catholic Nicodemism in late sixteenth-century England. The range of accommodations to enforced Anglicanism is clear in the memoirs of the English Jesuit John Gerard, who differentiates between recusants, who refused to attend Anglican services and often paid punitive fines for doing so, and schismatics, who secretly aided priests and fellow-believers, but who attended established worship with their neighbors. Gerard vacillates between treating the recusants as "real" Catholics and the schismatics as merely potential members of the Roman Church, and considering both recusants and schismatics true Catholics (*John Gerard: The Autobiography of an Elizabethan*, trans. Philip Caraman [New York: Longmans, Green, and Co., 1951]).

57. For an excellent account of Familist practice and the exasperation it occasioned in orthodox Anglicans, see Janet E. Halley, "Heresy, Orthodoxy, and the Politics of Religious Discourse: The Case of the English Family of Love," *Representing the English Renaissance*, ed. Stephen Greenblatt (Berkeley: University of California Press, 1988), pp. 303–25.

founder Hendrik Niclas, than a woman coerced to perform sexual acts was guilty of unchastity.

Catholic and radical Protestant responses to the problems of practicing a minority faith differ in predictable ways. The Catholic mode makes a space for private conviction by insisting upon a traditional distinction between the domains of secular and ecclesiastical authority, rendering unto Caesar what is Caesar's and reserving for God what is God's. There is nothing in the Catholic doctrine that identifies religious conviction as necessarily private or interior. Rather, such conviction becomes private and interior in the inhospitable environment of a Protestant state, which forbids the public demonstration of rightful allegiances. When Catholics, as Persons writes, "live amid so many difficulties and dangers and amid so much desolation and have hardly any human consolation," the demands of their faith must be reinterpreted to make allowances for their parlous circumstances. The radical Protestants instead typically contrast an unmediated relationship between God and man, a relationship celebrated for its intrinsic inwardness, with the empty corporeality of external secular affairs.

In practice, however, various persecuted religious minorities tend to find similar solutions to their similar dilemmas. From the Anglican point of view, papists and sectarians could seem to be allied with one another despite their contrary doctrinal premises; they were even accused of collaborating with the hope of toppling the English political and ecclesiastical system.[58] To oppose this perceived threat, the Elizabethan regime in the later decades of the sixteenth century devised an unprecedented domestic espionage system under the auspices of Francis Walsingham, which infiltrated heterodox and possibly subversive religious groups. It is difficult to know at this historical remove whether the aggressions of the state produced furtiveness in its enemies or supposed enemies as a defensive reflex, or whether the secretiveness of the heterodox necessitated the regime's attempt at surveillance. Whatever the original causal relationship, the effect was a spiraling paranoia on both sides accompanied by a sharply higher awareness of the practical advantages of secrecy. Significantly, the ecclesiastical authorities found invisible religious minorities threatening not because the authorities rejected the assump-

58. For analogies between Catholics and Puritans in the Anglican mind, see, for instance, the *Works* of Elizabeth I's Archbishop of Canterbury, John Whitgift, ed. J. Ayre (London: Parker Society, 1851–53), 3:300–315.

tions upon which dissidents based their arguments, but because, on
the contrary, they wholeheartedly accepted them—because a tranquil
and orderly society seemed to depend not merely upon the "outward
observance" and "external conformity" of its subjects, but upon their
"heartfelt love" and "sincere conviction." It was because hypocrisy
was so easy that it was so dangerous.

⅏ THE RAPID URBANIZATION of English literate culture must
have powerfully exacerbated many of the tensions just described. Despite periodic ravages of the plague, a persistently high mortality rate,
and a lower-than-average birthrate, sixteenth-century London bur-
geoned. The population grew from seventy thousand to two hundred
thousand people between 1550 and 1600, and doubled again in the
next half-century. Most of the increase was attributable to migration
from the provincial towns and villages; there was also a significant
influx of religious refugees from the Continent.[59] The centralization
of literary production was even more marked. Monastic libraries were
dispersed, and old regional centers lost their prestige as the Crown
consolidated its power and its patronage networks, and as the
increasing importance of foreign trade concentrated wealth in the
capital city.

Consequently producers and consumers of late sixteenth- and
early seventeenth-century literature were likely to have some experience with city life, even while retaining some memory—perhaps
their own, perhaps their parents'—of an earlier rural order. Whereas
the inhabitant of a small village would have been acquainted with the
same limited group of neighbors from birth, the city-dweller had to
interact with a dramatically larger number and variety of people. The
changes were qualitative as well as quantitative. The new urbanite
needed to learn to manage a wider spectrum of familiarities: from
almost anonymous interactions with unknown persons, to casual at-
tachments with acquaintances, to the intimate relationships among
family members and close friends. If, as apparently often happened,
a "vertical" change in class status accompanied "horizontal" or geo-
graphical displacement, the resulting disorientation must have been
even more acute.

Clues to such disorientation emerge in accounts of late sixteenth-

59. These population estimates are Roger Finlay's in his sophisticated study *Population and Metropolis: The Demography of London 1580–1650* (Cambridge: Cambridge
University Press, 1981).

century London life. In *A Notable Discovery of Cosenage*, Robert Greene describes how a couple of schemers plot to relieve a dupe of his money. Their preferred victim is a provincial: "a welchman . . . being a mere stranger in London, and not well acquainted with the English tongue," or "a plain country fellow well and cleanly apparelled, either in a coat of homespun russet, or of freize."[60] One of the group strikes up a conversation with this innocent, who guilelessly reveals his name, his place of residence, his kinsmen, and the names of his neighbors. The interlocutor conveys this information to an accessory, who approaches him separately and accosts him by name.

> The poor countryman hearing himself named by a man he knows not, marvels, and answers that he knows him not, and craves pardon. Not me goodman Barton, have you forgot me? Why I am such a man's kinsman, your neighbor not far off: how doth this or that good gentleman my friend? Good Lord that I should be out of your remembrance, I have been at your house diverse times. (19–20)

Greene's coseners self-consciously exploit rustic modes of identity formation based upon kinship relations, reputation among one's neighbors, and reciprocal acts of hospitality. They counterfeit social intimacy with one for whom that intimacy involves obligations; the "countryman" is led to feel that he *must* share a drink with a man whom he fails to recognize, but who knows his name and the names of his neighbors. The wiliness of the thieves is, Greene emphasizes, a distinctively urban trait, a product of the distance between emerging and traditional ways of life.

In what does this distance consist? Greene does not suggest that relationships in the city are consistently remote, or that each individual is isolated from all others. The coney-catching tracts testify to the efficient and profitable collusion among close-knit companies of rogues, giving samples of the dialect they use among themselves, their cryptic methods of recognizing one another, and so forth. The rustics are vulnerable, in fact, because they *imagine* that in London they are anonymous, unscrutinized, and thus free to indulge impulses of lust and greed they would prudently contain at home. In the trick called the "cross-bite," for instance, a prostitute lures a visiting bumpkin into her bed. Then a man with whom she is in collusion bursts into the room and claims to be her husband. He threatens legal reprisals,

60. Robert Greene, *A Notable Discovery of Cosenage* (London, 1581), ed. G. B. Harrison (New York: Barnes and Noble, 1966), pp. 31, 18.

but is eventually mollified by an additional payment. The cross-bite first extracts money from the dupe by allowing him to imagine himself as free of social controls, liberated into the pleasurable secrecy of the city. Then it suddenly reimposes those controls, and extracts money again. In another version of the trick, the whore's male accomplice pretends to be a summoner or parator—a representative of the ecclesiastical courts—whom the client bribes to overlook his offense and protect his good name. The criminals of Greene's coney-catching tracts circulate in a city not big enough to assure complete anonymity, but big enough to generate disproportions and unevenness in human beings' knowledge of one another. A person's reputation will naturally "carry" only so far, and beyond that circle he can plausibly improvise an identity which is difficult to corroborate. In such an environment it is not surprising that self-display and self-withholding should become calculated tactics, or that the art of self-deployment, though it might seem more naturally at home in courtly circles, should penetrate far down the social scale.

ℨ III ℬ

EARLIER I MENTIONED that some new-historicist and cultural-materialist critics of early modern English literature have tended to deny or downplay the significance of a rhetoric of inwardness in early modern England, even though evidence abounds for its importance in the period. I believe that this denial arises from, or is symptomatic of, a false sense of what is necessitated by the premises of cultural-materialist and new-historicist criticism. Despite differences in the details of their approaches, such critics characteristically work from philosophical positions that reject as illusory the possibility of a subjectivity prior to or exempt from social determination. That is, they are making a claim not only about English Renaissance subjectivity, but about subjectivity *tout court:* a claim "that the self," in Annabel Patterson's words, "is always necessarily a product of its relations."[61] At the same time, they want to resist speciously imputing modern assumptions about "the self" to a historically distant culture: they are especially suspicious of the kind of triumphantly individualist rhetoric that used to characterize a good deal of Renaissance history and literary criticism. Admitting the significance of conceptions of per-

61. Annabel Patterson, *Censorship and Interpretation: The Conditions of Writing and Reading in Early Modern England* (Madison: University of Wisconsin Press, 1984), p. 139.

sonal inwardness for the English Renaissance, they imagine, would be tantamount to embracing a naive essentialism about human nature.

This consequence simply does not follow, however. Perhaps the historicist argument makes the philosophical argument seem more plausible; for if our intuitions about subjectivity are demonstrably absent in other cultures or periods, then those intuitions are unlikely to represent transhistorical constants, or to reflect stubborn facts about human nature. But the philosophical argument does not need to be made in historicist terms—and in fact, in some of its most influential formulations is not so made—nor does the historicist project require this particular philosophical agenda.[62] The difference is worth keeping in mind, because philosophical claims about the necessarily social constitution of *any* subjectivity, Renaissance or modern, sometimes seem to get confused with historicist claims about an early modern form of subjectivity supposedly less inward-looking than our own.

Since, as we have seen, the idea of "inward truth" in early modern England is intimately linked to transcendental religious claims, antagonism to those claims perhaps contributes to the recent tendency to underestimate the conceptual importance of personal inwardness in this period. I share the religious incredulity of many new-historicist and cultural-materialist critics. I suspect, however, that if the religious categories in which the English Renaissance tried to comprehend itself often seem to us to involve glaring mystifications of social and political dynamics, so too our secularist interpretive axioms may blind us to their own explanatory limitations. Perhaps our suspicion of privacy, inwardness, subjectivity, soul, and so forth—our conviction that such terms beg to be debunked—has less to do with their inherently unsatisfactory features than with our sense of what counts as a satisfactory explanation. Perhaps it is not the people of early modern England but we, the postmodern academic heirs of Witt-

62. Various forms of the philosophical argument are made in general terms by such writers as Freud, Marx, Foucault, Lacan, Derrida, Dewey, and Wittgenstein; except in the case of Foucault, perhaps, their arguments do not stand or fall upon a particular reading of Renaissance culture. Anne Ferry makes a historicist argument without, apparently, sharing the philosophical agenda that motivates such critics as Barker or Belsey—although she, too, regards Renaissance conceptions of interiority as relatively undeveloped: "Only some poets, and those almost exclusively in sonnets, seemed to have concerned themselves with what a modern writer would call the *inner life*" (*The 'Inward' Language: Sonnets of Wyatt, Sidney, Shakespeare, Donne* [Chicago: University of Chicago Press, 1983], p. 14).

genstein, Lacan, Marx, Austin, and Foucault, who experience difficulty thinking of individuals apart from external matrices, who imagine "the supposedly 'private' sphere . . . only through its similarities and dissimilarities to the public world," and who are attracted to the notion that selves are void. If so, it is disingenuous to pretend that by discovering the externally constituted nature of Renaissance selves we have identified one feature of a great gulf set between "them" and "us."

So distinguishing between what I would call a "philosophical" argument and a "historical" one seems important. And this distinction is related to another: the difference between the origins of an idea and its effects once it becomes culturally available. The new-historicist critique insists, correctly in my view, that the "self" is not independent of or prior to its social context. Yet that critique often seems to assume that once this dependence is pointed out, inwardness simply vaporizes, like the Wicked Witch of the West under Dorothy's bucket of water. It may well be true that Renaissance notions of interior truth turn out to be philosophically defective: they are rarely elaborately or rigorously argued for. But lack of rigor neither limits the extent of, nor determines the nature of, the power such ideas can exert. Murkiness and illogicality may, in fact, enhance rather than limit their potency.

Instead of dismantling Renaissance distinctions between inward and outward, public and private, then, or evaluating their theoretical acceptability, I shall undertake a more pragmatic enterprise, analyzing some of the ways the distinction matters, and some of the ways in which it is used. What is at issue—ethically, politically, epistemologically, theologically—when someone in early modern England appeals to a difference between external show and form internal, or between outer and inner man? How are the boundaries drawn that separate what counts as "inside" from what counts as "outside"? How does the existence of such categories help shape thought and behavior? These investigations need not comprise a rejection, but rather an attempt to refine and advance a historically self-conscious discussion of the early modern period.

The range of materials I have briefly surveyed in this chapter already begins to suggest the importance in English Renaissance culture of two fantasies: one, that selves are obscure, hidden, ineffable; the other, that they are fully manifest or capable of being made fully manifest. These seem to be contradictory notions, but again and again they are voiced together, so that they seem less self-canceling than symbiotically related or mutually constitutive. Thomas Wright insists that "we cannot enter into a man's heart" in *The Passions of the Mind,* a treatise devoted to the techniques of mind-reading. Ralegh argues for the incommensurability of animal with human perception, and then guesses at what cats and goats might see as they look out of their peculiar eyes. Hamlet claims that theatrical externals conceal an inaccessible inwardness, but stages a play to discover his uncle's secrets. James I writes that a king "can never without secrecy do great things" only a couple of pages before describing him "as one set on a scaffold, whose smallest actions and gestures all the people gazingly do behold."[63] Thus the public domain seems to derive its significance from the possibility of privacy—from what is withheld or excluded from it—and vice versa. "Counsels if they be wrapped up in silence," writes the essayist Robert Johnson, "are very fortunately powerful in civil actions, but divulgated lose their force."[64] Just so, the revelatory power of theater is predicated upon disguising; just so, divine omniscience indicates, even as it repairs, the limitations of mortal vision.

The elaboration in early modern England of this dialectic of vision and concealment is surely an important chapter in the history of self-conceptions, whether we are inclined to see that history in terms of rupture or of continuities. At the same time I would emphasize that it is merely a chapter, not the whole story. For the "idea of the subject" is, in fact, not *an* idea, nor is it simply commensurate with the "inwardness" that is the subject of this book. "Subjectivity" is often treated casually as a unified or coherent concept when, in fact, it is a loose and varied collection of assumptions, intuitions, and practices that do not all logically entail one another and need not appear together at the same cultural moment. A well-developed rhetoric of inward truth, for instance, may exist in a society that never imagines that such inwardness might provide a basis for political rights. The intuition that sexual and family relations are "private" may, but need not, coincide with strong feelings about the "unity of the subject," or with convictions about the freedom, self-determination, or uniqueness of individuals, or with the sense that the self constitutes a form

63. James I and VI, *Basilikon Doron* (Edinburgh, 1595), pp. 119, 121.
64. Robert Johnson, *Essays* (London, 1601), F8ʳ-G1ʳ.

of property. It seems to me a mistake to assume that all these matters can be discussed at once, that they are necessarily part of the same cluster of ideas.

As will become clear in the chapters that follow, various forms of "privacy," "inwardness," and "individuality" are indeed sometimes associated, sometimes because they loosely imply one another, sometimes for purely contingent reasons. Yet their conceptual separability makes that association highly precarious, and they may diverge or come into conflict at critical junctures. As we shall see, for instance, both Kyd and Marlowe dramatize what might be called "individualism," but they differ drastically in what they consider an individual to be. Likewise, Jonson and Shakespeare both construe the sexual domain as a kind of metonymy of inward truth, but their notions of what that inwardness comprises are radically at variance.

My specific interest in the early modern rhetoric of inwardness, and my conviction that this interest is not commensurate with an interest in "subjectivity" per se, has significant methodological consequences. When I began thinking about the issues that shall concern me in this book, I gravitated toward psychoanalytic modes of explanation.[65] Psychoanalysis offered highly elaborate and specific ways of discussing the formation of subjectivity; distinguished critics had already demonstrated its usefulness to the analysis of Shakespearean drama and of spectatorial positioning in drama and film.[66] As my

65. In Katharine Eisaman Maus, "Horns of Dilemma: Jealousy, Gender, and Spectatorship in English Renaissance Drama," *ELH* 54 (1987): 561–83. Although some have argued that psychoanalysis is anachronistic when applied to Renaissance texts, that fact does not seem very compelling, since almost all our critical terminologies could be so criticized.

66. For influential book-length psychoanalytic accounts of Shakespeare plays, see, for instance, Janet Adelman, *The Common Liar: An Essay on Anthony and Cleopatra* (New Haven: Yale University Press, 1973) and *Suffocating Mothers: Fantasies of Maternal Origin in Shakespeare's Plays, Hamlet to the Tempest* (New York: Routledge, 1992); C. L. Barber and Richard Wheeler *The Whole Journey: Shakespeare's Power of Development* (Berkeley: University of California Press, 1986); Coppelia Kahn, *Man's Estate: Masculine Identity in Shakespeare* (Berkeley: University of California Press, 1981). For psychoanalytically inflected accounts of the experience of spectatorship in film and theater, see, for instance, Laura Mulvey, *Visual and Other Pleasures* (Bloomington: University of Indiana Press, 1989); Teresa de Lauretis, *Alice Doesn't: Feminism, Semiotics, Cinema* (Bloomington: University of Indiana Press, 1984) and *Technologies of Gender: Essays on Theory, Film, and Fiction* (Bloomington: University of Indiana Press, 1989); Barbara Freedman, *Staging the Gaze: Postmodernism, Psychoanalysis, and Shakespearean Comedy* (Ithaca: Cornell University Press, 1991).

sense of my project consolidated, however, I found psychoanalytic ways of thinking increasingly irrelevant to the particular problems I wished to investigate. Whereas my considerations are primarily epistemological (how can one person know another?), the primary concerns of psychoanalysis are developmental (how does a person constitute him or herself, or find him or herself configured by family dynamics and the processes of maturation). The etiological specificity of the psychoanalytic account—its privileging of the infant's early experience within the nuclear family, the supreme significance it accords to sexuality—eventually seemed too baroque and too tendentious for my purposes. Although I have no serious methodological quarrel with psychoanalysis, I simply found it dispensable, and usually unhelpful for describing the ubiquitous, powerful, culturally important, but ultimately fairly simple concepts I wanted to investigate.

In other ways, too, my project is a restricted, closely focused one. Since an anxiety about the epistemology of inwardness is not exclusively, or even primarily, a theatrical phenomenon, my emphasis upon dramatic literature in the following chapters to some extent reflects merely my own expertise and interests. In addition, however, the issues I investigate have a particular pertinence to the drama of the English Renaissance. Theater tends to be an art of collectives: groups of actors playing before large and varied groups of auditors. It would not be surprising if the complexities of intersubjective comprehension should be closer to the surface here, presented more immediately by the conditions of the performance, than they are in literary forms composed with particular patrons in mind, or designed to be enjoyed without any direct encounter between purveyor and consumer. Theater involves, too, a deliberate, agreed-upon estrangement of fictional surface from "truth": the plebeian actor concealing his identity under the language and manner of a king, the prepubescent boy donning Cleopatra's sumptuous robes, friends from the repertory company butchering one another in a staged duel. The dramatic techniques favored by English Renaissance dramatists further aggravate the relationship between spectacle and truth. Unlike the writer of romance or epic or lyric poem, a writer for the theater must take into account the limits upon what can be presented onstage. Some dramatic traditions address this problem by narrowing the range of appropriate plots and subjects: Continental neoclassicists endorse the unities of time and place, for instance, on the grounds that following these rules increases plausibility. But few English Renaissance playwrights accept such restrictions. Ambitious and wide-ranging, they inevitably encounter a gap between their limited theatrical resources and the extravagant situations they dramatize. English Renaissance theatrical method is thus radically synecdochic, endlessly referring the spectators to events, objects, situations, landscapes that cannot be shown them. We are provided not with pitched battles between rival armies but with "alarums within" and short representative skirmishes; not with people on horseback but with descriptions of people on horseback; not with an actual sexual act but with the preliminaries or consequences of a sexual relationship.[67]

In other words, the English Renaissance stage seems deliberately to foster theatergoers' capacity to use partial and limited presentations as a basis for conjecture about what is undisplayed or undisplayable. Its spectacles are understood to depend upon and indicate the shapes of things unseen. Critics like Francis Barker and Catherine Belsey, who have claimed that the Renaissance lacked a conception of inwardness, have pointed to the dominance of the theatrical mode in this period to support their point, connecting that dominance with a faith in the ultimate validity of what is displayed. I would argue just the opposite: that in a culture in which truth is imagined to be inward and invisible, and in which playwrights seem perversely to insist upon parading the shortcomings of their art, theatrical representation becomes subject to profound and fascinating crises of authenticity.

My focus upon the epistemological puzzles and pleasures of a performed art makes a particular range of extraliterary cultural phenomena especially relevant to my claims. Historians of private life, literary critics who analyze the development of a "speaking subject," often find it natural to dwell upon the moments in which intimacy seems to flower: examining such forms as the diary or the erotic lyric; such architectural developments as the bedroom, private dining room, or walled garden. But inwardness as it becomes a concern in the theater is always perforce inwardness displayed: an inwardness, in other words, that has already ceased to exist. The cultural institutions with which I shall concern myself, then, are those which share the peculiar

67. In "Falstaff Uncolted," *Shakespeare and the Revolution of the Times: Perspectives and Commentaries* (Oxford: Oxford University Press, 1976), pp. 121–30, Harry Levin shows how self-consciously Marlowe and Shakespeare play with the convention that horses never appear on stage. Tamburlaine harnesses men to his chariot. In *Richard III*, it is a foregone conclusion that no horse will materialize even when the hero is willing to trade his kingdom for one.

drawbacks and anxieties of the theatrical situation: they are highly public procedures of revelation, and the interiors they unveil often seem to be structured as much by those procedures as by their prior hidden content. Several chapters concern themselves with legal and quasilegal protocols for dealing with classes of crimes that surge in apparent importance and frequency in the early modern period. I think it is no coincidence that a period of great theater should also be "a great age of litigation," as Martin Ingram calls it, in which "the importance of law and legal institutions . . . is hard to exaggerate."[68] I should emphasize, however, that I do not insist upon a direct or unequivocal *influence* either from the theater to the courtroom or vice versa. Our relative lack of information about the details of most Renaissance trials renders this kind of claim tenuous or impossible to make. In chapter 4, for instance, I discuss Jonson's fascination with the impotence trial in *Epicoene*, a procedure with which he clearly had some familiarity—but the only extended record of an English impotence trial that has descended to us is the Essex divorce trial, conducted four years after *Epicoene*'s composition. Rather I would argue that the offenses of heresy, witchcraft, treason, impotence, fornication, and defamation, in the specific forms in which they were conceptualized in the Renaissance—by their elusiveness and susceptibility to camouflage, by the ease with which charges could be reversed, and by the paranoia consequent upon that elusiveness and reversibility—generate particular challenges to investigatorial procedures. In those very challenges, they clarify and complicate Renaissance paradigms for inward truth. It is those shared paradigms I wish to investigate, in their theatrical and extratheatrical manifestations.

The nature of my topic, because it requires collusion in the structures I am investigating, exacerbates the hermeneutically circular difficulties inherent in any process of interpretation. Inwardness, inaccessibility, invisibility, all seem to lose their authenticity as soon as they are advertised to or noted by another. The student of inwardness—playwright, inquisitor, or critic—annihilates the material, like a physicist who explodes subatomic particles in order to reveal the structure they supposedly used to possess. Moreover, the kinds of literary and theatrical phenomena I discuss are often impossible to recover with certainty even when they are not in principle

68. Martin Ingram, *Church Courts, Sex and Marriage in England, 1570–1640* (Cambridge: Cambridge University Press, 1987), pp. 27–28.

unknowable. Difficulties of retrieval have often been noted by historians interested in the mute inglorious majority of human beings in the English Renaissance—by scholars of women's history, for instance, or by those who attempt to investigate the vast, illiterate laboring classes.[69] Similar gaps and silences trouble anyone who wants to explore the epistemological problems posed in an art form for which we have few detailed contemporary accounts. What was it like to sit in the Globe or the Swan, to witness an early performance of *The Spanish Tragedy* or *Volpone?* Theater historians have helped establish some rough parameters for the experience, but most theater historians and virtually all critics of Renaissance plays commit themselves implicitly or explicitly to claims that necessarily exceed the archeological evidence. They speculate about what kinds of people attended the theater and what such people were likely to notice. They make assumptions about the ways in which plays structured the experience of spectators, and about the ways in which spectators may have resisted the imposition of that structure. My own methods are unavoidably involved in the same combination of suspicion and inductive empathy I shall be endeavoring to discuss. Perhaps, in fact, my interest in the purportedly omniscient but in fact deeply compromised and entangled investigator, an authorial self-characterization of endless appeal to Renaissance writers, fascinates me because of the self-reflexive insights it offers into my own critical operations upon a necessarily evanescent subject.

69. See, for instance, Peter Laslett, *Family Life and Illicit Love in Earlier Generations* (Cambridge: Cambridge University Press, 1977), pp. 15–24; Lawrence Stone, *Family, Sex, and Marriage in England: 1500–1800* (New York: Harper and Row, 1977), pp. 10–14; Susan Amussen, "Two Elizabeths," plenary lecture at the conference "Attending to Women," University of Maryland, November 1990.

ꙮ 2 ꙮ

MACHIAVELS AND FAMILY MEN

ꙮ I. The Age of Discovery ꙮ

On the English Renaissance stage the exorbitantly crafty "machiavel" personifies a radical, unprincipled estrangement of internal truth from external manifestation. A durable dramatic conception, the stage machiavel adapts himself to comedy as well as to tragedy, to bitter Jacobean satires as well as to bloody Elizabethan revenge plots. Kyd's Lorenzo and Marlowe's Barabbas beget Shakespeare's Richard III, Iago, and Edmund, Jonson's Volpone and Face, Chapman's Monsieur, Tourneur's D'Amville, Webster's Bosola, Massinger's Giles Overreach, and a host of others. Some critics have argued that English Renaissance dramatists were shallowly acquainted, if at all, with the Italian political theorist; others ascribe to at least some writers, like Marlowe, a serious engagement with the moral and intellectual challenges Machiavelli poses.[1] Still other critics have emphasized instead the indigenous theatrical origins of the stage machiavel, whose descent they trace from the allegorical vice-character of late-medieval morality plays.[2]

None of these accounts seem entirely satisfying. If playwrights are

1. The *locus classicus* of this view is Edward Meyer's *Machiavelli and the Elizabethan Drama* (Weimar, 1897); see also Mario Praz, "The Politic Brain: Machiavelli and the Elizabethans," in *The Flaming Heart* (New York: Doubleday, 1958), pp. 90–145, and Irving Ribner, "The Significance of Gentillet's *Contre-Machiavel,*" *Modern Language Quarterly* 10 (1949): 153–57. Margaret Scott reconsiders the issue of Machiavelli's direct influence in "Machiavelli and the Machiavel," *Renaissance Drama* new series 15 (1984): 147–73. Victoria Kahn's discussion of Machiavelli's reception, *Machiavellian Rhetoric: From the Counterreformation to Milton* (Princeton: Princeton University Press, 1994), although it pays scant attention to the drama, makes it clear that many English intellectuals read Machiavelli closely and intelligently.

2. The most impressive and fully documented version of this thesis is still Bernard Spivack, *Shakespeare and the Allegory of Evil* (New York: Columbia University Press, 1958). Despite their general similarities, vices are not quite the same as machiavels: Shakespeare's Falstaff, for instance, is describable as a vice but not as a machiavel; Kyd's Hieronimo, in *The Spanish Tragedy,* as a machiavel but not as a vice.

ignorant of Machiavelli, why do they pretend to have read him? Or, if they do read Machiavelli, why do they construe his theatrical usefulness in such a restricted, even peculiar, way? Or again, why should playwrights continue to create "vice-characters" after the specific dramatic purposes those characters serve have evaporated, along with the entire allegorical framework in which they were originally conceived? The genealogies critics have provided helpfully specify the machiavel's characteristics, but they hardly provide adequate accounts of where Renaissance playwrights acquired their ideas and dramatic conventions.

In fact, the figure of the sinister hypocrite turns up again and again not merely in Elizabethan and Jacobean plays, or in their immediate dramatic predecessors, but in sixteenth- and seventeenth-century writing of all kinds, both "literary" and "nonliterary," both impeccably canonical and now largely unread. Investigating the reasons for the perennial popularity of the "stage machiavel," then, requires going beyond questions of theatrical or intellectual influence in the narrow sense, and framing questions about the general disposition of early modern culture. It also requires perusing texts that rarely, if ever, have been imagined to pertain to the history of the drama. These works are interesting not because they are influential in any direct sense, but because they testify to a paranoia about hypocrisy and surveillance much too widespread to derive from a single text or author.

In 1556, for instance, with Mary Tudor on the English throne, the Catholic Myles Haggard attempted to justify her severity toward religious dissenters in a series of treatises. Haggard was an artisan, not a clergyman or professional intellectual, and the homely, informal style of his polemic made him one of the most effective propagandists for Mary's cause. His best-known book, *The Displaying of the Protestants*, opens with an extended analogy.

> Which protestants may aptly be compared to Plato his Gyges, the tale of whom Tully reciteth in his third book of his offices. At the falling down from above of certain storms of weather, the earth opened in diverse places, by reason of the drought before. Gyges being a king's shepherd, entered into the earth at a great hole, and found a brazen horse (as the fables declare) in whose sides were doors, which being opened, he espied the corse of a dead man of wonderful hugeness, and a gold ring upon his finger, which as soon as he pulled off, he put it upon his own. The nature of the ring was this: that when he had turned the head toward the palm of his hand, he was invisible, and

seen of nobody, and yet saw everything: and turning the ring from him again, he was seen of everybody. And so using the advantage of the ring, he lay with the queen wife to Candaules king of Lydia. So the Protestants, when it pleased God to plague this our country for the sin of the people, with the unquiet storms of heresy, got them out of the company of other shepherds, and dispersed themselves into the earth, and at length entered into brazen horses, the houses of the chief governors then, abusing the same with false interpretation of God's word. ... Then these shepherds perceiving the chief magistrates prone to sundry alterations and novelties, began by little and little also to corrupt the consciences of the vulgar people, infecting the same with the poison of heretical doctrine, that at length they became altogether dead corses of wonderful hugeness. Then framed they rings to seem invisible to the world: then played they Gyges part, then ruled they the roost. (6–7)[3]

Haggard's allegorizing is ungainly, to say the least. He insists upon a point-by-point resemblance between Gyges and the Protestants, but that resemblance keeps breaking down in its details. The brazen horse, concealed in a hole, incongruously becomes a nobleman's house populated with magistrates. Gyges's solitary quest becomes a collective affair: numerous Protestant shepherds diverge in search of multiple brazen horses. Whereas Gyges finds a dead corpse with a ring on its finger, the Protestants poison people and manufacture magic rings.

Why, then, use the Gyges story at all? Several aspects of the narrative recommend themselves to Haggard. Gyges, an ordinary man, descends into a space trauma has made newly accessible. He enters interiors nested one inside the other: the cave, then the hollow horse. There he acquires a magical power by uncanny and perhaps unethical means (is the ring stolen, or is it his by rights?). His magic is a control over vision: "he was invisible, and seen of nobody, and yet saw everything." In Gyges's hands, such power disrupts fundamental social relationships: between subject and ruler, between husband and wife. Eventually, Haggard tells us later in his treatise, Gyges murders his king.

For Haggard, the Gyges legend is a story about hypocrisy, and about the particular challenge that the hypocrite presents to a Chris-

---

3. For an account of Haggard's career and a list of his surviving works, see J. W. Martin, "Miles Hogarde: Artisan and Aspiring Author in Sixteenth-Century England," *Religious Radicals in Tudor England* (London: Hambledon Press, 1989), pp. 83–105. The name is variously spelled Haggard, Haggarde, Huggarde, Hogarde.

tian world view. The hypocrite acts as if the only witnesses to his actions are human witnesses. If God exists, this working premise is an extremely dangerous one: "The liar," as Montaigne writes, "is a coward towards men and a boaster before God."[4] Yet the idea has its attractions. Now and then, it occurs to even the most convinced theists that the divine supervisor might not really be out there at all, or might not be watching on every occasion. Perhaps, in fact, the possibility of evaporation or inattention is irresistibly insinuated by the very idea of such a supervisor.

Renaissance Christians are obliged to withstand such subversive suggestions with all the faith they can muster. For once one's vivid sense of the divine witness is lost, most Renaissance religious writers agree, one plummets immediately into moral chaos. Only God's continuous discipline over the hidden interiors of human beings keeps them virtuous, for the innately corrupt human imagination can always find a way to evade or ignore frail external controls. That is the lesson of the Old Testament, which shows the Jews violating God's commandments again and again until God at last redrafts His covenant with man in the New Testament to emphasize renovation from within.

Thus the Catholic Haggard, taking the story of Gyges from a classical source, reformulates its message. Plato and Cicero use the story of Gyges to show what (and how rare) true virtue is. They contrast ordinary good behavior, grounded in the fear of getting caught, with real honesty, a radically untheatrical matter, requiring neither divine nor human onlookers. But for Renaissance Christians, virtue is the effect of a carefully cultivated paranoia. "There is not a more effectual means to persuade us to obedience," writes Thomas Cooper, "than that the eye of God is continually upon us."[5] Virtue requires God's surveillance in order to exist, as the falling tree needs to be overheard in order to make a sound. So hypocrisy becomes not merely the concealment of one's motives from other human beings, but an implicit denial of God's existence and a subversive assumption of the divine prerogative. Accordingly, Haggard makes another change in his source. In *De Officiis*, Cicero does not mention that Gyges's ring endows him with special powers of discernment; it merely makes him

4. John Florio, trans., *The Essayes of Michael Lord of Montaigne* (London: Grant Richards, 1908), p. 491. Francis Bacon quotes this apothegm in his essay "On Truth."
5. Thomas Cooper, *The romish spider, with his web of treason, woven and broken* (London, 1606), D4ᵛ.

invisible. Nor is it necessary that Gyges "see everything" in order to accomplish his aims. In Haggard's account, though, invisibility and omniscience go hand in hand, the inseparable divine attributes that the hypocrite attempts to commandeer.

Thus hypocrisy and atheism are often nearly synonymous in the Renaissance imagination. Hypocrites "say in effect, that none shall see them, and so they do put out the eye of God's providence, and thereupon conclude indeed, that there is no God."[6] Renaissance religious controversialists tend to accuse their antagonists of being knaves, not fools: artists of deception, not misguided enthusiasts or the victims of pernicious environments. Haggard warns that the Protestants "seem to the world to be godly, although in deed quite contrary to the thing they pretend."[7] For the Protestant J. Baxter, the Catholics are "foxes, wolves in sheep's clothing, false horned lambs, masking hypocrites, deceitful workmen, crafy companions, cosening knaves."[8] The Anglican Samuel Harsnett adheres to the *via media,* attacking the Jesuits on the one hand as "imposturing renegadoes," and the Puritan exorcist John Darrell on the other as "a counterfeiting hypocrite."[9]

What does the Gyges story reveal about the structure of hypocrisy? Gyges is merely a shepherd, but the magical ring he discovers in the secret interior allows him shocking liberty from the prescriptions of his social role. For Haggard, that lack of restraint is an essential connection between his story and the pretensions of the Protestants. Protestant children, Haggard tells us, revile their parents; wives defy the authority of their husbands; subjects rebel against their prince; the king replaces his wife with a strumpet: "The true religion of this realm ... of late was put to exile, and in stead of the same a strange and base woman called Heresy entertained, who hath so polluted this country with bastards and misbegotten children." In this passage the connection between Henry's divorce and his religious innovation is not merely coincidental, but absolutely intrinsic: Anne Boleyn and the "strange and base woman called Heresy" are one and the same. The Reformation disrupts social and familial relationships at every

6. Cooper, *The romish spider,* D3ʳ.
7. Myles Haggard, *The displaying of the protestants* (London, 1556), M7ʳ.
8. J. Baxter, *A toile for two-legged foxes, for encouragement against all popish practices* (London, 1600), p. 26.
9. Samuel Harsnett, *A declaration of egregious popish impostures* (London, 1603), A3ʳ; *A discovery of the fraudulent Practises of J. Darrel* (London, 1599), p. 78.

level, and Haggard offers that disruption as proof of Protestant depravity.

The general characteristics of Haggard's polemic have little to do with doctrinal differences between Catholics and Protestants. Protestant propaganda against Catholics in general and Jesuits in particular accuses them of precisely the same scandals Haggard associates with Protestantism. An anonymous anti-Jesuit tract advises its readers that the French superiors of the order "have vaults, yea they have secret places underground" in which they can practice all kinds of violence and sexual excess without being detected. One of them, Father Coton, possesses "a looking-glass of Astrology, wherein he made the King to see plainly whatsoever his Majesty desired to know, and . . . there is nothing so secret, nor anything propounded in the privy councils of other monarchs, which may not be seen or discovered by the means of this celestial or rather devilish glass."[10] Just as in Haggard, the effect of a Gyges-like combination of omniscience and concealment is an opportunistic disruption of kinship networks and social hierarchy. For Haggard, Protestantism is the interloping harlot who ruins the royal marriage between England and the Church. For Joseph Hall, Catholicism is "that courtesan of Rome" who "sets herself out to sale in tempting fashion; here want no colors, no perfumes, no wanton dresses; whereas the poor spouse of Christ can only say of herself, 'I am black, but comely.'"[11] Meredith Hamner, another Protestant polemicist, reproaches a Pope who "hath set the mother against her own son, the son to take armor against his own father, the subject against the prince, and the princes together at mortal wars."[12] English Catholics wander abroad and forget their native allegiances; Catholic priests use the privacy of the confessional to seduce wives and maidens, and to steal the patrimonies of whole families.

Such polemics postulate a kind of enemy whose inward truth is hidden: hypocrites, magicians, con men, whores. An identity predicated upon this sinister interiority competes with and undermines another kind of identity, founded upon the individual's place in social hierarchies and kinship networks. Thus in the polemical tracts, the hypocrite's realization of his internal resources seems profoundly

10. Anon., *A discoverie of the most secret and subtile practises of the Jesuites* (1610), B2ʳ.

11. Joseph Hall, *Quo vadis? A just censure of travell* (London, 1617), pp. 15–16.

12. Meredith Hanmer, *The great Bragge and challenge of M. Champion a Jesuite, commonly called Edmund Campion* (London, 1581), p. 17.

subversive. But none of the polemicists address, in abstract terms, the interaction between a subjectivity of inwardness and a subjectivity of relationship. Their avoidance of the topic is not surprising, because for neither Catholics nor Protestants are blood relations or social status ultimate determinants of identity. The Old Testament commands believers to "honor thy father and thy mother," and the Old Testament God chooses His people by their pedigree. But Christ, insisting upon the universality of his message, discounts the importance of kinship, bloodline, and status: "I have come to set a man against his father, and a daughter against her mother, and a daughter-in-law against her mother-in-law. . . . He who loves father or mother more than me is not worthy of me; and he who loves son or daughter more than me is not worthy of me"(Matthew 10:35–38).

In consequence, although all parties in sixteenth- and early seventeenth-century religious polemic decry their enemies' defiance of kinship obligations and social hierarchy, they are willing to encourage and admire that lack of respect in their coreligionists. In *Acts and Monuments* John Foxe dilates almost endlessly upon the martyrs' leavetaking of their families, friends, and congregations, reprinting their final letters, detailing their last farewells. When Rowland Taylor, a minister, is led out of jail toward the place of execution, his family waits by the roadside hoping to catch a glimpse of him.

> Elizabeth cried, saying, "O my dear father! mother, mother, here is my father led away." Then cried his wife, "Rowland, Rowland, where art thou?"—for it was a very dark morning, that the one could not see the other. Dr. Taylor answered, "Dear wife, I am here;" and stayed.
> . . .Then came she to him, and he took his daughter Mary in his arms, and he, his wife, and Elizabeth, kneeled down and said the Lord's prayer. At which sight the sheriff wept apace, and so did divers others of the company. After they had prayed, he rose up and kissed his wife, and shook her by the hand, and said, "Farewell, my dear wife, be of good comfort, for I am quiet in my conscience. God shall stir up a father for my children." (6.694)

This touching scene and its hundreds of variants in *Acts and Monuments* emphasize both that the martyr has something to lose and that he is willing to lose it; they focus the pathos and the heroism of his terrible choice. At a certain point even the closest and most loving human connections become impediments. When Nicholas Ridley is burned in Oxford, Foxe writes, his distraught brother-in-law stands beside the fire and heaps faggots upon him in a humane attempt to ensure that he is killed quickly. But he only succeeds in smothering the flames and prolonging the poor man's agony.

The Marian persecution, Foxe emphasizes, makes no distinction of class or gender in its victims: it condemns old and young, poor and exalted, men and women, ministers and laypeople. On the Isle of Guernsey, he informs us, the Catholics burn a mother and her two grown daughters, one of whom is pregnant. When the pregnant woman's torments induce her to give birth at the stake, one of the onlookers snatches the infant out of the fire and lays it upon the grass; but the bailiff orders it cast back upon the pyre.[13] In Derby, the Catholics burn a poor blind woman; in Barking, a sixty-eight-year-old cripple and a blind man. In London, Bishop Bonner whips an eight-year-old boy to death.

> I know not whether more to marvel at the great and unsearchable mercies of God (with whom there is no respect in degrees of persons, but he chooseth as well the poor, lame, and blind, as the rich, mighty and healthful, to set forth his glory), or else to note the unreasonable or rather unnatural doing of these unmerciful catholics . . . in whom was so little favor or mercy to all sorts and kinds of men, that also they spared neither impotent age, neither lame nor blind.[14]

A ghastly mirror-image of God's universal love, the inclusiveness of the Marian persecution both confirms the wickedness of the inquisitors and offers democratizing opportunities for heroism among the lower orders—"the poor, simple and inferior sort of people (I mean in degree, though God be praised, not in steadfastness)."[15] The hostile Haggard accuses lower-class Protestants of insolence, of trying by their grand deaths to escape the limitations of their class origins. Later in the century, such Protestants as Anthony Munday and Samuel Harsnett likewise attack "the glorious ostentation" of Catholic priests bound for execution.[16]

For Foxe, the heroism of the Marian martyrs testifies to the effectiveness of a Protestant doctrinal emphasis upon the inner man, and to its concern for a personal relationship to God unmediated by ecclesiastical hierarchy. He implies that Catholics, addicted to merely ex-

---

13. Foxe, *Acts and Monuments of these latter and perilous days* . . . (New York: AMS Press, 1965), 8.229–30.

14. Foxe, *Acts and Monuments*, 8.140.

15. Foxe, *Acts and Monuments*, 7.715.

16. Harsnett, *A declaration of egregious popish impostures*, A3ᵛ.

ternal gauds and shows, would not possess the personal resources to sustain such zeal. But Foxe can arrogate the heroism of martyrdom to his own cause only because he imagines the difference between true and false religion in a way that presupposes the empty frivolousness of the rival faith. In fact, the Catholic *Treatise of Renunciation* is just as firm as Foxe is in the order of its priorities.

> Where do we not see, that either parents by children, or children by parents: husbands by wives, or wives by husbands: one friend by another: the subject, by the superiors and superiors by subjects, are hindered from the service of God? . . . as though either wives had sold both body and soul to be by their husbands mortgaged to perpetual slavery of the devil; or parents had authority to kill the souls of their children over whose bodies they have no such power: or those which are as it were God's lieutenants in their several offices, might convert their forces to fight for hell, and lawfully constrain their soldiers and subjects to rebel against God; or finally as if there were any perfect friendship where there wanteth honesty.[17]

The martyr, or even the ordinary sincere Catholic, must be willing to renounce his nearest and dearest in order to remain true to convictions imagined as lodged in his depths. "He is a true pilgrim in this world, who like unto one of a strange language, amongst men of an unknown tongue, only dwelleth at home in the knowledge of himself."[18] Significantly, in these positive accounts of conscience pursued to its heroic limits, the subjectivity of inwardness and the subjectivity of social relationships are still imagined as mutually antagonistic, just as they are in the Gyges legend. The signs of moral valence have been reversed, but the structure of opposition remains the same.

The fact that Catholics and Protestants draw their rhetorical weapons from the same arsenal frequently produces marked peculiarities of tone. Haggard ferociously attacks the motives of Mary's victims, but has trouble showing how they differ from the Catholic martyrs under Henry and Edward, whom he holds up for admiration. In *The Fiery Trial of God's Saints* T. Purfoot attempts to justify the persecution of Catholics under Elizabeth and James, claiming that it has been insignificant compared to the persecution of Protestants under Mary. At the end of the volume, to prove his point, he lists by the year of

17. Anon., *A treatise of renunciation*, 1600, pp. 8–9. This treatise is convincingly attributed to Henry Garnet by Anthony Allison in "The Writings of Fr. Henry Garnet, S. J. (1555–1606)," *Biographical Studies* 1 (1951): 7–21.

18. *A treatise of renunciation*, p. 59.

their deaths all those who have been executed for religious crimes from the mid-sixteenth century to the first decade of the seventeenth century. The unintentional effect of his format is to indicate clearly how the oppression of Catholics accelerates in the 1580s and 1590s, and to make the later "traitors," the Jesuits and the recusants, look exactly like the Protestant "martyrs" with whom they are supposed to be contrasted. Even the typefaces in which their names are printed are identical.

In fact, the extravagant hypocrites of the religious polemics are the evil twins, as it were, of saints and martyrs. They personify the dark underside of a positive theology of interior conviction. Instead of the inner man, Gyges unearths a monstrous corpse, festering with subversive promise. The privacy of the self, the inaccessibility to others of the space in which one's innermost beliefs are lodged, is the precondition for a commitment to truths imagined to transcend evanescent social circumstances. But in this world, those commitments can be faked. The opposition between inside and outside is subject to manipulation and abuse.

The tactics of the religious polemicists, therefore, must be tactics of exposure. Haggard assaults the pretensions of the Protestants by "displaying" them, by making Gyges visible. Harsnett disables the impostures of the Jesuits by "discovering" them. Cooper, celebrating King James's delivery from the Catholic perpetrators of the Gunpowder Plot, prays that in his writing "the deepness of Satan may be discovered, and the inmost secret of the iniquity of his instruments may be thoroughly laid open."[19] A poetic account of the same event compares Catholics to owls, predatory at night, but after daybreak rendered powerless by the gaze of Protestant "light-embracing fowls."[20] The procedures of discovery bring socially acknowledged externals into alignment with internal truths.

The epistemological utility of "discovery" goes far beyond narrowly religious applications. Renaissance philosophical treatises, how-to manuals, miscellanies, jokebooks, accounts of crimes and scandals: all typically create powerful motives for readerly attention by rehearsing distinctions between external falsity and internal truth—and by rehearsing them, seeming to promise their erasure. They advertise themselves on their title pages as "brief discoveries,"

19. Cooper, *The romish spider*, K1ʳ.
20. H. I., *The Devil of the Vault* (London, 1606), C2ʳ.

"anatomies," "displayings," and "detections." They take as axiomatic the claim that "there is more peril in close fistulas, than outward sores, in secret ambush, than main battles."[21] Even vision itself can become the object of this kind of suspicion: George Hakewill, in a discussion of hallucinations and optical illusions, proposes "ripping up, and searching out the abuse of the eye."[22]

The first paragraph of Thomas Lodge's *Wit's Misery and the World's Madness* (London, 1596) is typical. "Conjecturing men's inward affections by their outward actions," Lodge concludes almost immediately that "the Epicure conceited not so many imaginary worlds, as this world containeth incarnate devils." Lodge imagines that his reader will dispute this claim. "Incarnate devils, quoth you; why there are none such." But of course, Lodge continues, incarnate devils are superficially indistinguishable from ordinary human beings. They look *exactly like us,* but in their incalculable depths they are wicked and alien.

Lodge may seem to be contradicting himself. At first he suggests that inward affections may be discerned by the evidence of outward actions, in which case the problem of falsification seems negligible. Then he maintains that it is not, in fact, possible to make inferences reliably, in which case his original assurance is called into question. But the argument is not meant to be logical. By representing the interior as simultaneously visible to the knowledgeable author and invisible to the innocent reader, Lodge lays claim to an expertise that makes his treatise seem worth perusing. Having aroused suspicion, he immediately promises to allay it: "Come, come, let us take the painting from this foul face, pull off the cover from this cup of poison, rip up the covert of this bed of serpents, and we shall discover that palpably, which hath long time been hidden cunningly. How? say you. Marry, thus, if you please." The strategies of "discovery" aggravate paranoia—how are readers to diagnose a "close fistula," or predict a secret ambush? But the same tactics alleviate uncontrolled suspicion, promising readers precisely the guidance they require.

As the veils are torn away, naive complacency, which leaves the

21. Stephen Gosson, *The schoole of abuse* (London, 1582), C4ᵛ. Devon Hodges, in *Renaissance Fictions of Anatomy* (Amherst: University of Massachusetts Press, 1985), provides a helpful discussion of some of the strategies of cutting open and unveiling that I discuss here, and an interesting account of the relationship between such popular rhetorical techniques and the new medical interest in the dissection of cadavers.

22. George Hakewill, *The vanity of the eye* (Oxford, 1615), p. 10.

reader vulnerable to all kinds of imposition, is replaced by the sophisticated pleasure of awareness. At such moments, knowledge-bliss can virtually overwhelm indignation. In Robert Greene's coney-catching pamphlets, satiric outrage dissolves into an affectionate celebration of London's minor criminals, as well as of the unexpected cunning of those victims who manage to turn the tables upon them. In Reginald Scot's *The Discovery of Witchcraft* the exposure of papistical frauds and unscrupulous charlatans becomes so detailed, and so blackly comic, that Scot needs to intervene to remind his readers and, probably, himself, that witchcraft prosecutions were matters of life and death for the defendants.

A tendency to get caught up in the elaborate secrets one is supposed to be obliterating is only one of the problems the discoverer confronts. At least as important is the problem of establishing his own reliability. For only if the author is himself omniscient is his "discovery" unimpeachable. Since false pretensions to omniscience are precisely what are being exposed, the object of investigation makes claims parodically close to the investigator's. When Haggard gives an overview of Gyges's career, in other words, he suspiciously resembles Gyges himself.

Often the polemicists try to shore up their authority by associating their discoveries with truths revealed by divine providence. For Catholics, the Protestant enemy is consummately personified by Francis Walsingham, Elizabeth I's master of espionage, who sets spies upon Catholics and suspected Catholics in order to gather evidence against them. Walsingham is, for a time, the successfully unseen spectator, the terrifying Gyges who turns his secret knowledge to worldly gain. But on his deathbed, urine erupts from his nose and mouth.[23] At the last moment, God presses Walsingham's stinking interior out into common view.

Of course, claims of divine assistance can be pretenses too. They are routinely counterfeited by one's enemies. Thus when Samuel Harsnett accuses Catholic priests of forging exorcisms, he aligns himself with the authority of the omniscient God who discovers their devilish duplicity. But the Catholics reply that Harsnett himself is in the devil's service: that he is possessed by spirits of lust and envy, who deny his need for their exorcising rituals. And the Puritan John Darrell re-

---

23. Anon., *A declaration of the true causes of the great troubles presupposed to be intended against the realm of England* (1592), p. 54.

sponds to Harsnett's "discovery" with *A Detection of That Sinful and Ridiculous Discourse of S. Harsnett*. Satirical exposure would like to demonstrate the difference between truth and its structurally similar parodies, a difference which must be grounded in a transcendental truth. But the transcendental truth is by its nature absent, and hence always a subject for dispute. The frenzied rhetoric of religious polemic recognizes this endlessly regressive hermeneutic dilemma, even as it attempts to ward off its implications.

⟡ II. MYSELF ALONE: RICHARD III AS STAGE MACHIAVEL ⟡

THE RELIGIOUS CONTROVERSIES I have been discussing were waged intermittently throughout the sixteenth and seventeenth centuries, but the polemical battles grew particularly heated in the latter part of Elizabeth's reign. In 1571, the Papal bull *regnans in excelsis* excommunicated Elizabeth and pronounced that her subjects were no longer bound to acknowledge her authority. In the following three decades, various Catholic plots to dethrone Elizabeth in favor of Mary Queen of Scots, the influx of English Jesuits trained on the Continent, the dispatch of the Spanish Armada, and a series of open exhortations to rebellion by some English Catholics living in exile, all sharpened Protestant paranoia about Catholicism and intensified the persecution of English Catholics. At the same time, left-wing Protestants were mounting a different kind of threat, organizing secretly in an attempt to take over the institutions of the Church of England from within.[24] The Renaissance public theater originates during these ideologically turbulent years, and I think it is no coincidence that the major achievements of this theater offer occasions to reflect upon the same epistemological perplexities that afflict doctrinal controversy in the period.

Like religious polemic which ascribes political and epistemological disruptions to malignant hypocrites, the drama imagines such perplexities as in the first instance problems about the structure of character. The "machiavel" in English Renaissance theater is a *kind of person,* not primarily an exponent of particular political views. Like Gyges, the stage machiavel uses his own inwardness, his invisibility to others, to undermine social networks and the kinds of identity that

24. For a discussion of this effort, called the *classis* movement, see M. M. Knappen, *Tudor Puritanism: A Chapter in the History of Idealism* (Chicago: University of Chicago Press, 1970), pp. 284–302.

can be founded upon those networks. Religious controversialists emphasize that the hypocritical adherents to the enemy faith promote dissent because they personally benefit from social unrest, presumably at the expense of the majority. Likewise, the ambitious machiavels who populate Renaissance plays are often those whose marginality or subjugation gives them little motive to acquiesce in the status quo: racial or class interlopers, bastards, displaced gentlemen. Yet even machiavels who seem most privileged by the established social system, like Kyd's Lorenzo or Jonson's Volpone, insist upon their own distance from other people.

Shakespeare's Richard III, a particularly clear and well-elaborated example of the stage machiavel, disowns his kin in a typical gesture well before he obtains the throne:

> I have no brother, I am like no brother;
> And this word 'love', which greybeards call divine,
> Be resident in men like one another,
> And not in me. I am myself alone.
> (*3 Henry VI* 5.5.80–83)

Richard sets himself apart from other men in two related senses. "Love," as an emotional characteristic and as a relationship, both makes men similar to one another and makes them seek one another out. An intuition of sameness allows them to deny or bridge the gaps among them. Richard's difference from other men creates and is constituted by an absolute barrier between self and others, all imagined as equally remote: "Be resident in men like one another, / And not in me." This is self-description, but it is also a command; Richard banishes love even as he claims he does not possess it. Being "myself" thus entails being "alone." The self-interestedness of the machiavel is bound up with a particular, restricted notion of what selves might be: atomized, alienated, concerned with other people only insofar as they can be intimidated, manipulated, or astonished. But the machiavel's self-interest is simultaneously bound up with a restricted notion of what selves might *need*. If one's requirements were understood differently—if, for instance, one craved intimate and trusting relationships with other people more than one craved power over them—then self-interestedness, too, would have to be differently defined.

In the *Henry VI* plays, Shakespeare shows such a self-conception in the process of evolution. Although in retrospect both Richard and his victims enjoy describing him as morally defective from birth, in fact his "machiavellianism" emerges rather slowly. The initial hostilities in the Wars of the Roses pit the Lancasters against the Yorks, two branches of the same extended family. At this stage, fierce coterie allegiances seem to compensate for the neglect of larger-scale, more distant forms of confederation. Individuals pour their energies into securing the triumph of their particular factions, identifying themselves by red and white roses, the totemic emblems of their clans. The young Richard thus figures as a loyal, if ruthless, son to Richard of York, and brother to Edward, Clarence, and Rutland.

A combination of fidelity to the small family unit and treachery to the large is, however, a highly unstable social configuration. In the middle of *Henry VI, Part 3*, it begins to collapse. Having secured a victory over King Henry, King Edward sends his most loyal supporter, Warwick, on an ambassadorial mission to obtain the princess Bona of France as his queen; but while Warwick is away, Edward impulsively marries a commoner. Offended, Warwick revolts to King Henry's side, temporarily joined by Edward's brother Clarence, who marries Warwick's daughter. Under these circumstances, with kinship lines hopelessly entangled and compromised, the logic of the family feud becomes impossible to sustain. Just at this point, Richard begins to articulate his "machiavellianism"; in other words, he becomes a machiavel when his brothers' actions destroy the possibility of an identity founded upon an allegiance to the nuclear family. The pattern resembles Haggard's story of Gyges: social trauma, by forcing or allowing individuals to venture from the group, makes available a kind of inwardness that, in turn, powerfully outrages social order.

By recognizing, or constructing, a boundary isolating himself from other people, the machiavel enables himself to organize his behavior on the basis of the difference between what he knows about himself and what others can learn of him. In relation to the other characters, he exploits the invisibility of his own interior.

> Why, I can smile, and murder while I smile,
> And cry 'Content!' to that which grieves my heart,
> And wet my cheeks with artificial tears,
> And frame my face to all occasions.
> I'll drown more sailors than the mermaid shall;
> I'll slay more gazers than the basilisk;

I'll play the orator as well as Nestor,
Deceive more slily than Ulysses could
And, like a Sinon, take another Troy.
                              (*3 Henry VI* 3.2.18–90)

Openly violent earlier in the play, Richard learns to elaborate an innocuous surface while pursuing his aggressions where they cannot be detected. This new skill enables him, like the invisible Gyges, to circumvent the ordinary social restraints upon his behavior, and his subsequent career rehearses Gyges's almost exactly: the seduction of a predecessor's wife, regicide, usurpation. In *Richard III*, malevolent hypocrisy is not merely an attribute of the tyrant, but virtually the definition of tyranny as it is exercised in the play: a private whim executed in secret without regard to publicly accepted laws.

We have already seen that when the true interior is conceptually separated from the visible exterior, problems of evaluating the truth of any claim about that interior immediately arise. The religious controversialists endlessly accuse their enemies of fraudulence, but the ascription can never be proven, and is always susceptible to reversal. Richard routinely capitalizes upon this hermeneutic dilemma for his own purposes, hypocritically telling Prince Edward, for instance, that Edward's immaturity prevents him from recognizing the hypocrisy of Richard's enemies. Richard's courtship of Anne relies even more brazenly upon the same strategy. He presents himself to her as a strong silent type on the verge of breakdown. None of the disasters of war—his brother's death, or his father's—were able to make him weep:

                    In that sad time
        My manly eyes did scorn an humble tear.
                              (1.2.163–64)

But Anne's beauty, he maintains, has "drawn" from him, has "exhaled" (that is, pulled out) both tears and pleas.

Richard's soldierly, undemonstrative surface conceals, he claims, an enormous tenderness; but of course if his surface were really entirely undemonstrative, that tenderness could never declare itself. Richard must theatrically parade his own supposed emotional repression at the moment of its putative release. He weeps what Eve Sedgwick, in her analysis of early twentieth-century sentimentality, sarcastically calls "the sacred tears of the heterosexual man." His overwrought stoicism incarnates what Sedgwick describes as the exemplary instance of the sentimental: "the body of a man who . . . physically dramatizes . . . a struggle of masculine identity with emotions or physical stigmata stereotyped as feminine."[25] The power of this dramatization, in the sixteenth century or in the twentieth, lies in its privileging of a putative interior. The tears are moving not for their own sake—they are almost by definition trivial—but because they hint thrillingly at huge mute passions lurking just beneath the surface.

Richard kneels at Anne's feet, asking her to open him up.

> If thy revengeful heart cannot forgive,
> Lo, here I lend thee this sharp-pointed sword,
> Which, if thou please to hide in this true breast
> And let the soul forth that adoreth thee,
> I lay it naked to the deadly stroke.
>
> (1.2.173–77)

Of course Richard's interior does not exist, at least not as he has constituted it in this speech, but Anne cannot know whether it does or not, and Richard knows that she cannot know. Baring his breast to her, pleading for a murderous "discovery," Richard devises a false theater of exposure. Anne recognizes the possibility of hoax:

> ANNE: I would I knew your heart.
> RICHARD: 'Tis figured in my tongue.
> ANNE: I fear me both are false.
> RICHARD: Then never was man true.
>
> (1.2.192–95)

But by this point she is close to capitulation, having allowed herself to be distracted from her initial clearheaded focus upon Richard's previous butchery to a futile inquiry into the undecidable depths of his inner nature. One irony here is, of course, that Richard's nature is actually fully apparent: "as crooked in thy manners as thy shape," Clifford calls him in 2 Henry VI (5.1.158). In fact, Richard's external distortion bodies forth moral deformity. Yet the theoretical separability of the inside from the outside means that the equivalence can never be made with any certainty.

Richard's downfall results not from tactical inconsistency or loss of nerve, but because contradictions in the way his inwardness is con-

25. Sedgwick, *The Epistemology of the Closet* (Berkeley: University of California Press, 1990), pp. 144–45.

stituted become increasingly oppressive. From the hypocrite's point of view, the most obvious problem with the personal interior is that everybody can have one. The stupider characters in the play find this elementary fact difficult to grasp. Even after he has perjured himself Hastings cannot imagine that other people share his capacity for prevarication, and so he trusts the Richard he thinks he knows:

> I think there's never a man in Christendom
> Can lesser hide his love or hate than he,
> For by his face straight shall you know his heart.
>
> (3.4.50–53)

Richard takes advantage of Hastings' ingenuousness, accusing him, in a typical act of cunning displacement, of "daubing his vice with show of virtue," and packing him off to execution. Nonetheless, as the play grinds on, other people learn to use Richard's tactics against him. Queen Elizabeth successfully bluffs in the marriage negotiations for Princess Elizabeth. As civil war breaks out once more, "doubtful hollow-hearted friends," most notably Lord Stanley, desert to Richmond's side.

Another increasingly urgent problem is the tendency for the liberated, alienated subjectivity to convert itself into guilty secrecy. Imprisoned in the Tower, the claustrophobic setting for many of the deaths in *Richard III*, Clarence dreams prophetically of his own drowning shortly before his murderers arrive.

> often I did strive
> To yield the ghost; but still the envious flood
> Stopped in my soul, and would not let it forth
> To find the empty, vast, and wandering air,
> But smothered it within my panting bulk,
> Who almost burst to belch it in the sea.
>
> (1.4.36–41)

Drowning, for the secretly culpable Clarence, entails a desperate but futile attempt to get free of a "smothered" interior he identifies with life itself, but which at the same time seems to be killing him. Pain is not the consequence of dying—imagined literally as an expiration, a release of breath into emptiness—but of being compelled to remain conscious and individuated by a frightful pressure from the outside.

This paradoxical torment is not Clarence's alone. Representations of the afterlife in *Richard III* seem flatly contradictory. On the one hand the dead are consigned to the silent, solitary confinement of the grave, as cramped and dark as the "guilty closures" of Pomfret or the Tower of London. On the other hand the dead have a weird unfastened quality: troubled ghosts, released from their bodies, wander without apparent destinations. The disparity registers quite precisely the incongruous position of hypocritical soul, liberated by the same maneuvers that compress it tightly within its bounds. Since the machiavel bears the traces of the transcendental system of which he is the dark obverse, his ambitions are not merely larger than they should be; they are infinite, insatiable. But his own carefully guarded interior gives him no object for that ambition, nothing ultimately to value or desire.

In *Richard III*, what happens inside the machiavel's strict subjective boundaries is nightmare. The liability of many of the characters, especially the sinful ones, to prophetic dreams seems to privilege the truth of the interior realm. (For what could be more personal, less available to others than a dream, in traditional philosophical skepticism the very criterion of an unshareable inwardness?) But that liability also suggests an encroachment by supernatural and providential agencies undeterred by the individual's frail defenses. Richard's attempts to define a "self" without reference to external allegiances of any kind turn into tautologies and contradictions: "Myself is not myself"; "Thyself is self-misused"; "Myself myself confound." "Richard loves Richard: that is, I am I"—but then, "I myself / Find in myself no pity to myself." At the same time, everything Richard thought he had put outside himself keeps covertly reentering. The more he struggles to constitute an inwardness by excluding alternative, "relational" modes of determining identity, the more he finds himself unwillingly entangled in a relational mode. The Renaissance theater presents, again and again, both the incommensurability of these two methods of self-definition and the impossibility of separating them. The Jew of Malta is betrayed by a daughter and an adopted slave, Iago by his wife, D'Amville by his sons, Giles Overreach by his daughter and his servant, Richard by kin who finally join together to destroy him. He perishes alone, encased within and encumbered by his armor, lacking the horse that would spirit him to safety. His death allegorizes the collapse of a strictly bounded but nonetheless impossibly complete autonomy.

What does it mean that Richard's rise and fall takes place in the theater? Many critics have noted Richard's blatant theatricality, his special intimacy with the audience.[26] Ordinarily, in fact, although the stage machiavel's intentions are "hidden" to the other characters, they are wholly available to the theater spectators: we see Anne taken in by a false display of inward truth, but we are confident that Richard's self-disclosure to *us* is entirely reliable. Barabbas, Richard, Lorenzo, Iago, Edmund, Volpone, Mosca, D'Amville, and all that company are masters of the soliloquy and the aside, urgently communicating their "close intent" to the audience. They love to exhibit their cleverness, even though exposure means downfall. The theatrical situation, distinguishing sharply between the privileged viewpoint of the theater spectators and the impercipience of onstage colleagues, is thus a convenience for the machiavels, allowing them both audience and scope for action. Yet the same situation reproduces the Christian providential scheme the machiavel defies, with its contrast between divine omniscience and mortal myopia. The fact that the machiavel's machinations are *witnessed* guarantees both our delight and his undoing. That delight, moreover, is partly due to the highly flattering role the spectators are asked to play, successfully standing in for the deity the machiavel will ultimately fail to imitate or replace. The almost reassuring, "comic" quality of many stage machiavels as they plot their cruelties is entirely consistent with the fantasies of immunity and omniscience theatergoers are encouraged to entertain, as we are given safe, enticingly godlike access to fictional hiddenness. We trump, as it were, the Gygean ambitions of the onstage villain.

Of course, the pleasure such fantasies provide is directly proportional to the strength of the anxieties they temporarily allay. In *Richard III* Shakespeare puts us not only on God's side but in God's place, in the position of "the high all-seer" in the providential drama of history. The play protects its audience from the crises of authority that haunt the "discoveries" of Renaissance polemical writers like Haggard and Harsnett—protects it so well that even twentieth-century scholars must struggle to separate the historical Richard III from Shakespeare's vivid animation of Tudor propaganda. The epistemological self-assurance of *Richard III* is its ultimate fiction, its most effective seduction scene.

26. See, for example, M. M. Reese, *The Cease of Majesty: A Study of Shakespeare's History Plays* (New York: St. Martin's, 1961), pp. 207–25; A. P. Rossiter, *Angel with Horns* (London: Longman, Green, 1961), pp. 19–22; Anne Righter, *Shakespeare and the Idea of the Play* (London: Chatto and Windus, 1962), pp. 89–100.

ॐ III. *THE SPANISH TRAGEDY,* or, the Machiavel's Revenge ॐ

THE ENDS OF MACHIAVELLIAN INWARDNESS are emphatically not contemplative: we have already seen how Gygean invisibility repudiates divine authority, and it manifestly defies secular masters as well. The machiavel exploits his self-awareness by undertaking a *coup d'état.* What, then, is the relationship between inwardness and rebellion?

The significance of the machiavel's disruptiveness depends, of course, upon what he is disrupting: upon the context in which he acts. By the end of the War of the Roses in *Richard III,* every claimant to the throne is a kind of usurper, even Richmond, who must miraculously revive a sense of legitimate entitlement almost hopelessly compromised by preceding events. While radical social breakdown makes Richmond's task more difficult in some ways, it also preserves him from the taint of treason, a crime which can only occur in a world where there are allegiances to violate. Richard's "illegitimacy"—his personal defectiveness and his faulty title to the throne—both helps justify Richmond's action and strongly implies that English institutions may be rescued simply by installing a more deserving person as England's king. Although there is indeed something the matter with Richard, there is nothing the matter with the monarchy that a personnel change will not repair.

Like the usurper, the hero of English Renaissance revenge tragedy comes to self-consciousness by first experiencing, and then effecting, a profound alteration in his relationship to authority. Revengers are driven to their bloody task because a ruler has failed to punish injustice properly, usually because he himself or members of his family are implicated in the wrongdoing. Most conspicuously, revengers assault the body of the sovereign or the bodies of his close kin. Less obviously, the revenger's outlaw legalism commandeers the monarch's exclusive prerogative over the prosecution of felonies, which were defined as crimes to which the crown was always supposedly a party. The grounds for the revenger's aggression, however, differ from Richard's or Richmond's. Although rulers in revenge plays are incompetent or wicked, no one denies their title to their offices: that the King in *The Spanish Tragedy* is the rightful monarch, that Lussurioso is heir to the dukedom in *The Revenger's Tragedy*—or even that Claudius is really King of Denmark, having been, as Hamlet tells us late in the play, *elected* to his throne. Thus revengers, despite their corrosive attack on royal power, are not primarily concerned with establishing their own claims to the throne. Most are too obsessed with retaliation to concern themselves with their personal prospects afterwards, and at any rate their own deaths follow so quickly upon the wreaking of vengeance that they have no time to install themselves in place of their enemies. In consequence the relative optimism of *Richard III* rarely seems plausible in the revenge play, where the institutions of government, not merely the persons who happen to inhabit those institutions, seem irremediably defective. A revenger can exterminate a particular criminal ruler, but the general difficulty posed by hierarchical social organization—the vulnerability of inferiors to irresponsible superiors—seems endemic and intractable.

These differences in the way sovereignty is conceived translate into differences in the way "machiavellianism" is structured and motivated in the revenge play. In Kyd's *Spanish Tragedy* these differences are already fully apparent. The few scenes devoted to the court of Portugal contain the play's simplest episode of lethal insincerity. When Villuppo maliciously accuses Alexandro of murdering Prince Balthazar, Alexandro has no alibi with which to counter his confident account. The unexpectedness of the accusation hardly constitutes evidence for Alexandro's innocence: just the opposite, in fact. For a noble bystander, the occasion brings to mind the familiar distinction between inward truth and external manifestation:

> I had not thought that Alexandro's heart
> Had been envenomed with such extreme hate;
> But now I see that words have several works,
> And there's no credit in the countenance.
>
> (3.1.15–18)

Since the signs of Alexandro's integrity speak equally plausibly to his guilt, Villuppo replies to the nobleman by cleverly drawing attention to, rather than minimizing, Alexandro's apparent forthrightness and loyalty:

> No; for, my lord, had you beheld the train
> That feignéd love had colored in his looks,
> When he in camp consorted Balthazar,
> Far more inconstant had you thought the sun,

That hourly coasts the center of the earth,
Than Alexandro's purpose to the prince.

(3.1.8–23)

When a seemingly loyal and straightforward subordinate commits treason, he subverts not only an individual superior, but more fundamentally, the publicly shared perceptions upon which any social structure relies. The traitor clever enough to erase the evidence of his crime in the very act of committing it is—like the "incarnate devils" of Lodge's *Wit's Misery*—both supremely dangerous and indistinguishable from an innocent man.

In fact, Villuppo's tactics develop out of and exacerbate a paranoia identical to that simultaneously paraded and assuaged by the authors of "discovery" literature, who claim to possess knowledge of cunningly concealed vice. The only way to defend oneself against such an accusation is to turn it back upon the accuser. Like the mutual recriminations of Catholics and Protestants, or like Richard's reproach of Hastings, Villuppo's indictment is curiously transitive: his treason consists in accusing another of betrayal. (In chapters 4 and 5 we shall deal at more length with this multiplication of inwardnesses, and then confusing displacement and substitutability: one person's traitorous intentions for another's loyal "conscience"; one person's guilty dreams for another's supposed secrets.) The Viceroy has no criterion for deciding between Villuppo's avowal and Alexandro's defense, but his "nightly dreams" support Villuppo, and he sentences Alexandro to death. The fortuitous arrival of the Ambassador with news of Balthazar's prospects in Spain saves Alexandro at the last minute. But the troubling issues raised by Villuppo's accusation hardly vanish so easily.

Indeed, they are echoed and immensely amplified in the main plot of *The Spanish Tragedy*, which concerns a violent struggle between male members of the aristocratic and professional classes over the competing claims of birth and merit. Strength and beauty of mind and body are, of course, the traditional markers of aristocratic status, but in *The Spanish Tragedy*, they are better exemplified by persons of unremarkable lineage. Don Andrea and Horatio's valor in battle surpasses that of their superiors, and their reward is Bel-imperia, who contemptuously ignores the obligation of highborn women to await arranged marriages to suitable patricians. The moments of escape into meritocratic utopia are brief, however; class distinctions are oppressively reinforced almost as soon as they are overthrown. Andrea excels in battle until Prince Balthazar's henchmen bayonet his horse's belly, and Balthazar unchivalrously presses his advantage and kills him. Horatio defeats Balthazar, but partial credit goes to Lorenzo. Bel-imperia dallies with her lowborn lovers, but both are slaughtered, and she eventually is forced into a dynastically advantageous wedding to a man she abhors.

It is easy to imagine the heavy investment of a man like Thomas Kyd—a gifted, bankrupt scrivener's son—both in Hieronimo's nightmare of injustice and in his retaliatory triumph. It is also easy to see allegorized in the struggle between Lorenzo and Hieronimo the conflict between an old-fashioned aristocratic esteem for inherited status and a new emphasis on the intellectual and practical accomplishments demanded by the recently centralized Tudor bureaucracy.[27] The relationship of *Spanish Tragedy* to a historically momentous, personally experienced class conflict means that Kyd's conception of machiavellian inwardness differs from Shakespeare's in *Richard III*.

As we have seen, Richard commences his career as a machiavel when loyalty to people or causes outside himself no longer seems possible. He forthwith announces his isolation and uniqueness, and fortifies the boundary between himself and others. *The Spanish Tragedy* similarly chronicles the disintegration of social ties, but the dynamic which produces machiavellian inwardness is considerably more complex. Early in the play, matters are neither so bleak nor so clearly delineated as they later become. The fathers and uncles—the King, Castile, Hieronimo—provide hints of a bygone order in which inherited and acquired entitlements were not imagined to be at odds. Even when, in the first act, Lorenzo and Horatio both lay claim to the capture of Balthazar, an equitable settlement seems possible. The King's meticulous division of the spoils, although it appears to give more credit to Lorenzo than he deserves, seems to content all parties. By the same token, Hieronimo's pride in his son, and his faith that Horatio will be rewarded and advanced, do not mean that he expects Horatio to take Lorenzo's place at court. Rather he hopes that his son's "merit" will earn him a position of respect much like Hieronimo's

27. For this change in attitude during the sixteenth century, see Mark H. Curtis, *Oxford and Cambridge in Transition* (Oxford: Clarendon, 1959), esp. pp. 265–81; Joan Simon, *Education and Society in Tudor England* (Cambridge: Cambridge University Press, 1961), pp. 333–68; and Laurence Stone, *The Crisis of the Aristocracy* (Oxford: Clarendon, 1965); pp. 672–724.

own. Hieronimo is proud, not mortified, when the King holds a banquet for Prince Balthazar, Horatio's prisoner of war, and asks Horatio to wait upon their cups.

The safety of the competent professional class is, however, a function not only of its own restricted aspirations but of the self-confidence of the aristocrats who employ professionals. Once Horatio begins to seem a rival to people like Lorenzo and Balthazar, his very excellences make him vulnerable. Horatio's courage on the battlefield diminishes Lorenzo's triumph, his erotic success displaces Balthazar. As his lynched body dangles in the arbor, Lorenzo quips:

> Although his life were still ambitious-proud,
> Yet is he at the highest now that he is dead.
>
> (2.4.60–61)

Since Balthazar, Lorenzo, and their henchmen stab Horatio to death, the hanging itself is technically superfluous, but symbolically satisfying for the aggressors, who thereby assign an ignominious death to a perceived transgressor of social hierarchy.

Thus although Lorenzo is quite as ruthless and manipulative as Shakespeare's Richard, his "machiavellianism" contrasts markedly from Richard's in its motivation and its goals. Lorenzo curiously combines the revolutionary possibilities of amoral individualism with intense class pride. Far from attacking wholesale the structure of the aristocratic order, Lorenzo attempts to preserve it for those born into it, against the pretensions of those who practice its ancestral virtues. To effect this preservation he actually disregards his individual interests, narrowly conceived.[28] For if his sister remains unmarried, or marries a commoner, or irremediably disgraces herself, he may well inherit the Spanish throne; but one of the provisions of the nuptial treaty between Balthazar and Bel-imperia provides for the passage of the kingdom directly to their male issue. Therefore Lorenzo's father, trying to puzzle out Lorenzo's hostility to Hieronimo, supposes that it obscurely reflects Lorenzo's desire to "intercept" Bel-imperia's marriage—whereas in fact Lorenzo is its principal contriver.

---

28. In a paper written in 1976 but not published until 1994, William Empson finds this point so curious that to account for it he proposes that the printed text of *The Spanish Tragedy* is a version massively cut by the censor. See *Essays on Renaissance Literature, Volume Two: The Drama*, ed. John Haffenden (Cambridge: Cambridge University Press, 1994), pp. 41–65.

Lorenzo's rigorous enforcement of class boundaries, however, decisively redefines class relationships. With Balthazar's collaboration, Lorenzo estranges traditional aristocratic privilege—the license to behave as one pleases—from the traditional aristocratic obligation to support loyal or talented subordinates. Hieronimo, who has not previously conceived the possibility of separating duties from entitlements, is hurled over the brink of madness by this moral innovation. The Knight Marshal mourns the loss not only of his son, but of an implicit contract between social classes so basic to his life and work that it seems to underlie rationality itself.

Hieronimo's own birth into machiavellian cunning thus represents—as it does in Haggard or Shakespeare—an adaptation to a drastic crisis of authority, a crisis that seems both to necessitate and to enable circuitous illegalities. As in *Richard III*, the immediate formal consequence of Hieronimo's transformation is a new preference for soliloquy: for speech too conspiratorial, too intimate, or too unbalanced for another's ear. Alone onstage in act 3, scene 13, he lays his devious plans:

> I will revenge his death.
> But how? Not as the vulgar wits of men,
> With open, but inevitable ills,
> As by a secret, yet a certain mean,
> Which under kindship will be cloaked best.

> (3.13.20–25)

"Kindship"—both "benevolence" and "blood-relatedness" in Renaissance English—once wholly determined Hieronimo's sense of identity. Now, however, "kindship" is hollowed out, a mask behind which the alienated subject works his treachery. In this respect Hieronimo differs little from the monsters imagined by religious polemicists. Moreover Hieronimo's estrangement and duplicity, like Richard III's, proceeds from a perception of defectiveness. As Richard must contend with his deformity, Hieronimo must accommodate his tactics to his relatively low status:

> Nor aught avails it me to menace them,
> Who, as a wintry storm upon a plain,
> Will bear me down with their nobility.
> No, no, Hieronimo, thou must enjoin
> Thine eyes to observation, and thy tongue
> To milder speeches than thy spirit affords.

> (3.13.39–44)

Like Gyges, Hieronimo makes himself unseen—or at least unnoticed—but whets his own perspicacity, a strategy that allows him an access to power he would otherwise not possess.

At the same time, just as Lorenzo's "machiavellianism" is founded upon a primary allegiance not to "himself alone" but to a particular social order, Hieronimo's "machiavellianism" redeploys rather than repudiates family and class ties. His task, after all, originates in a paternal responsibility to find and punish his son's murderers, and more generally "his anguished need for vengeance," as C. L. Barber remarks, "is a function of the violation of an original investment of social piety."[29] Not surprisingly, then, the Knight Marshal resorts to procedures that reflect the values and competences of his caste. Whereas Lorenzo derives his claim to power over others from his noble rank, Hieronimo grounds his on the intellectual superiority of the court professional. Eager to differentiate himself from "vulgar wits" who cannot settle important legal cases, write court masques, or effect clever reprisals, he cultivates an intellectually elitist connoisseurship of violence, privileging secret ingenuity over open brutality.

In fact, the key to Hieronimo's triumph lies in class-bound differences in the way *The Spanish Tragedy*'s battling machiavels develop their fantasies of masterful secret knowledge. Lorenzo thinks of power in old-fashioned aristocratic terms, as emanating from an immediate physical presence. He refuses to trust secondhand reports. When Pedringano informs him that Horatio is Bel-imperia's lover, he does not simply accept the account as true, but confirms it by eavesdropping upon the couple in person. Conversely, he assumes that other people's power will be neutralized by their bodily absence. His matter-of-fact advice to the lovelorn Balthazar sounds like the solution to a problem in elementary engineering:

> Some cause there is that lets you not be loved;
> First that must needs be known, and then removed.
>
> (2.1.31–32)

Once Horatio and Pedringano are dead, once Bel-imperia is hustled out of the way, Lorenzo assumes they need no longer be feared. And he is right that in the Spanish court, where authority is highly personalized, out of sight seems to be out of mind: Castile does not inquire after his missing daughter, nor the King after his young war hero.

29. C. L. Barber, *Creating Elizabethan Tragedy: The Theater of Marlowe and Kyd* (Chicago: University of Chicago Press, 1988), p. 143.

Lorenzo's manipulation of the conditions of visibility and invisibility, however, turns out to be too simple in its premises. He ignores incentives and effects that do not require physical presence: specifically, the ghostly mechanisms of memory, which insistently bring the dead or absent before the minds of the living, and the equally ghostly art of writing, which permits the dead or absent a voice. It fails to occur to Lorenzo that Bel-imperia's loyalty to Don Andrea may make Balthazar a target for her hatred even before Horatio's murder. Nor does he anticipate Hieronimo's refusal to forget his son. His only concern for a document is a pretense: the nonexistent pardon he promises Pedringano in order to buy his silence.

Hieronimo, by bureaucratic training and by bitter experience, is more sophisticated. His literary productions—the masque he produces for the Portuguese ambassador and the play he directs at Bel-imperia's wedding—both purport to derive from the history of the Iberian peninsula, reanimating the past in the present.[30] This revivalism and concern for precedent, the Renaissance-humanist proclivities of a poet and a lawyer, likewise sustain Hieronimo's desire for a revenge that protests against equating the past with the forgotten, that returns obsolete calamities to a traumatized present. Specific connections between revenge and literacy are made throughout the play not only in imagery insistently linking blood and ink, but in the practical details of Hieronimo's eventually successful criminal investigation. Hieronimo depends heavily upon the written testimony of Bel-imperia and Pedringano for his enlightenment. No more than Lorenzo is he willing to trust unsupported rumor and conjecture: Bel-imperia's letter does not verify its own claims, but puts him on his guard.

> I therefore will by circumstances try
> What I can gather to confirm this writ.

> (3.2.48–49)

But Hieronimo's conception of what can count as relevant "circumstances," and his procedures for acquiring crucial information, are

---

30. For an alternative view *contrasting* Hieronimo's activities as a court entertainer with his activities as a lawyer, see Kay Stockholder, "'Yet Can He Write': Reading the Silences in *The Spanish Tragedy*," *American Imago* 47 (1990): 93–124. Despite Stockholder's strange and logically superfluous insistence that the whole play constitutes Hieronimo's dream, her analysis of class relationships in *The Spanish Tragedy* is very acute.

more extensive and flexible than Lorenzo's. Likewise he exploits his own familiarity with textual possibility, and the corresponding naiveté of his opponents, to effect his revenge in the final act.

Kyd's versions of the machiavel thus significantly redelineate the distinction I made earlier between a subjectivity of inwardness and a subjectivity defined by kinship and social place. Whereas in religious polemic personal inwardness, whether subversive or centered upon God, is contrasted with an identity centered upon social relationships of all kinds, in *The Spanish Tragedy* the characters constitute their interiors by selectively introjecting socially available materials and attitudes. Even Bel-imperia's defiance of patriarchal mandates is not invented out of whole cloth. Both her boldness and her calculating use of inferiors are thoroughly aristocratic qualities; she bears a strong family resemblance, in fact, to the brother she so violently resents.

> Yes, second love shall further my revenge.
> I'll love Horatio, my Andrea's friend,
> The more to spite the prince that wrought his end.
> (1.4.66–68)

Likewise Hieronimo's apparently unexceptionable demand for "justice" seems a product of his particular social positioning, a professional advocate's idealization of a law that promises to compensate individuals on the basis of behavior rather than on the basis of rank. The meticulous contextualization of Kyd's characters makes it difficult to associate his intriguers with the unfettered, presocial morality-play Vice to whom some stage machiavels, like Richard III, are arguably indebted.[31] The implications of Kyd's characterology are close, in fact, to the claims of recent critics like Stephen Greenblatt, Jonathan Goldberg, Jonathan Dollimore, and Catherine Belsey, who maintain that the structure of personality is a "cultural artifact" that derives from social structures, rather than anteceding or escaping them.[32]

It is, I would argue, no accident that the contemporary critics

---

31. See, for instance, Bernard Spivack, *Shakespeare and the Allegory of Evil.*

32. See Stephen Greenblatt, *Renaissance Self-Fashioning* (Chicago: University of Chicago Press, 1981); Jonathan Dollimore, *Radical Tragedy: Religion, Ideology, and Power in the Drama of Shakespeare and His Contemporaries* (Chicago: University of Chicago Press, 1984); Catherine Belsey, *The Subject of Tragedy.* The phrase "cultural artifact" is Clifford Geertz's in *The Interpretation of Cultures* (New York: Basic Books, 1973).

whose views most resemble Kyd's should treat traditional religious claims with frank incredulity. One consequence of Kyd's distinctive construal of machiavellian inwardness is that the characters of *Spanish Tragedy* occupy a very different relationship to transcendental truths than do the martyrs and hypocrites of Renaissance religious polemic. Orthodox Renaissance doctrine imagines earthly justice as a pale, flawed derivative of a perfect divine pattern. In this arrangement, God presides over the ultimate court of appeal, definitively punishing criminal secrecy and vindicating obscure righteousness. This attractive conception is not entirely absent from *Spanish Tragedy*. Shortly after his son is murdered, Hieronimo's conviction that the world is a "mass of public wrongs" naturally leads him to reflect upon another world in which those wrongs might be corrected. The grief-stricken Isabella envisages her slaughtered boy singing hymns among the cherubim. Alexandro, too, puts his hopes in heaven, confident at the point of death that a divine overseer will confirm his undisplayable innocence:

> As heavens have known my secret thoughts,
> So am I free from this suggestion.

> (3.1.45–46)

All the virtuous characters, in fact, console themselves in adversity with the thought of a vaguely Christian otherworld presided over by a just, all-knowing God.

The induction and entr'actes, however, give us not the fair, clear-sighted heavenly jurisdiction that Alexandro, Isabella, and Hieronimo in some moods piously anticipate, but a pagan underworld, capriciously administered. In the courts of Spain and Portugal, categories of class, gender, and merit become blurred as male aristocrats degenerate, and females and underlings aspire to heroic status. It seems unlikely that remedies for the resulting inequities will be forthcoming from the bumbling divine bureaucrats of the induction, graveled as they are by the elementary challenge Don Andrea's case presents to the infernal classification scheme. More vigorous, and more providentially supervisory, is the ominous figure of Revenge.[33] Revenge, however, sleeps through much of the action: allegorically expressing the occult workings of vengeance, but also, surely, its blindness to the details of its victims' offenses. The rough, partisan justice that

33. For another view of this issue, see Geoffrey Aggeler, "The Eschatological Crux in *The Spanish Tragedy*," *JEGP* 86 (1987): 319–31.

concludes the play condemns Castile, an innocent bystander, as harshly as the true villains, and assigns inapposite penalties even to the real offenders: punishing Lorenzo, for instance, as an aspiring erotomaniac. In *The Spanish Tragedy* "the absorption of the human into the divine justice machine," G. K. Hunter writes, "is the destruction of the human."[34] Hunter is correct in the sense that Kyd's otherworld fails to exemplify humane ideals of justice, and in that Hieronimo is brutalized by being made an instrument of vengeance. In another sense, however, Kyd's "divine justice machine" is all too human. Kyd seems to share with his more orthodox contemporaries a conviction that the otherworld has an especially intimate relationship to the personal interior. But just as the inwardness that might conceivably provide an escape from an oppressive social formation in *Spanish Tragedy* turns out merely to duplicate its flaws, so Kyd's otherworld reproduces in grander form the favoritism, irrationality, and sheer carelessness of earthly rule.

As Hieronimo increasingly loses faith in procedures of justice he has always taken for granted, the supervenient authority that had seemed to guarantee just outcomes early in the play simply evaporates. The King, alert and responsive to his subjects in the first act, becomes strangely distracted and unreachable. At the same time it occurs to Hieronimo that the cosmic order from which the King has supposedly derived his legitimacy suffers the same defects:

> Yet still tormented is my tortured soul
> With broken sighs and restless passions,
> That, winged, mount, and, hovering in the air,
> Beat at the windows of the brightest heavens,
> Soliciting for justice and revenge:
> But they are placed in those empyreal heights,
> Where, countermured with walls of diamond,
> I find the place impregnable; and they
> Resist my woes, and give my words no way.
>
> (3.7.10–18)

In place of the orthodox scheme, in which justice cascades downward from god to king to commoner, Hieronimo imagines the demand for equity, and an intuition about what justice means, erupting from below. The action of the play bears him out: the relatively powerless,

34. G. K. Hunter, "Ironies of Justice in *The Spanish Tragedy*," *Renaissance Drama* 8 (1965): 101.

violently silenced Bel-imperia and Pedringano provide evidence against Lorenzo and Balthazar, and the disregarded Hieronimo exacts the penalty. The weak *need* justice, Kyd seems to suggest, whereas the strong can obtain what they want by any number of means.

The Renaissance conception of machiavellian hypocrisy, as we have already noted, closely associates power with spectatorial prowess. Even as Kyd calls the nature and efficacy of such power into question, he populates his play with supervisory figures, constructing, again and again, scenarios in which voyeurs suppose themselves unseen, but prove actually visible in ways they do not suspect. Thus the courtship of Bel-imperia and Horatio is watched by Lorenzo and Balthazar, who are observed by Revenge and Andrea, who are themselves displayed for the theater spectators. The spectatorial dynamic in which persons are imagined to achieve their reality is not eradicated—if anything, it is all the more oppressively enforced—but the reassuring connections *Richard III* implies between that dynamic and an ultimately beneficent universe are ruptured. For unless omniscience is linked with the effective administration of transcendental justice, it threatens rather than fortifies human hopes for personal vindication. To keep Pedringano from informing upon him, Lorenzo cynically sends him a boy with a pardon supposedly enclosed in a black box. But the boy surreptitiously opens the box and finds it empty. The box that pretends to contain an authoritative, salvific text may be understood as a figure for the opaque, perjured subjectivity of the machiavel, but also, perhaps, as a comment upon the hollow promises of a Christianity *The Spanish Tragedy* both evokes and renounces.

The skepticism, even nihilism, of *The Spanish Tragedy* makes the machiavellian adaptation to hostile circumstances seem more justified than it does in *Richard III*. In a Christian universe, in which virtue imitates a divine pattern, the machiavel is a scandalous aberration. His blindness to supervising power must be elaborately accounted for: as an innate depravity commensurate with physical deformity, as a punishment for the sins of a whole society, as the perverse logic of an individual traumatically alienated from normal affiliations and affections. In the world of *The Spanish Tragedy*, riddled from the top down by hypocrisy and manipulation, Hieronimo's behavior seems the comprehensibly desperate adaptation of a decent man to a bad world. What replaces the missing omniscience is a struggle among competing, incommensurable perspectives, all demonstrably limited,

all conditioned by habit, bias, and self-interest. Without any transcendental guarantee of absolute equity, without any hope of an all-
knowing supervisor in whom justice and mercy are miraculously
combined, intuitions about just treatment become not imperfect human reflections of the divine perfection, but fallible forms of myopic
and narcissistic special pleading that may or may not happen to be
rewarded. The mystery in *Spanish Tragedy*, then, is not where "machiavellianism" originates, but rather where convictions about order,
virtue, and justice derive.

For the weird persistence of those convictions, despite their apparent groundlessness, help determine Hieronimo's calamitous course of
action in the final act of the play. It is worth looking carefully at his
final, extravagantly brutal display to see what it suggests both about
his own vengeful endeavor, and about Kyd's conception of his theatrical project. The nuptials between Balthazar and Bel-imperia are supposed harmoniously to combine affection with expediency, passion
with dynastic ambition. As such they are no different from most
court spectacles, which ordinarily depict a seamless convergence between the subject's desires and the sovereign's interests. Everything
that resists this complacent vision must be rigorously suppressed: in
The Spanish Tragedy, the deserving subordinate's unaddressed demand for justice, and the bride's abiding hatred of her criminal bridegroom. Hieronimo's "Tragedy of Soliman," then, voices what has
been silenced, releases what has been thwarted. A form traditionally
designed to depict the world as seen from the perspective of the rulers
is turned upside-down to express the perspective of the ruled. The
effect is to deny the comprehensiveness of the sovereign's vision, and
to insist upon the significance of the subject's occluded point of view.
The playwright's hidden plot begs to be set against the ideologically
motivated concealments of court spectacle, his ferocity against the
violence with which the two victim-conspirators have been stifled
and overridden. Just as Kyd's machiavels do not disavow their social
positioning, but rather create their interiors by a process of introjec-
tion, Hieronimo does not simply renounce court spectacle, but *infil-
trates* it in order to turn it against itself.

To their betters, Hieronimo and Bel-imperia do not count; that is,
they do not constitute independent centers of consciousness that
need to be taken seriously. Thus Hieronimo's revenge consists not
merely of killing Horatio's murderers, but of enlightening his oppres-
sors in the significance of their mistake. In order to convey such

a lesson, Hieronimo must establish some common ground with them—must attempt to make them see him as like themselves. In an earlier scene, Hieronimo had discovered a capacity to cross class boundaries and commiserate with Bazulto, a powerless and impoverished old man whose son had, like his own, been slaughtered.

> Here, take my handkercher and wipe thine eyes,
> Whiles wretched I, in thy mishaps, may see
> The lively portrait of my dying self.
>
> (3.13.83–85)

The force of empathy seems to propel the confrontation into the register of the aesthetic: the Old Man is Hieronimo's "portrait." The ambiguous word "lively," which could mean either "living" or "lifelike," suggests that mimetic representation heightens rather than diminishes real-life pertinence. The uncanny interview with the Old Man conflates the diverse intensities of actual suffering and fictional contrivance.

In the last act, in a fable that turns out to be true, Hieronimo attempts to enforce upon the rulers of Spain and Portugal the acknowledgment of likeness that had overcome him spontaneously in his encounter with Bazulto—as if sharing his affliction will make them comprehend his plight.

> As dear to me was my Horatio,
> As yours, or yours, or yours, my lord, to you.
>
> (4.4.168–69)

Ranging the corpse of his socially inferior son alongside the bodies of the heirs apparent, Hieronimo stages and voices a radically leveling sentiment: that one dead child is very like another, that paternal love feels essentially the same for noble and commoner, that his suffering is worth as much as the suffering of princes.

> With soonest speed I hasted to the noise,
> Where hanging on a tree I found my son,
> Through-girt with wounds, and slaughtered as you see.
> And grieved I, think you, at this spectacle?
> Speak, Portuguese, whose loss resembles mine:
> If thou canst weep upon thy Balthazar,
> 'Tis like I wailed for my Horatio.
> And you, my lord, whose reconciléd son
> Marched in a net, and thought himself unseen . . .
> How can you brook our play's catastrophe?
>
> (4.4.110–16)

Hieronimo's strict talion—son for son, spectacle for spectacle, wail for wail—ignores disparities between one person and another, insisting upon equivalence and substitutability. Balthazar and Lorenzo are higher in rank than Horatio, but just as dead by the end of Hieronimo's play. The climax of his stagecraft is the sudden and surprising revelation of Horatio's corpse—not a verbal recollection, but an actual corporeal presence. His stubborn emphasis on the body and its vicissitudes in the final scene of *Spanish Tragedy* relies upon an intuition which, as we shall see, Shakespeare will find attractive in later plays: that human beings despite their differences share an experience of embodiment, a "common human lot" that can provide a basis both for social cohesion and for theatrical pedagogy.

One effect of Hieronimo's seditious infiltration of court spectacle, then, is to suggest an alternative to what has become, in the course of the play, the radically atomized individualism of the Spanish court. In this respect his theatricality differs fundamentally from Richard's: whereas Richard's theater, reveling in trickery, insists upon the distance between himself and others, Hieronimo's obliterates, in a sumptuously bloody catastrophe, the ideological gap between royal and subjected flesh. Kyd apparently recognizes that such drama of fellow feeling, although it may seem to rely upon a communal impulse, hardly conduces to the maintenance of social stability: just the opposite, in fact, insofar as granting the full humanity of one's inferiors tends to call into question the naturalness and propriety of disproportionate entitlements. English theater in the decades after Kyd seizes enthusiastically upon this conundrum, cultivating empathy in a large, diverse group of spectators with unprecedentedly naturalistic characters across boundaries of class, sex, and nationality. This theatrical tradition is continually drawn to plots of usurpation and revenge, plots which insist upon the capacity of the marginalized and the alien for independent agency. Its formal indecorousness, its mingling of kings and clowns, thus often seems almost per se leveling or subversive, even when the overt lessons of such mingling seem to reinforce authoritarian hierarchies.

In *Spanish Tragedy,* however, Hieronimo's theater fails to educate its audience in the way he claims he has intended it to do. "Soliman and Perseda" is, in fact, virtually guaranteed to miscarry. Hieronimo arranges for each of the characters to speak a different language: unintelligible to one another and to the audience, sundered, as in the Babel legend Hieronimo himself invokes, from originary or conclusive sources of meaning. Even while "Soliman and Perseda" urges the parallel between Horatio's vulnerability and the vulnerability of his superiors, between Hieronimo's grief and the grief of kings and princes, it simultaneously emphasizes the irreducible separateness of revenger and victim, between one who punishes and one who endures castigation. To show the King and Castile what the death of a son feels like, Hieronimo has to harden himself to the prospect of their suffering, to refuse to acknowledge a pain his own experience has uniquely qualified him to anticipate. Likewise, and unsurprisingly, his onstage audience resists his invitation to see his grievances duplicated in their own. "Why hast thou done this undeserving deed?" ask the King and the Viceroy, after Hieronimo has spent seventy-five lines explaining his reasons, and Lorenzo's and Balthazar's deserts. The apparent obtuseness of the royal audience at this moment has led some editors to suspect textual corruption:[35] but perhaps Kyd is merely dramatizing a hopeless inability to grasp Hieronimo's theatrical point. The King, Castile, and the Viceroy imagine that an erstwhile loyal servant has shown himself to be radically alien. They cannot conceive of him as a suffering father like themselves but only as a "traitor," a "damnéd, bloody murderer," a "wretch."

As pedagogy, then, Hieronimo's playlet is a failure; but as insurrection it is eminently successful. The denouement of *Spanish Tragedy* suggests that for Kyd, the connection between a challenge to authority and a highly developed sense of personal inwardness is not accidental but absolutely intrinsic. Recognizing what one does not share with one's superiors—the significance of experiences that are irreducibly one's own—upsets the deference to others' interests that is the essence of subordination. Understanding, at the same time, what one *does* share with one's superiors—a common bodily vulnerability—provides the basis of an effective defiance. Pressed to reveal more than he wishes to, Hieronimo first bites out his tongue and then uses a penknife to kill himself: violently repudiating first verbal and then written means of expression. Hieronimo's suicide "ruptures," in his word, the transfer of inside to outside, protecting his hard-won privacy. A creature that seems wholly realized through forms of theatrical and rhetorical display finally declares the insufficiency of those forms. It is a twist in Kyd's conception of his art that Shakespeare

35. See, for instance, Philip Edwards, ed., *The Spanish Tragedy* (London: The Revels Plays, 1959) and Andrew Cairncross, ed., *The First Part of Hieronimo and The Spanish Tragedy* (Lincoln: University of Nebraska Press, 1967).

MACHIAVELS AND FAMILY MEN

may recall when he eventually bases his own revenge play on a Kydian prototype and creates a character who repudiates "trappings and suits" in favor of "that within."

There is despair in *The Spanish Tragedy*, as there is in *Richard III*, but there is also, strangely, a kind of triumph. If a beneficent providence does not exist, there is little hope for the redress of injustice in this world or the next; at the same time, divine punishment for self-assertion is less automatic and thus perhaps less fearsome. Instead of reassuring his audience with a theologico-theatrical fiction of beneficent omniscience, Kyd acquaints it with the disquieting possibility that it is caught in the same ironies that doom his characters, victims of powers that are not necessarily either just or merciful, and whom they are incapable of understanding. If *Richard III* more faithfully reproduces the spectatorial economy of late sixteenth-century religious polemic, *The Spanish Tragedy* more effectively stages its deepest fears.

3

HERETICAL CONSCIENCE AND THEATRICAL RHETORIC: THE CASE OF CHRISTOPHER MARLOWE

I

AT THE END OF THE FIRST ACT of Marlowe's *Massacre at Paris*, the Catholic Duke of Guise and his henchmen are butchering Huguenots. They burst into the study of Peter Ramus, the famous logician. "O good my lord," cries their victim, "Wherein hath Ramus been offensious?" Guise replies:

> Was it not thou that scoff'st the *Organon*,
> And said it was a heap of vanities?
> He that will be a flat dichotomist
> And seen in nothing but epitomes,
> Is in your judgment thought a learned man;
> And he, forsooth, must go and preach in Germany,
> Excepting against doctors' axioms,
> And *ipse dixit* with this quiddity,
> *Argumentum testimonii est inartificiale.*
> To contradict which, I say, Ramus shall die;
> How answer you that? Your *nego argumentum*
> Cannot serve, sirrah. —Kill him.
>
> (1.7.27–38)

In this curious passage, Guise objects to the challenge Ramus's influential logical system has mounted to Catholic scholastic philosophy, which was based on Aquinas's adaptation of Aristotle. His dagger provides a "refutation" which is at once a black parody of logical disputation and its most effective implementation. By slaying his opponent, he makes his argument literally unanswerable.

Over and over again in Marlowe's plays, persuasion or a simulacrum of persuasion converts to violence. Tamburlaine's words are swords, and his sword plays the orator; his courtship of Zenocrate is also a capture. "The high poetry in *Tamburlaine* is not shaped to express what is but to make something happen," as C. L. Barber com-

[72]

ments.[1] Similarly, Faustus is seduced, and ultimately doomed, by the coercive languages of contract and magic. Even as these languages are represented as sources of power, however, the nature of that power is called into question. We no sooner begin to ascribe Tamburlaine's success to his rhetorical fluency than the downfall of the equally grandiloquent Bazajeth demystifies the relationship between language and strength. In *Doctor Faustus* the force of the contract with the devil is never clear in the play, and critics dispute whether and at what point Faustus's deed of gift becomes irrevocable. Magical language is similarly problematic. It seems to put the physical world at the disposal of the desiring mind: merely verbalizing a wish will make it come true.

> The iterating of these lines brings gold,
> The framing of this circle on the ground
> Brings thunder, whirlwinds, storm and lightning.
> (*Doctor Faustus* 1.5.62–64)

But it quickly becomes obscure whether the world is really at the command of the magician, or whether its apparent responsiveness is a devilish illusion. When Faustus first raises Mephistophilis, he exults in the efficacy of magical processes:

> How pliant is this Mephistophilis!
> Full of obedience and humility,
> Such is the force of magic and my spells.
> (1.2.29–31)

But Mephistophilis insists that "I came now hither of mine own accord." Faustus asks:

> Did not my conjuring speeches raise thee?
> Speak.
> MEPHISTOPHILIS: That was the cause, but yet *per accidens*;
> For when we hear one rack the name of God,
> Abjure the scriptures and his savior Christ,
> We fly in hope to get his glorious soul.
> (46–49)

In other words, Faustus does not compel Mephistophilis, but merely awakens his interest.

1. C. L. Barber, *Creating Elizabethan Tragedy: The Theater of Marlowe and Kyd* (Chicago: University of Chicago Press, 1988), p. 53.

The relationship between coercion and language in Marlowe has been an issue for critics ever since Ben Jonson praised Marlowe's "mighty line" in his poem to Shakespeare. Marjorie Garber has discussed Marlowe's "performative utterances" from a deconstructive perspective; Constance Kuriyama, A. L. Rowse, and Karen Cunningham ascribe Marlowe's fascination with violence to his turbulent personality or to the bloody tastes of the Elizabethan theater public.[2] In this chapter I want to look at the issue from another point of view. I shall argue that Marlowe's plays reflect some of the dilemmas that arise from Renaissance conceptions of personal inwardness, and from the questionable inquisitorial methods developed for disclosing, regulating, and modifying that inward domain from the outside.

৶ II ৬

IN THE ENGLISH RENAISSANCE, and in particular at the end of the 1580s when Marlowe's career was at its brief zenith, the theater was a highly controversial institution. Both critics and apologists agree, however, that theater, even more effectively than other art forms, inculcates patterns of behavior in the audience. That is its promise and its danger, depending upon one's point of view. Defenders of the theater claim that heroic examples on stage produce heroic behavior in the audience and that bad examples repel the audience from foolishness and vice. The superiority of theater over other forms of instruction is said to be the compelling quality of these examples—that theater does not merely inform, but actually changes the spectators. Thus Philip Sidney praises the "sweet violence" of tragic drama and ranks poetry higher than philosophy because poetry can "strike, pierce [and] possess the sight of the soul." "Moving is of a higher degree than teaching," he argues. "It is not *gnosis*, but *praxis* must be the fruit."[3] Thomas Heywood likewise claims that "lively and well spirited action . . . hath power to new mold the hearts of the spectators and fashion them to the shape of any noble and notable at-

2. Marjorie Garber, "'Here's Nothing Writ': Scribe, Script, and Circumspection in Marlowe's Plays," *Theatre Journal* 36 (1984): 301–20; Constance Kuriyama, *Hammer or Anvil: Psychological Patterns in Christopher Marlowe's Plays* (New Brunswick: Rutgers University Press, 1980), pp. 213–32; A. L. Rowse, *Christopher Marlowe: A Biography* (London: MacMillan, 1964); Karen Cunningham, "Renaissance Execution and Marlovian Elocution: The Drama of Death," *PMLA* 105 (1990): 209–22.
3. Philip Sidney, "Defense of Poetry," *Prose Works*, ed. Albert Feuillerat (Cambridge: Cambridge University Press, 1963), pp. 24, 14.

tempt."[4] Antitheatricalists like Stephen Gosson, arguing the opposite side of the question, represent theatrical compulsion in negative terms. Lust and violence on stage, they maintain, produce lust and violence among the spectators, whose powers of resistance crumble before the seductions of spectacle.

> Delight being moved with a variety of shows, of events, or music, the longer we gaze, the more we crave, yea so forcible they are, that afterwards being but thought upon, they make us seek for the like another time.[5]

The word that keeps recurring in these discussions is "force"; irresistible rhetorical energy imagined as effecting a corresponding "movement" in the spectators. Both pro- and antitheatricalists dwell upon the ways in which persuasion becomes coercion: the same process that Marlowe seems obsessively to stage.

That certain kinds of speech might be understood in terms of physical duress is hardly a new idea in the Renaissance; it is a staple of classical rhetorical theory.[6] The intimacy between speech and coercion in Marlowe, then, can be seen as a form of literary self-consciousness. Yet it is not only that. Sixteenth-century debates about the theater take place in a cultural arena in which the relationship of persuasion to coercion has become an especially acute problem. As religious schism endangers a political order that had seemed to be grounded upon unanimity of faith, every European government and every ecclesiastical organization, both Protestant and Catholic, must formulate a position on how to deal with dissenting elements. The potential for covert rebellion, as we have already seen, generates a particular kind of troubled inwardness in members of oppressed groups. At the same time, the nature of their rebelliousness poses a number of largely intractable difficulties for the agents of orthodoxy.

The traditional method for dealing with religious dissent is the heresy trial. In the pre-Reformation period, such trials had represented themselves as enforcing a unanimous socioreligious consensus

---

4. Thomas Heywood, *An apology for actors* (London, 1612), B4ʳ.
5. Stephen Gosson, *Plays confuted in five actions* (London, 1582), G6r.
6. For an interesting account of Renaissance rhetoricians' self-consciousness of this issue, see Neil Rhodes, *The Power of Eloquence and English Renaissance Literature* (New York: Harvester Wheatsheaf, 1992). On pp. 69–117 Rhodes discusses Marlowe's attraction to the idea of rhetorical coercion, although his method, emphases, and conclusions are very different from mine.

against the scandalous aberrations of individual eccentrics. Even in these cases, the premise was sometimes implausible. The suppression of the Albigensians in the thirteenth century, for instance, did not involve the selective eradication of a few idiosyncratic thinkers, but the repression of a widely dispersed belief system by one that was even more powerful. Nonetheless, while the universal Church retained its prestige such claims were not altogether absurd. In the sixteenth century, however, as waves of reformation and counterreformation sweep through Europe, the credibility of the heresy trial, as originally conceived, slowly erodes along with the idea of religous unity that had sustained it. Not that heresy trials for that reason disappear: in fact, religious turmoil enormously multiplies the occasions for them. But the loss of religious homogeneity, as a fact if not yet as an ideal, draws widespread attention to some peculiar features of heresy and its prosecution that might otherwise have gone unremarked.

In particular, it becomes obvious that in the heresy trial, the relationship between coercion and persuasion becomes complicated in a variety of ways. Heresy is not a crime that is first committed and then punished. Instead it must involve conscious, protracted recalcitrance on the part of the accused. Impetuous murderers, thieves, traitors, counterfeiters, or witches who repent of their actions after having performed them are not for that reason excused from paying the penalty for the crime. But the heretic must be examined three times, at length, by ecclesiastical authorities not themselves entitled to discipline the offender, but merely to hand him over to "the secular arm" for punishment. If, during the course of this examination, the heretic becomes convinced of the error of his ways, he is made to undergo a public ceremony of penitence, and welcomed back into the church with a warning not to transgress again. (This seems to have been by far the commonest outcome of English heresy trials before the Reformation.)[7] However, if the accused remains obdurate, the secular power carries out (or occasionally, refuses to carry out) sentence of death by burning. At the place of execution, the convicted heretic is once again offered a pardon on the condition that he or she publicly recant and agree to conform to accepted views. Heretics who reject this final offer are bound to the stake and set afire. Those who accept, even at this late date, are supposed to be spared.

7. Ralph Houlbrooke surveys the surviving "act books" to come to this conclusion in *Church Courts and the People during the English Reformation 1520–1570* (Oxford: Oxford University Press, 1979), pp. 222–25.

The inquiry into heretical opinions thus involves a series of examinations structured as a progression of more and more aggressive attempts to elicit compliance, like Tamburlaine's succession of increasingly ominous flags—white, red, and black—posted outside a city he intends to seize. Intellectual heretics, like the Oxford martyrs Cramner, Ridley, and Latimer, are commonly "invited" to debate their views publicly with orthodox scholars. Of course, participation in these exchanges is hardly optional; and when they end the orthodox side is predictably declared victorious, and the losers sentenced to perish in torment. So the fiction of free scholarly inquiry is quite transparent. It is interesting, however, that it is felt to be required at all—that the authorities cannot simply annihilate the bothersome deviant without explanation or apology. Their power over the body of the heretic is never in doubt, but their resort to violence needs elaborate justification, often to the inquisitors themselves, apparently, as well as to the numerous spectators present at trials, debates, and executions. Only when every persuasive resource seems to have failed can the champions of orthodoxy rationalize deploying the ultimate weapon of physical coercion.

This last step is tricky, too, however, for it relies upon an assumption which the heresy proceedings themselves call into question—the assumption that the fate of the body and the fate of soul are identical. The flames in which the heretic dies are supposed to be the earthly prelude to the hellfire in which his soul will suffer for eternity; they are the visible, corporeal, and earthly allegory of an invisible, spiritual, extraworldly event. By punishing the heretic, the forces of orthodoxy hope to amplify solidarity among the legions of the faithful, not merely by enhancing their terror of transgression but by encouraging a vicarious or not-so-vicarious participation in the rituals of ostracization. In fact, however, the spectacular attempts to isolate and stigmatize the heretic are profoundly equivocal. While his dreadful fate demonstrates the power of orthodoxy, it simultaneously demonstrates the limitations of orthodoxy. The powers-that-be have failed in their attempts at persuasion; their logic is not irresistible. No power on earth, it seems, can force the truly resolute believer to change his or her allegiance.

The authorities and the heretic collide in their assessment of the facts—facts which, it became increasingly clear in the course of the sixteenth century, are not subject to universally acknowledged proof or disproof. Either transubstantiation does or does not occur; the

Pope either is or is not the supreme head of the church on earth: but how might the truth or falsity of such propositions possibly be established once a social consensus about them has broken down? To a modern agnostic, Renaissance heresy trials often seem to be games of chance played at very high stakes. If the state is right, the heretic is a hell-bound outcast. If the heretic is right, then his doom manifests not only the failure to coerce but the oppressive *difference* between coercion and persuasion, a difference supposedly coordinated with the disparity between a corrupt mundane order and a perfect divine one. The outcast's degradation and pain transform themselves into signs of the martyr's heavenly prestige.

It is impossible absolutely to exclude the second interpretive option. The more terrible the death, the more complete seems the triumph of secular power over the smoking flesh of the condemned, the more likely it is, in fact, that the very distinctions between persuasion and coercion, soul and body, that the punishments for heresy try to erase become as a result of these efforts all the more visible. John Foxe shows clearly how, at a breathtaking price to themselves, the Protestants turn the rituals of ostracization into propaganda for their cause. When Ridley and Latimer are burned, Foxe writes:

> Surely it moved hundreds to tears, in beholding the horrible sight; for I think there was none that had not clean exiled all humanity and mercy, which would not have lamented to behold the fury of the fire so to rage upon their bodies. Signs there were of sorrow on every side.[8]

Julius Palmer, a Catholic fellow of Magdalen College, converts on the spot and is later burned himself.[9] The sensational impact of these public burnings is such that in *The Displaying of the Protestants*, Myles Haggard accuses the Protestants of going to the stake merely to get sympathetic attention.[10] Nor is this effect merely the consequence of some Protestant doctrinal advantage; for a quarter-century later, the brutal treatment of Jesuits and recusant Catholics under Elizabeth encourages converts to Catholicism. At Edmund Campion's execu-

---

8. John Foxe, *Acts and Monuments of these latter and perilous days . . .* (New York: AMS Press, 1965), 7:551.

9. See D. M. Loades, *The Oxford Martyrs* (New York: Stein and Day, 1970), p. 220. Loades maintains that the effect of the Marian persecution in England was to alter public sentiment decisively in favor of the Protestants: accomplishing, that is, exactly the opposite of what Mary wanted to achieve.

10. Myles Haggard, *The displaying of the protestants* (London, 1556), E7ʳ-F1ʳ.

tion, guards unsuccessfully attempt to hold back relic-seeking crowds. When Henry Garnet is to be hanged and then disemboweled alive, onlookers impressed by the speech and behavior of the condemned prevent the hangman from cutting him down from the gallows until after he is dead.

The suppression of religious dissent in a Christian society, then, may be inexpedient. It poses theoretical difficulties as well for a religion supposedly founded upon the rule of charity. Even zealous foes of schism can recoil from the incongruity of professed Christians torturing and slaying other professed Christians. In *A Dialogue Concerning Heresies*, Thomas More's interlocutor laments:

> I would all the world were all agreed to take all violence and compulsion away upon all sides, Christian and heathen, and that no man were constrained to believe but as he could be by grace, wisdom, and good words induced.[11]

More replies that the threat heretics and infidels pose to the common good renders this clemency impractical. But he shares his opponent's uneasiness with the shedding of blood in a religious cause, emphasizing the distinction between the ecclesiastical judgment and the secular punishment of heretics in order to excuse, however flimsily, the participation of clerics in heresy prosecutions. Although as Lord Chancellor in the late 1520s More vigorously prosecutes the followers of Luther and Tyndale, his Utopia, conceived in an earlier and more tranquil decade, is a place where

> it should be lawful for every man to follow the religion of his choice, that each might strive to bring the others over to his own, provided that he quietly and modestly supported his own by reasons nor ... used any violence.

Forcible conversions are improper, the Utopians reason, because "if the struggle were decided by arms and riots, since the worst men are always the most unyielding, the best and holiest religion would be overwhelmed."[12] Other sixteenth-century writers, like John Foxe, argue more consistently that the use of severe punishments in matters

11. *The Complete Works of Thomas More*, vol. 6, part 1, ed. Thomas M. C. Lawler, Germain Marc'haudor, and Richard C. Marius (New Haven: Yale University Press, 1981), p. 407.
12. *The Complete Works of Sir Thomas More*, vol. 4, ed. Edward Suarez and J. H. Hexter (New Haven: Yale University Press, 1965), p. 221.

of faith is never appropriate, drawing a rigorous moral distinction between attempts at persuasion and corporal duress.

The force of this moral distinction pervades the disputes between religious majorities and minorities all through the sixteenth century. Typically a persecuted group accuses an important establishment figure of inflicting outrageous bodily pain in the course of investigating dissenters; the authority responds by publicly denying the charge. In the 1520s, when Protestants accuse More of beating suspects, tying knotted cords around their heads, and so forth, he publishes a lengthy *Apology* protesting his own gentleness. In the 1580s, when imprisoned Catholics complain that they have been tortured and forced to go without food, Burghley declares indignantly that they starved themselves out of obstinacy and were only "lightly" racked.[13] Those accused of persecution, in other words, attempt to disavow or at least mitigate their reputations for physical ferocity rather than to defend the legitimacy of such tactics. Even Robert Persons, a militant Jesuit who condemns Mary Tudor as a ditherer and advocates the armed invasion of England by Spain, prefers to achieve religious conformity by nonviolent means. "Matters of religion," he claims, "of all other affairs, is the point that most requireth liberty, both of judgment and will, and least beareth the force of straining."[14] Accordingly he proposes that after Catholicism is reintroduced into England, the Church spend several years persuading and instructing Protestants in the ways of the true church, instead of introducing the Inquisition posthaste.

Thus, although sixteenth-century religious conformity cannot be achieved without force, the use of compulsion in such matters seems to vex even those who continually resort to it. By the time Elizabeth succeeds Mary Tudor, heresy inquisitions are in very bad odor, and the 1559 Act of Supremacy drastically reduces the grounds upon which such prosecutions may be undertaken. When in the 1580s Elizabeth is faced by challenges to her ecclesiastical authority from both

13. William Cecil, Lord Burghley (attrib.), *A declaration of the favorable dealing of her majesty's commissioners* (1583). In *Lord Burghley and Queen Elizabeth* (New York: Alfred A. Knopf, 1960), p. 251, Conyers Read questions the usual attribution, holding that the pamphlet was written by Thomas Norton, one of Campion's examiners, with Burghley's sanction. More's behavior as an interrogator of heretics is still a matter of dispute among his biographers; for a balanced consideration of the evidence on both sides, see Richard Marius, *Thomas More: A Biography* (New York: Alfred A. Knopf, 1984), pp. 386–406.

14. Robert Persons, *News from Spain and Holland* (1593), D5r.

Catholics on the right and Puritans on the left, she charges her most important opponents not with heresy but with sedition or treason; while they maintain to the contrary that they suffer not for their political activities but purely for their religious beliefs. Edmund Campion, one of the first Jesuits to be tried and executed, claims that

> I never had mind . . . to deal in any respect with any matter of state or policy of this realm, as those things appertain not to my vocation, and from which I gladly estrange and sequester my thoughts.[15]

In print and at his trial, Campion and those who followed him to the scaffold seek to establish a space for "conscience" defined as an apolitical, nonactivist, purely spiritual entity.

The Catholics' task, like that of Protestants under Mary, is in some respects the mirror image of the authorities'. The establishment maintains that its resources are not merely secular, that its authority, deriving from God, rests upon more than mere physical strength. Its material power, it claims, expresses rather than produces its divine mandate: to think otherwise is to make legitimacy attend upon brute force, a doctrine variously excoriated as "tyrannical," "atheistical," or "machiavellian." Meanwhile the dissidents rely upon the same double scheme, drawing a similar, often barely tenable distinction between nonrevolutionary "resistance" of conscience and an outright rebellion against the existing political order.

⅋ DEVELOPING HERE is a conception of the difference, important in modern liberal democracy, between holding or expressing an opinion and wreaking havoc. This difference relies upon the separation of an arena of opinions—figured as conscience, mind, or spirit, and ascribed to an interior realm—and an "external," secular arena of actions in which the body is involved. These two arenas are imagined to be addressed by different means: persuasion is the appropriate means of addressing the spiritual realm, coercion appropriate to the body. The problem for Christians, then, even Christians who are willing to undertake heresy prosecutions, is that forcible tactics may be unsuitable or pointless in matters of religious conviction, insofar as that conviction is imagined as a spiritual property. When

15. Campion's open letter to the Privy Council, written and circulated before his arrest, was often reprinted both by Catholics and by Protestants seeking to refute his claims. For an example of such a point-by-point discussion see William Charke, *An answere to a seditious pamphlet lately cast abroade by a Jesuite* (London, 1581).

resolutely held, as we have already seen, a position that rigorously separates the coerced body from the persuaded soul implies that no one can be constrained to believe anything.

Several factors disturb the simplicity of this conceptual scheme. The first is that persuasion and coercion are not merely equivalent activities in separate-but-equal domains. Rather, coercion often is simply a more effective way of obtaining swift compliance. It is also, to the degree that it is more effective, morally more dangerous. (Even Tamburlaine, therefore, erects his white tent before his red or black one.) The relationship between persuasion and coercion can seem less a dichotomy of aim and method than a seamless progression from gentle, respectful means of encouragement to atrociously painful forms of violation.[16] This sense of sequence underlies the regular procedure, throughout the early modern period, for the interrogation of suspected criminals on the Continent: the accused is first asked questions without compulsion, then shown the instruments of torture and questioned again, then subjected to those instruments in a regular order meant to inflict increasingly intense suffering. At some point along this scale of pain, most but not all of those questioned begin to give the interrogators the answers they want. Even as the bodily ante is upped, however, the validity of the investigation is compromised, as we have already seen, by the possibility that something unconstrainable may have escaped, that the shattering of the body is not the same as the opening of the soul. One reason torture never becomes common in England is that lay jurists are chronically skeptical of the reliability of evidence obtained by such means.[17] Thus coercion and persuasion seem on the one hand theoretically separable but on the other hand part of the same continuum, on the one hand morally incommensurate but on the other hand a distinction without a difference.

In the early modern period, a second difficulty is posed by the

16. This problem is a modern one as well, as numerous legal and ethical cases suggest; in fact the gray areas between persuasion and coercion become more important insofar as the distinction between the two activities underlies a democracy that conceives itself as founded upon consent rather than tyranny. What degree of physical discomfort can investigators inflict upon recalcitrant crime suspects from whom they want to obtain confessions? Is it appropriate to sleep with a student or employee if he or she expresses willingness to do so, or does subordinate status inevitably contaminate the mechanisms of consent?

17. See, for example, the account in James Heath, *Torture and English Law* (Westport, Conn.: Greenwood Press, 1982).

practical inextricability of religion and politics, which tends to make hash of attempts to distinguish between what is God's and what is Caesar's by a simple mind/body dichotomy. Elizabeth's career at the head of the Church of England testifies both to the allure and the tenuousness of such distinctions. Elizabeth begins her reign by attempting to persuade a religious consensus. Her religious settlement demands not absolute and wholesale agreement, but merely superficial conformity. Although attendance at established church services is statutorily required, the language of those services is deliberately rendered vague enough to satisfy widely differing construals. When Parliament overwhelmingly passes a statute in 1563 defining two refusals to take the Oath of Supremacy as treason, Elizabeth forbids the administration of the oath to Mary's former clergy without her express permission. The Queen represents herself as willing to compromise—in Bacon's words, "not liking . . . to make windows into men's hearts and secret thoughts, except the abundance of them did overflow into overt and express acts and affirmations."[18] This formulation relies upon a distinction between the secret and the overt, between the contents of the heart and the express acts that make those contents publicly available. It allows the subject the privilege of an inward life uninvaded by sovereign power. For the purposes of social order, the young Elizabeth seems to declare, apparent consensus and "real" consensus are the same thing.

In the latter part of Elizabeth's reign, however, manifold challenges to her authority from both the right and the left undermine the confidence of her regime. The sanguine assumption that good outward behavior is all that a queen can reasonably require increasingly transforms itself into a paranoid anxiety that good outward behavior is merely the cloak and pretext for subversive conspiracies. This anxiety is only exacerbated by the willingness of Catholic casuists and Protestant radicals to exploit the hiddenness of the interior realm by resorting to various forms of equivocation. Violating common law precedent, Elizabeth's government begins to subject Catholics to torture in the 1580s, using bodily compulsions as a way to discover the truths of the soul. The careful demarcation between inside and outside, covert and obvious, soul and body, God and Caesar, persuasion

18. Bacon, *Certain Observations Made Upon a Libel Published this Present Year, 1592*, in James Spedding, *Letters and Life of Francis Bacon*, vol. 1 (London: Longmans, Green, and Co., 1890), p. 178. This treatise replies to the Catholic *Declaration of the true causes of the great troubles*, cited in chapter 2, note 23.

and coercion, threatens to collapse, even though those distinctions had been made earlier by Elizabeth's government itself, and continue to be insisted upon by religious dissidents politically loyal to her regime.[19] The conceptual crisis that results is suggested by the inconsistent way in which Elizabeth's government prosecutes Catholics. While the missionary priests are routinely found guilty of treason and savagely executed, vestiges of the heresy trial remain. Burghley arranges a mock debate between Edmund Campion and chosen Protestant divines, reminiscent of the debates between Mary's prelates and Ridley or Latimer several decades earlier—and finds, like his predecessors, that the effect of such a spectacle is highly equivocal: "The meek demeanor of their opponent, unprepared as he was, broken by the rack and his memory failing him, aroused unexpected sympathy among the anything but friendly audience."[20] Similarly, lay Catholics who aid and abet the priests are usually treated more like heretics than like the traitors the government claims them to be. Since they are accessories to the priests' treason their lives ought to be forfeit, but those who publicly renounce their Catholicism are regularly pardoned and released.

Yet a further problem is posed by the content of the religious disputes themselves, insofar as that is distinguishable from the ways in which conformity might be enforced or resisted. The dilemmas that arise from attempts to ensure religious conformity eventually seem— in post-Restoration England, in revolutionary America—to require a separation of the secular from religious sphere, and the placing of strict legal limits upon the use of bodily coercion to obtain mental agreement. However, that solution requires an intuitive consensus upon what pertains to the body and what to the mind or spirit: agreement often hard to obtain nowadays, and in the sixteenth century, precisely the point at which various sects find themselves drastically at odds. Central to the Marian heresy examinations is a discussion of the text *hoc est corpus meum*, seemingly transparent both to

19. For a description of the Catholic loyalist position and the way it differed from the militant Catholicism of William Allen and Robert Persons, see Arnold Pritchard, *Catholic Loyalism in Elizabethan England* (Chapel Hill: University of North Carolina Press, 1979), pp. 11–72, and Peter Holmes, *Resistance and Compromise: The Political Thought of Elizabethan Catholics*. For a useful discussion of the complementary way torturers and victims comprehended their respective situations, see Elizabeth Hanson, "Torture and Truth in Renaissance England," *Representations* 34 (1991): 53–84.

20. Alan Gordon Smith, *William Cecil* (New York: Haskell House, 1971 [reprint of the 1934 edition]), p. 199.

examiner and examinee, but rendered ambiguous by their disagreement. An exchange from the trial of Lady Jane Grey is wholly characteristic:

> FECKNAM: Why, does not Christ speak these words,
> 'Take, eat, this is my body?' Require you any plainer
> words? Doth he not say, it is his body?
> JANE: I grant, he saith so; and so he saith, 'I am the
> vine, I am the door,' but he is never the more for
> that, the door or the vine. Doth not St. Paul say, 'He
> calleth things not, as though they were?'[21]

Renaissance heresies typically veer from orthodoxy by ascribing materiality to the things orthodoxy calls spiritual, or spirituality to things orthodoxy insists are material. Anglicans revile Catholics for overemphasizing the external and the material aspects of religion, but reject with equal vigor those who believe that the Bible recounts mere allegories rather than actual occurrences, or who maintain that bodily decorum is unnecessary to the practice of religion. At issue is not merely whether the body is separate from or continuous with the mind, but what the terms "mind" and "body" mean: what their respective domains are, how and where they intersect.

❧ III ❧

RECENT CRITICS OF RENAISSANCE LITERATURE have emphasized the extremely close proximity of the aesthetic and political aspects of Renaissance art. This proximity seems to be borne out by sixteenth-century English literary theory, which derives its assumptions and categories from the openly political arts of classical rhetoric. But since the lessons of sixteenth-century politics are themselves ambiguous, the inextricability of art from politics merely complicates the issues under discussion here, as they affect the work of writers like Marlowe. On the one hand, rhetorical theory, gauging the value of language in terms of its manipulative efficacy, tends to elide conceptual differences between mind and body and between language and physical force. In religious disputes, on the other hand, just where effective rhetoric is most urgently necessary, that elision seems quite possibly inappropriate.

Philip Sidney, who like Marlowe was both highly trained as a rhetorician and deeply concerned with *realpolitik*, wittily invokes these

21. Foxe, *Acts and Monuments*, 6:416.

difficulties when he describes two kinds of female beauty in *The New Arcadia:*

> Methought love played in Philoclea's eyes and threatened in Pamela's; methought Philoclea's beauty only persuaded—but so persuaded as all hearts must yield; Pamela's beauty used violence—and such violence as no heart could resist.[22]

Without a clear difference between persuasion and violence, Sidney's contrast between the two sisters makes no sense. Philoclea is charming and submissive, Pamela dignified and imperious. At the same time, Sidney continually muddles the very distinction upon which he seems to rely. The irresistibility of Philoclea's persuasion makes it equivalent to coercion; the splendor of Pamela's violence makes it tantamount to enticement. Throughout the *Arcadia* this deliberate conceptual ambiguity informs Sidney's account of erotic love among princes, love equivocally poised between a voluntary resolution and a helpless compulsion, and between a private preoccupation and a political act.

In Marlowe, the difficulties seem even more acute and inescapable. Of the spotty information biographers have unearthed on Marlowe's life and career, a surprising proportion suggests his participation in dangerously unconventional beliefs and practices, dating from his undergraduate days to the weeks immediately preceding his violent death. Each individual testimony or datum might be unreliable, and each has indeed been challenged, particularly by critics who view Marlowe as subscribing to an impeccably orthodox worldview.[23] The sinister informer Richard Baines may have ulterior motives when he accuses Marlowe of reckless impieties, initiating an official investigation that is suspended after Marlowe's death. Marlowe's roommate Thomas Kyd, arrested and tortured when a heretical manuscript is found in his lodgings, certainly has sufficient reason to ascribe its possession to his associate. Robert Greene's claim that Marlowe was an "atheist" may be spiteful, and at any rate the term was employed very loosely in the period. Perhaps Marlowe rebels against his theo-

22. Sir Philip Sidney, *The Countess of Pembroke's Arcadia (The New Arcadia),* ed. Victor Skretkowicz (Oxford: Clarendon, 1987), p. 17.

23. For critics who see Marlowe's sensibility as essentially orthodox see, for example, Roy Battenhouse, *Marlowe's Tamburlaine* (Nashville: Vanderbilt University Press, 1941); and John Wilkes, *The Idea of Conscience in Renaissance Tragedy* (London: Routledge, 1990), pp. 144–69.

logical training at Cambridge, treasonously studying at the Jesuit college in Rheims, as Cambridge authorities claim when they try to withhold his degree. Perhaps, however, as some biographers have speculated, he really serves as a spy upon recusant Catholics on the behalf of Francis Walsingham (though such endeavors hardly prove him a zealous adherent of the Church of England). Perhaps Marlowe is personally acquainted with, and influenced by, the notoriously freethinking Giordano Bruno during Bruno's sojourn in England. Perhaps he associates with purported skeptics like Walter Ralegh and Thomas Hariot, as part of a religiously dissident "School of Night." Or perhaps he does not. Episodes in Marlowe's plays and poems lend credence to the contemporary allegations of homosexuality—a preference Elizabethans associate with religious deviance.[24] But here again, twentieth-century biographers and critics have little but speculation to go on.

Despite these uncertainties, the cumulative record implies that Marlowe is likely to take a highly personal interest in the complicated situation of the late sixteenth-century heretic. In the remainder of this chapter I shall argue that the nature of theater in Marlowe's plays is refracted through what I would call a "heretical conscience." This "heretical conscience" does not, however, merely refer to Marlowe's own actual, now irrecoverable, opinions or behaviors. Nor is it simply a matter of his use of precedents—the influence upon him, for instance, of Foxe's *Acts and Monuments*, one of the sources for *Tamburlaine* and *Dr. Faustus*. Rather it is a matter of Marlowe's recognizing that the primary political and religious crises of his time are closely related to the issues that make the Renaissance theater seem so promising and so dangerous.

In *Dr. Faustus*, Marlowe adapts an indigenous morality drama that in its original or pure form seems to fulfil all the criteria of pedagogical theater as the protheatricalists Sidney and Heywood imagine it. Dramas like *Everyman* attempt to convey lessons to the audience about problems of general concern. Everybody is going to die. Everybody worries about it, or ought to. The effect of universality in the morality play is intensified by its allegorical technique. Groups of people may be represented by a single character, like John Commonweal in Lindsay's *Satire of the Three Estates*. On the other hand, the

24. Alan Bray, *Homosexuality in Renaissance England* (London: Gay Men's Press, 1982).

traits, moods, or psychic components of an individual may be dispersed into various allegorical personifications, like Fancy, Despair, and Good Hope in Skelton's *Magnificence,* so that the message of the play seems to be reinforced by an entire community of characters. This dramaturgy is the product of a culture in which the difference between an individual and a group has not become highly charged, in which the boundaries between one individual and another are neither rigid nor ethically decisive. In the theatrical universe of the morality play, it is reasonable to imagine the audience as an essentially unanimous group that sees exemplary versions of itself mirrored in the abstract, generalized situations acted before it.

Well before Marlowe's time, however, morality drama had begun to change. Sixteenth-century morality plays are increasingly likely to treat relatively specialized topics, like the dilemma of the youthful prodigal or of the unwise ruler. As Bernard Spivack writes, "The human situation . . . is treated from some partial point of view, and restricted to the vices characteristic of some mode or station of life."[25] This particularizing tendency begins to confound the rather simple kinds of identification between character and spectator that Renaissance defenders of the theater take for granted. For instance, Heywood recommends chronicle history plays for stirring the patriotism of English kings:

> What English prince should he behold the true portraiture of that famous King Edward the third, foraging France . . . and would not suddenly be inflamed with so royal a spectacle, being made apt and fit for the like achievement.[26]

In the same vein, Sidney reminds us that Alexander took his copy of Homer with him on his campaigns, in order to be inspired by the example of Achilles. It might be obvious why Alexander would learn from Homer, or why an English king would be thrilled by a play about Edward III, or why every man would want to see *Everyman.* It is less obvious what a butcher, or a merchant's wife, or an apprentice would find compelling about the *Iliad,* or about a history play that deals entirely with the lives of the nobility. Sidney and Heywood presume that the social usefulness of theater flows from audiences' perception of a close resemblance between their own lives and the

25. Bernard Spivack, *Shakespeare and the Allegory of Evil* (New York: Columbia University Press, 1958), p. 207.
26. Heywood, *An apology for actors,* B4ʳ.

lives depicted onstage. As I mentioned in the last chapter, however, the unprecedented successes of the English Renaissance theater are grounded upon the surprising willingness of mass audiences to interest themselves in situations and in kinds of characters remote from anything they encountered outside the Globe or the Swan. Although, as we have seen, Kyd muses upon the curious workings of fellow feeling in *The Spanish Tragedy*, nothing in late sixteenth-century writing about the theater explicitly acknowledges the challenge contemporary dramaturgy poses to conventional accounts of audience response.

Marlowe, however, seems to recognize that his innovative theater must work its sweet violence from an oblique angle. At the conclusion of *Dr. Faustus*, the fate of the protagonist is described as straightforwardly edifying:

> Regard his hellish fall,
> Whose fiendful fortune may exhort the wise
> Only to wonder at unlawful things,
> Whose deepness doth entice such forward wits,
> To practice more than heavenly power permits.
>   (5.3.23–27)

But what, exactly, are spectators supposed to learn from Faustus? It is not clear that his "fortune" fits the pattern of exemplary instruction upon which the epilogue depends. In the play's opening lines, the Chorus announces his uniqueness in ways that suggest limitation:

> Not marching in the fields of Thrasimene,
> Where Mars did mate the warlike Carthagens,
> Nor sporting in the dalliance of love
> In courts of kings where state is overturned,
> Nor in the pomp of proud audacious deeds,
> Intends our muse to vaunt his heavenly verse.
>   (Prologue 1–6)

Faustus's story is only one among many possible stories, marked off grammatically ("not . . . nor . . . nor") and generically from epic, erotic, or chivalric plots. The Chorus emphasizes disparities, not similarities, among possible theatrical protagonists; so that Faustus's own tendency to cast himself as Everyman seems characteristically egoistical and myopic. If, however, each individual's story is different from every other's, then the exhortatory value of other people's experiences becomes questionable.

Throughout *Faustus*, Marlowe makes the individualist and naturalistic conventions of tragedy collide abruptly with the collectivist, allegorical procedures of the morality play, deliberately emphasizing the irreconcilability of the two genres.[27] The generic dislocation creates a series of dilemmas or equivocations where none seemed to exist before. W. W. Greg does not know what to make of Faustus's body: on the one hand Faustus seems to become a "spirit" upon signing the contract with the devil; on the other hand, much later in the play, Faustus "commits the sin of demoniality [with Helen], that is, bodily intercourse with demons."[28] Likewise Wilbur Sanders disapproves of Marlowe's inconsistent representation of Hell.[29] As the play proceeds toward its terrifying climax the physical location of hell and its corporeal horrors are increasingly emphasized, particularly in the B version, even though Mephistophilis earlier maintains that hell is not a place, but a state of mind: "Why, this is hell, nor am I out of it" (1.3.78). Such complaints may seem merely obtuse, since hell may be for the orthodox believer simultaneously a physical place and a state of mind, and damnation both a material and spiritual condition. Inadvertently Greg and Sanders identify, however, a consistent strain of inconsistency in *Faustus:* equivocations structured by theologico-political disputes over the relationship between bodies and minds, matter and spirit. These are the very controversies that, as we have already seen, dominate the heresy trial and its conceptualization by dissident and orthodox alike.

The imagery of Communion in *Faustus,* for instance, works in the same ambiguous way.[30] It is entirely consistent with Marlowe's tactics elsewhere in *Faustus* that the two quasisacramental moments in which the facts of the body seem most vividly present are also possibly but not necessarily moments of delusion: when Faustus's blood clots on his arm, and he momentarily sees "*homo fuge*" written there,

27. For a contrary view, which sees *Faustus* as essentially continuous with the morality tradition and its "movement . . . therefore inevitably towards orthodoxy rather than iconoclasm," see Michael Hattaway, "The Theology of Marlowe's *Dr. Faustus,*" *Renaissance Drama* new series 3 (1970): 51–78.

28. W. W. Greg, "The Damnation of Faustus," *Modern Language Review* 41 (1946): 97–107.

29. Wilbur Sanders, *The Dramatist and the Received Idea: Studies in the Plays of Marlowe and Shakespeare* (Cambridge: Cambridge University Press, 1968), pp. 194–242.

30. C. L. Barber notes the importance of Communion imagery in "The Form of Faustus' Fortunes Good or Bad," *Tulane Drama Review* 8 (1964): 92–119. The essay is republished in *Creating Elizabethan Tragedy.*

and then again when Christ's blood streams in the firmament, apparently forever out of reach. For here again, contemporary debates focus upon whether the elements undergo a material change (the Catholic position) or a change in spiritual character (the Lutheran position) or merely a transformation in the minds of the believers (the Zwinglian position). Renaissance disputes over the nature and power of devils run along similar lines. Some argue that devils can bring about material changes; others that they are at best masters of illusion; others that devils are pure hallucinations, projections of a guilty imagination.[31] These debates involve not merely disagreements about the source and efficacy of supernatural phenomena, but disagreements over the nature of, and the possibility of interaction between, matter and spirit. Thus when Faustus is dismembered and then reconstitutes himself in the comic scenes with the Horse-Courser, or when "Helen passes over the stage"—perhaps a resurrected historical Helen, perhaps a devil inhabiting Helen's corpse, perhaps a devil metamorphosed as Helen's duplicate—the uncanny fluidity of supernaturally controlled bodies obscure what exactly is happening and also, at the same time, whether the categories for specifying what might be happening are even appropriate. As in the heresy trial, it is not just a matter of labeling particular phenomena, of dividing or refusing to divide the realm of the body from the realm of the spirit, but of deciding what the terms of such classification are to signify.

The two texts we have of *Faustus*, the relative authority of which is endlessly debated among textual editors, inflects the action in opposite directions: the largely inner and spiritual struggles of the A text become extroverted, theatrical, and corporeal in the B text. The different versions exploit, that is, alternative interpretive options for the allegorical, psychomachic conventions of the morality play: one which tends to imagine the action as essentially internal to a single mind, the other of which tends to reify the allegorical abstractions and treat them as agents in their own right. The Good and Evil Angels, the Old Man, the mysterious force that holds Faustus down as he attempts to leap up to his God, even Mephistophilis himself: are these to be considered "natural persons," characters in their own

---

31. For the first of these three positions see, for instance, Jean Bodin, *De la Demonomanie des sorciers* (Paris, 1580); for the second, see Lewis Lavater, *Of ghostes and spirites walking by nyght* (London, 1572), and Lambertius Danaeus, *A dialogue of witches* (1575); for the third, see Reginald Scot, *The Discovery of Witchcraft* (1584).

right, or are they allegories, or are they guilty illusions? Perhaps these seem silly or hairsplitting questions: asked of an ordinary morality play, they would certainly be beside the point. And Renaissance drama, like its morality predecessors, often deliberately obscures the difference between natural and symbolic characters, so much so that the attempt to make the distinction itself can seem naive. But Marlowe makes it hard to discard such categories, unsatisfactory as they may be. Central to the critical debate about *Faustus* have long been the play's entirely ambiguous, but nonetheless unavoidable, claims about the freedom of Faustus's will.[32] Is he coerced, or is he persuaded? Is he responsible, or is he not? Is his fate in his own power, or is it imposed upon him? It is impossible to answer these questions, or even to ask them, without some rough rules for differentiating between what is proper to Faustus and what is not. But even as the distinctions are made they destabilize themselves, just as they do in the sixteenth-century heresy trial.

Both texts of *Faustus* employ allegorical conventions in deeply unsettling ways, dissolving any intuitions about "natural" or universally accepted boundaries between inside and outside, between soul and body, between self and other, even while insisting upon the importance of those boundaries. Marlowe wants it both ways, dramatizing a story of individual autonomy and radical alienation, but at the same time subjecting the assumptions upon which that story seems premised to a rigorous, suspicious critique.

❧ IV ❧

THE TWO *TAMBURLAINE* PLAYS pose even more clearly than *Faustus* the problem of what exemplary theater might mean in a world of radically diverse individuals. Zenocrate, spokesperson of pious orthodoxy, constantly underscores the connections among human beings:

---

32. For a variety of views on this issue, attempting to align Marlowe's view with a range of possible doctrines, see, for example, Lily Campbell, "Dr. Faustus: A Case of Conscience," *PMLA* 67 (1952): 219–39; Douglas Cole, *Suffering and Evil in the Plays of Christopher Marlowe* (Princeton: Princeton University Press, 1962); Richard Waswo, "Damnation, Protestant Style: Macbeth, Faustus, and Christian Tragedy," *Journal of Medieval and Renaissance Studies* 4 (1974): 63–99; Roy T. Eriksen, 'The Form of Faustus Fortunes': A Study of the Tragedy of Dr. Faustus (1616) (New Jersey: Humanities Press International, 1987), pp. 26–58.

> I fare, my lord, as other empresses
> That, when this frail and transitory flesh
> Hath sucked the measure of that vital air
> That feeds the body with his dated health,
> Wanes with enforced and necessary change.
>
> (*Tamburlaine II* 2.4.42–46)

Zenocrate sees herself as hemmed in by ordinary human weakness. Her days are numbered, her changes enforced and necessary. Her sense of fellow feeling proceeds, moreover, from a conception of her own body and the bodies of others as "frail and transitory": subject to capture, rape, torment, death. This frame of mind encourages her to derive lessons from the spectacles of those around her, especially when those spectacles emphasize physical vulnerability. In part I, for instance, she comes upon the corpses of Bazajeth and Zabina, and moralizes upon their fate:

> Those that are proud of fickle empery
> And place their chiefest good in earthly pomp,
> Behold the Turk and his great emperess!
> Ah, Tamburlaine my love, sweet Tamburlaine,
> That fights for sceptres and for slippery crowns,
> Behold the Turk and his great emperess!
>
> (*Tamburlaine I* 5.2.291–96)

Zenocrate behaves as Sidney or Heywood would expect a theater spectator to behave, generalizing from specific vivid cases in order to apply them to her own situation.

Zenocrate is not, however, at the hub of *Tamburlaine*. Her lover and husband dominates the plays, a man entirely insensitive to the sufferings of others, because he considers himself to be of a different kind. The stars that reigned at his birth, he declares, will never conjoin again until the end of the world. Whereas the body signifies common human weakness for Zenocrate, it expresses in Tamburlaine's case a transcendence of ordinary human frailty. Other bodies are wounded, but Tamburlaine's remains miraculously unscathed. Menaphon describes him as taller, larger, stronger, than anyone else: "in every part proportioned like the man/ Should make the world subdued to Tamburlaine" (1.1.27–28). Even at the moment of his death Tamburlaine imagines not a failure, but a reconfiguration of the body to allow a more perfect expression of and reward for the "fiery spirit" that no longer consents to terrestrial confinement.

[93]

In vain I strive and rail against those powers
That mean t'invest me with a higher throne,
As much too high for this disdainful earth.
(*Tamburlaine II* 5.3.121–23)

Tamburlaine refuses to be bound by precedent or to be intimidated by the fates of his own victims. By and large, he turns out to be right. Bazajeth's fate or Orcanes's fate is not Tamburlaine's fate. Fortune's wheel never turns—never, as his myriad enemies predict, grinds him back into servitude. The perennial victor does not merely happen to be callous to the examples of others. Rather empathy makes no sense to him, requires a kind of experience he never has.

The fundamental lack of reciprocity that characterizes human relationships throughout the two *Tamburlaine* plays necessarily typifies the rhetorical sphere as well. Tamburlaine convinces others, but they do not convince him, because none of the ways in which influence might be gained over him can possibly be effective. His fearlessness arms him against a rhetoric that attempts to terrify him, as Bazajeth's does. His mercilessness renders him equally incomprehending of the appeals of the weak. The virgins of Damascus desperately attempt to redefine empathy as characteristic of the strong man:

Pity our plights! O, pity poor Damascus!
Pity old age, within whose silver hairs
Honor and reverence evermore have reigned!
Pity the marriage-bed, where many a lord
In prime and glory of his loving joy,
Embraceth now with tears of ruth and blood
The jealous body of his fearful wife.
(*Tamburlaine I* 5.2.17–23)

But the whole play speaks against them. Tamburlaine cannot mistake the frail, dignified elders or the hopeful young lords for himself—cannot even recognize a similarity between himself and the bridegrooms of Damascus. In his world, an ability to enter imaginatively into the experiences of others is inextricable from the experience of being coerced or imagining oneself coerced.

Tamburlaine does not, however, renounce theatricality. Rather than killing his most significant foes, he keeps them captive for their curious entertainment value.

Now you shall feel the strength of Tamburlaine,
And, by the state of his supremacy,
Approve the difference 'twixt himself and you.
(*Tamburlaine II* 4.1.137–39)

Serving as Tambulaine's footstool or chariot horses, the conquered kings "approve" the difference between conqueror and conquered: a word that in Renaissance English signifies the giving of both testimony and consent. By enduring and displaying the effects of Tamburlaine's power, the kings are imagined to agree to it. Tamburlaine refuses to distinguish power over bodies from power over minds. In this paradigm coercion and persuasion are the same thing: it matters not why the subject obeys, but only that he does obey.

Tamburlaine's cruel theater dramatizes his particular form of individualism, in which his uniqueness is defined by the absolute disparity between master and slave, winner and loser, spectator and spectacle.[33] For their part, the slaves, losers, and spectacles resist as vigorously as they can their reduction to the degraded term of these binaries. Refusing to acknowledge the legitimacy of Tambulaine's power, they shower their conqueror with floods of abuse.

> ZENOCRATE: My lord, how can you suffer these
> Outrageous curses by these slaves of yours?
> TAMBURLAINE: To let them see, divine Zenocrate,
> I glory in the curses of my foes.
>
> (4.4.28–29)

The ultimate torment Tamburlaine visits upon his enemies is the recognition that their fiercest hatreds swerve helplessly into celebration and applause: that the more vehemently they protest, the more blithely their defiance is discredited. The "difference 'twixt himself and you" that Tamburlaine forcibly brings home to them is not the kind of difference that allows a principled toleration of incommensurate subjectivities, but one that so successfully exterminates all possibility of resistance that the existence of a rival perspective is hardly worth noticing.

Tamburlaine's nonchalance in the face of his victims' maledictions

---

33. Constance Kuriyama, *Hammer or Anvil* (New Brunswick: Rutgers University Press, 1980), draws attention to Marlowe's interest in this essentially competitive individualism, although I would want to distance my argument from her homophobic claims.

marks an important difference between him and Tudor monarchs. In sixteenth-century England utterances disrespectful or defiant of the sovereign power are prosecutable as treason. In fact political insolence, like religious schism, is a context-dependent offense, punished harshly when circumstances are unstable and tacitly permitted when it seems unlikely to do damage.[34] In the latter part of her reign, Elizabeth's precarious control over her subjects often forces her to take verbal defiance seriously, as the token of an insurrectionary will capable at any moment of challenging her government or endangering her person. By contrast Tamburlaine, whose power is virtually unlimited, need not fear such challenges and thus need not ordinarily bother to police his subjects' speech.

The exception that proves this rule is the case of Agydas, who by counseling Zenocrate to scorn her captor's love attracts Tamburlaine's murderous wrath. Agydas calls Tamburlaine's treatment of Zenocrate an "offensive rape,"[35] and points out that she is "supposed his worthless concubine." His formulation conflates, in thoroughly traditional fashion, the crimes of abduction and sexual violation: a conflation premised upon the assumption that any kidnapper with a woman at his mercy will inevitably ravish her. In fact, however, although Tamburlaine has no scruples about capturing Zenocrate, he refuses to proceed to the "obvious" next step: "For all blot of foul inchastity," he boasts to her father in 5.2, "I record heaven, her heavenly self is clear." Sexually forcing Zenocrate would spoil her suitability as Tamburlaine's consort, and would shatter, besides, his highly self-gratifying romance-hero pose. What he wants from Zenocrate—her love and her promise to marry him—can only be secured by her consent, a consent that requires Tamburlaine to make an entirely untypical discrimination between acceptable and unacceptable force. For once unable to "go all the way," Tamburlaine feels himself uncharacteristically vulnerable, and naysayers become as alarming to him as they are to Marlowe's sovereign. Eventually Tamburlaine wreaks poetic justice

34. For detailed discussion of the prosecution of seditious utterances in the Tudor period, see G. R. Elton, *Policy and Police: The Enforcement of the Reformation in the Age of Cromwell* (Cambridge: Cambridge University Press, 1972), pp. 263–425, and John Bellamy, *The Tudor Law of Treason* (London: Routledge and Kegan Paul, 1979), pp. 9–82.

35. Mary Beth Rose has drawn attention to this detail of Agydas's language in *The Expense of Spirit* (Ithaca: Cornell University Press, 1989), pp. 106–7, though her conclusions differ from mine.

upon Agydas by forcing him to commit suicide, a reluctant but technically voluntary act: forces him to acknowledge, in other words, the absolute ruler's power to abrogate consent as well as to open up a space for it.

Tamburlaine's pitiless egoism is part of a long tradition that, depending upon one's point of view, either demonstrates the superiority of Western forms of government or lays bare the West's actual reliance upon the same tactics that the East supposedly employs without mystifying overlay. From Herodotus's description of Xerxes' attempt to invade Greece, to network coverage of Saddam Hussein in the 1991 Iraq war, the "Oriental despot" as imagined by Western commentators characteristically neglects or tramples the moral difference between persuasion and coercion, consent and compulsion, citizenship and slavery. The Grand Turk, the Czar, the Emperors of China and Japan, all are imagined to found their power on the unembarrassed subjugation of their people's bodies rather than upon what Elizabeth I was fond of calling "the loving hearts" of her subjects. Marlowe subversively suggests, however, that a triumphant tyrant, secure in the knowledge that he can pulverize his opposition, is likely to be more tolerant of dissent than a narrowly empowered authority dependent upon the fickle consent of the governed.

Tamburlaine's power is thus distinguishable both from the "legitimate" forms of control sought by Western rulers and from the power wielded by Gyges, that other usurpatory shepherd, as it was discussed in the previous chapter. The power of the machiavel—Gyges, Richard, Lorenzo, Volpone—is an eminently social power, the ability to orchestrate what other people can and cannot perceive. Tamburlaine plays a few primitive tactical tricks of this kind early in his career, when his position is still uncertain, but thereafter nothing about his consciousness seems hidden from anyone. He always says exactly what he means, because an absolutely unrivaled ruler has no reason to hide anything, no motive for inwardness. One need only resort to "machiavellianism" when it matters what other people think: when it is necessary to evade their powers of surveillance, or to enlist their help against their true interests. Thus Marlowe's machiavel Barabbas, in The Jew of Malta, is a trader dependent upon the interpersonal exchanges of the marketplace, who must participate in an ineradicably social world despite his misanthropy and others' ostracism. Next to Tamburlaine's straightforwardness the machiavel's concealed menace looks like—and is—an admission of debility, insofar as it acknowledges both the existence of possible competitors and the need of accomplices.

The *Tamburlaine* plays seem to ask what would happen if the constraints the machiavel must plot to evade were simply absent from the start. If the figure of the machiavel raises spectres of skepticism, suggesting that other people are inaccessible, the figure of the absolute despot raises spectres of solipsism, suggesting that other people hardly matter. The individuating, interiorizing tendencies of heresy persecutions are differently inflected by Marlowe and Kyd. What "individualism" means in *The Spanish Tragedy* is an incommensurability among different people's aims and interests. Incommensurability produces conflict; but the theatrical violence that concludes the play suggests that human beings share, at least, a capacity for bodily suffering. In its backhanded way, *Spanish Tragedy* acknowledges a ground of similarity among different human beings.

In *Tamburlaine,* by contrast, the priority given to a single individual is so overwhelming that the possibility of genuine conflict seems to evaporate, and at the same time empathy is rendered a useless accessory of powerlessness. Yet it is important to recognize that Tamburlaine's power to change the world he lives in is not unlimited, that some things cannot be forced. In the second play, particularly, he and his allies confront predicaments that resist their paradigms of conquest. Nothing Tamburlaine can do will keep Zenocrate alive, or will fashion Calyphas into a suitably virile heir. Nothing Theridamas can do will make Olympia love him. Their almost automatic murderousness in these situations thus signifies frustration rather than triumph. They fail not because they use the wrong tactics, but because the problems they face are intractable ones, not susceptible to strategies of force *or* to strategies of persuasion.

Like Faustus, Tamburlaine presents a very unlikely vehicle for the kinds of exemplary instruction so hopefully described by Renaissance defenders of the theater. In a world in which, as we have already seen, all liability to persuasion is figured as capitulation, to be capable of terror and pity is to acknowledge oneself fatally vulnerable. The kind of theatrical responsiveness that Sidney and Heywood celebrate is precisely what Marlowe's Scythian defines himself as being able to resist. To the extent that they can "identify" with Tamburlaine, the theater spectators seem to declare themselves unlike him, to become—like so many others—his victim or subordinate.

> Won with thy words and conquered with thy looks,
> I yield myself, my men, and horse to thee.
>
> (1.2.228–29)

Conversely, the possibility of identification with or imitation of the hero seems to void the claim to singularity upon which Tamburlaine's appeal originally rests. The awkward situation of Tamburlaine's sons clarifies the problem. Calyphas, refusing to follow in his father's footsteps, recapitulates Tamburlaine's own rejection of the paternal vocation, but his "difference," like that of Tamburlaine's other victims, is necessarily a fatal one. Meanwhile Amyras and Celebinus, eagerly mimicking Tamburlaine's terrifying prototype, relinquish any claim to their father's singularity, and by forfeiting their uniqueness threaten his legacy.

Perhaps, however, the relationship between the theater audience and the world of *Tamburlaine* operates according to laws different from those which govern the interactions among characters onstage. The prologue to *Tamburlaine I*, both tentative and equivocal, seems to offer to the spectator options unavailable to Theridamas, Bazajeth, or Zenocrate:

> From jigging veins of rhyming mother-wits
> And such conceits as clownage keeps in pay,
> We'll lead you to the stately tent of war,
> Where you shall hear the Scythian Tamburlaine
> Threatening the world with high astounding terms,
> And scourging kingdoms with his conquering sword.
> View but his picture in this tragic glass,
> And then applaud his fortunes as you please.
>
> (1–8)

As in *Faustus*, Tamburlaine's unique career, Tamburlaine's strange play, is pointedly contrasted to other careers, other plays, other genres. He is introduced as a figure of tremendous power: astounding with his words, scourging with his sword. Nonetheless, the prologue does not imitate his tactics, but employs an ingratiating courtesy: "View but his picture." The theater spectators are addressed as honored guests at a massacre. Their evaluations of Tamburlaine are certainly not imagined as coerced by the spectacle; instead, they may employ whatever standards of evaluation they choose: "And then applaud his fortunes as you please."

David Thurn has pointed out the analogies between Tamburlaine's tactics and the tactics of a dramatist, his "determination to stage his power by making it fully visible."[36] Yet the *difference* between what Tamburlaine can do and what Marlowe can do finally seems at least as important. Part of the pleasure of watching Tamburlaine on stage is that the theater spectators, poised outside the represented world, are exempted from its terrifying rules. For them persuasion, theatrical rhetoric, remains distinct from real violence. The privilege of that exemption means that the audience's relationship to Tamburlaine's example cannot be forced and is necessarily quite unscripted. When Ben Jonson deplores Tamburlaine's "scenical strutting and furious vociferation" or T. S. Eliot condescends to Marlowe's "pretty simple huffe-snuffe bombast,"[37] they are exercising their entitlement as members of Marlowe's audience to spurn the importunities of the Scythian shepherd. "Bombast," after all, is a language the pretensions to power of which can be successfully resisted or ignored. This is not to say that theater has no power to move an audience, no coercive or seductive resources—just that these resources as Marlowe exercises them in *Tamburlaine* obey the logic of neither the antitheatricalist nor the protheatricalist position as outlined by Stephen Gosson or Philip Sidney. Both the standard positions insist upon the unbroken continuity between theatrical spectacle and the world: Marlowe insists upon their disparity.

In other plays, too, Marlowe suggests that theater may elicit something other than a predictably edified response. In *Dr. Faustus*, Satan's playlet of the Seven Deadly Sins distracts Faustus from thoughts of repentance. In *Edward II*, Gaveston contemplates strengthening his hold over Edward by means of Italian masques, comedies, pleasing shows. These spectacles powerfully impress those who witness them, but their effect depends not upon the inescapable moral violence of stage representation, but upon the interpretive preferences of the individual spectator. When theater is used expediently by Satan or by Gaveston, the possibility of apparent misreading is precisely the point. Satan knows Faustus well enough to know that he will be diverted from, not strengthened in, his resolve to repent by the very

---

36. David Thurn, "Sights of Power in *Tamburlaine*," *English Literary Renaissance* 19 (1989): 3–21.

37. Ben Jonson, *Timber, or Discoveries*, in C. H. Herford and Percy and Evelyn Simpson, *Ben Jonson* (London: Oxford University Press, 1952); T. S. Eliot, *Essays on Elizabethan Drama* (New York: Harcourt Brace and World, 1932), p. 58.

theater that is supposed to encourage his religious compunctions. Gaveston knows Edward well enough to know that when he sees naked boys performing the story of Actaeon, he will not recall that the myth was commonly glossed as an allegory about the unfortunate consequences of forbidden desire, or alternatively as a warning against the unreliability of sycophants. The flatterer—Satan or Gaveston—cannily tailors his theater to a highly specific rhetorical situation. Conversely, Marlowe shows Gaveston's instinctive perceptiveness eluding his nemesis, the blustering Mortimer, who contrives to kill Edward by sending an unpunctuated note to his keepers:

> This letter, written by a friend of ours,
> Contains his death, yet bids them save his life:
> (*Reads*) *Edwardum occidere nolite timere bonum est,*
> *Fear not to kill the king, 'tis good he die.*
> But read it thus, and that's another sense:
> *Edwardum occidere nolite timere bonum est,*
> *Kill not the king, 'tis good to fear the worst.*
> Unpointed as it is, thus it shall go.
> That, being dead, if it chance to be found,
> Matrevis and the rest may bear the blame,
> And we be quit that caused it to be done.
>
> (5.4.7–16)

Exulting in the letter's grammatical ingenuity, Mortimer forgets that what matters is not whether it *can* be construed as exonerating him, but whether young Edward III, once he succeeds his deposed father, *will* construe it that way. In the event the new king, rightly convinced of Mortimer's guilt, pays no attention to the note's punctuation and has the usurper hauled off to execution regardless.

Satan and Gaveston, devising amusements for individual clients, might be described as successful patronage poets. When Marlowe writes *Dr. Faustus* or *Tamburlaine* for a professional repertory company, he is participating in a new kind of literary economy that aims to make a profit by supplying entertainment to a large, miscellaneous audience. It would be surprising if the differences in the two kinds of enterprise did not occur to him—if he were not, as a practical matter, alert to the special challenges of appealing spectators who come to the theater with unpredictably various interests, capacities, and beliefs. A good deal of Marlowe criticism has undertaken to eliminate the interpretive instability of the plays by attempting, explicitly or tacitly, to retrieve the mentality of their original audiences: they were or were not repelled by cruelty, they were or were not convinced Christians, they did or did not possess aspiring minds. Such critics assume that it is possible to make blanket generalizations about Elizabethan theatergoers, even when they admit that "in modern viewers and readers . . . we would expect to encounter a considerable variety of personal reactions."[38] Similarly, many of Marlowe's important modern critics, even when they stress Marlowe's subversiveness, assume that it fits into the context of a simple Manichean division between an orthodox majority and the unorthodox minority, between the godly and the damned. Harry Levin's Marlowe is a talented overreacher fighting a doomed battle against human limitation; Stephen Greenblatt's an ineffective saboteur fighting a doomed battle against the overwhelming forces of Renaissance cultural discipline.[39] Both battles seem always already lost, owing to the immense disproportion between tiny Marlowe on one side and the rest of the world solidly unified against him on the other. In fact, however, the heresy disputes in the sixteenth century reveal a splintering of belief into infinite shades of opinion, and an active struggle, once again conducted both by force and by persuasion, not merely to endorse or deny a static orthodoxy but to control and revise what counts as orthodox in the first place.

Appealing to an audience of his contemporaries may have seemed a considerably trickier endeavor to Marlowe than it does to us: a distance of four hundred years makes it easy to overlook or downplay the significance of differences that loomed large at the time. As a kind of recompense, however, the existence of those differences probably made Marlowe's own situation seem considerably less desperate to him than it does in long retrospect, to critics fixated, as Marlowe of course could not be, upon his violent and untimely end. Reported by Richard Baines and Thomas Kyd to believe that the Bible revealed Moses to be a juggler, Mary a whore, and Christ a homosexual, Mar-

38. Richard Levin, "The Contemporary Perception of Marlowe's *Tamburlaine*," *Medieval and Renaissance Drama in English* 1 (1984): 51. Levin claims convincingly, pp. 51–70, that no one whose response to *Tamburlaine* has come down to us saw the play as a consistent exercise in deliberately intended authorial irony. But this is only one, very restricted, way in which the play might elicit a mixed response. The very passages Levin quotes to buttress his claim suggest a wide range of evaluations of the hero and of the play, ranging from enthusiasm to anger to condescension.

39. Harry Levin, *The Overreacher: A Study of Christopher Marlowe* (Cambridge: Harvard University Press, 1952); Stephen Greenblatt, *Renaissance Self-Fashioning* (Chicago: University of Chicago Press, 1981), pp. 193–221.

lowe clearly knows how to read, as we say, against the grain of the text. But once reading "against the grain" becomes possible, a deep skepticism about meaning and where it inheres may result. Under the gaze of multiple spectators, interpretations proliferate uncontrollably, and in place of consensus one is left with myriad perspectives, each one unique, but none authoritative. Just as the incineration of a heretic may produce a terrified recantation of unorthodoxy in one spectator and an increased confidence in the rightness of the heretic's cause in another, so the displays of Marlovian theater are never self-evident, because the responses of individuals are unpredictable, because one person's orthodoxy is another person's heresy, because no external methods of compelling belief are assured of success. The debate about the morality of theater in the late sixteenth century, like the concurrent debate about heretical opinion, nostalgically and implausibly imagines a collective social body constituted through consensus. Marlowe, however—contemptuous of received interpretations himself, highly individual in his own convictions—does not address his audience as a unanimous totality, an "interpretive community" of any kind. What he sees as the sheer diversity of his audience complicates his rhetorical task; where everyone is a patron, one cannot count upon anything, even upon the reliable perversity of an Edward or a Faustus. This is a theatrical analogue to the religious Reformation taken to its radical conclusion, a conclusion to which, I suspect, Marlowe is wholly willing to pursue it.

ॐ 4 ॐ

PROOF AND CONSEQUENCES:
OTHELLO AND THE CRIME
OF INTENTION

ॐ I ॐ

AT HIS TRIAL on a trumped-up treason charge in 1603, Sir Walter Ralegh complained that the prosecutors had "not proved any one thing against me by direct proofs, but all by circumstances." Justice Warburton responded:

> I marvel, Sir Walter, that you being of such experience and wit, should stand on this point; for so many horse-stealers may escape, if they may not be condemned without witnesses. If one should rush into the king's privy chamber, whilst he is alone, and kill the king . . . and this man be met coming with his sword drawn all bloody: shall he not be condemned to death?[1]

Warburton's explication of English legal custom is correct. On the Continent, the kinds and amount of evidence necessary for conviction were strictly prescribed. Two eyewitnesses, or a confession—which could be obtained under torture—were ordinarily required. In England, by contrast, evidentiary rules remained loose, almost chaotic. Under most circumstances torture was impermissible, but as John Langbein has pointed out, this apparent humanity was made possible by the fact that circumstantial evidence was all that was required for conviction. English courts made no rules about the admissibility of evidence, no qualitative distinction among kinds of proof, until well into the seventeenth century.[2] The power to convince the jury was all that mattered.

---

1. William Cobbett and Thomas Howell, *Cobbett's Complete Collection of State Trials* (London, 1809), 2:15.
2. For a discussion of the difference between the regular Continental use of judicial torture (that is, torture employed during the evidence-gathering stage) and its relatively infrequent use in England, see James Heath, *Torture and English Law* (Westport, Conn.: Greenwood Press, 1982). In *Torture and the Law of Proof* (Chicago: University of Chicago Press, 1977), Langbein connects the Continental practice with strict eviden-

Less than a year after Ralegh's trial, the King's Men performed *Othello* for the first time. A debate about evidence occurs virtually in the center of the play. To Othello's demands for "ocular proof" of Desdemona's infidelity, Iago maintains that Othello must content himself with "imputation and strong circumstances"—that is, with the kind of inferential proof upon which English courts often relied. Othello's eventual acceptance of this argument, of course, leads directly to his downfall. Why should Shakespeare figure the pivotal moment of the tragedy in these terms? What is the relevance of evidentiary concerns to the marital difficulties of a Moor and a Venetian? Why should a play about a disastrous sexual jealousy begin, as Robert Heilman noted long ago, "where some plays end, with a formal legal hearing that clears things up," and "advance by a series of scenes analogous to trials or court actions"?[3]

The answer lies in the similarity between some of the most fundamental issues of tragic subjectivity, as this play conceives them, and those raised by the procedures for criminal prosecution in Elizabethan and Jacobean England, procedures in many respects unique in Renaissance Europe. Recently, literary critics who have written on Eng-

---

lary rules; if one could convict only those criminals who confessed, one had a very strong motive to compel that confession. He shows both how the relative infrequency of torture in England, and its abolition on the Continent in the eighteenth century, are directly linked not to the greater humaneness of prosecutors but to the acceptance of a looser evidentiary standard. Despite this looseness, both Langbein and John Bellamy, in *Criminal Law and Society in Late Medieval and Tudor England* (New York: St. Martin's, 1984), argue that in the course of the sixteenth century, English courts begin to pay more attention to the orderly gathering of evidence and its presentation in court. In *Probability and Certainty in Seventeenth-Century England* (Princeton: Princeton University Press, 1983), pp. 163–93, Barbara Shapiro describes the way the belated development of the English law of evidence in the seventeenth century reflects changes in the general intellectual climate during this period; the origins of the phenomena she describes can be traced in accounts of sixteenth-century criminal trials.

3. Robert Heilman, *The Magic in the Web: Action and Language in Othello* (Lexington: University of Kentucky Press, 1956), p. 129. Heilman relates *Othello*'s legal scenes and metaphors to ironies of justice: 127–36; 152–68. Two sophisticated discussions of *Othello* treat the issue of legality in terms of a rhetorical tradition inherited from Cicero and Quintilian. In "'Preposterous Conclusions': Eros, *Enargeia*, and the Composition of *Othello*," *Representations* 18 (spring 1987): 129–57, Joel Altman discusses problems of probability in the play in terms of the figure of *hysteron proteron*. In "Dilation and Delation in *Othello*," in *Shakespeare and the Question of Theory* (New York: Methuen, 1985), 54–74, Patricia Parker analyzes the significance of narrative unfolding in response to accusatory interrogation. Both these essays have informed my own.

lish Renaissance crime and punishment have often followed Foucault's lead, concentrating upon the scene of public execution.[4] But with the notable exception of some executions for treason and heresy, English executions tended to be relatively unspectacular affairs. Hanging by the neck until dead was the uniform method of capital punishment for most felonies under common law. Hanging was not necessarily a humane form of execution—those whose necks were not broken immediately suffered slow death from asphyxiation—but neither did it have the cruel pertinence to a particular offense highlighted by French and German punishments. The difference between crude English methods and the more ferocious, more delicately calibrated forms of execution on the Continent attracted considerable comment from contemporaries.[5] On the other hand, while the Continental trial was conducted in secret and much of the testimony was presented in writing, in England the trial was a public, oral event, sometimes drawing large crowds, and detailed accounts of important

4. See, for instance, Jonathan Goldberg, *James I and the Politics of Literature* (Baltimore: Johns Hopkins University Press, 1983), pp. 2–6; Francis Barker, *The Tremulous Private Body* (New York: Methuen, 1984), pp. 13–25, 62–65; Leonard Tennenhouse, *Power on Display: The Politics of Shakespeare's Genres* (New York: Methuen, 1986), pp. 13–14, 115–46; Steven Mullaney, "Lying Like Truth: Representation and Treason in Renaissance England," *ELH* 47 (1980): 32–33. Foucault himself mentions the anomalies of the English system, *Discipline and Punish: The Birth of the Prison* (New York: Pantheon, 1977), p. 35.

5. Thomas Smith praised the relative humaneness of English common law in *De Republica Anglorum* (1583), ed. L. Alston (Cambridge: Cambridge University Press, 1906), 2.24; but the uniformity of punishment, and the illegality of torture under most circumstances, distressed commentators who thought it made insufficient distinction among crimes of varying degrees of heinousness. See, for example, the prefatory letter in W. W., *A true and iust recorde, of the information, examination, and confession of all the witches, taken at St. Oses in the countie of Essex* (London, 1582). According to Frederick Pollock and Frederick William Maitland, *A History of English Law before the Time of Edward I* (London: Cambridge University Press, 1968), 1:188–89, comments by English legal personnel on the distinctively English character of the common law begin shortly after the Norman Conquest. For a useful overview of the important procedural differences in English and Continental criminal prosecution, see John Langbein, *Prosecuting Crime in the Renaissance: England, Germany, France* (Cambridge: Harvard University Press, 1974). J. S. Cockburn's *A History of English Assizes 1558–1714* (Cambridge: Cambridge University Press, 1972), and John Bellamy's *Criminal Law and Society in Late Medieval and Tudor England* (New York: St. Martin's, 1984), give a more circumstantial account of the ordinary processes of English criminal justice in the sixteenth and seventeenth centuries. Thomas Andrew Green provides a helpful account of the development of the jury trial in *Verdict According to Conscience: Perspectives on the English Criminal Trial Jury 1200–1800* (Chicago: University of Chicago Press, 1985).

or sensational trials were printed shortly after they had occurred. Moreover, the English jury system, unique in Europe, made local laymen not only onlookers, but participants in the revelatory process. While France, Italy, and Germany put decisions about guilt or innocence into the hands of judges, in England the task of the bench was supposed to be restricted to "finding law," that is, to determining the applicable statutes and precedents. It was up to the English jury to "find fact," that is, to determine what had really occurred and to deliver a verdict.[6] If an English defendant was convicted by process of common law, his or her punishment was not, as it was on the Continent, what Foucault calls "the public support of a procedure that had hitherto remained in the shade."[7] Public punishment in England was rather the final episode in a considerably more protracted spectacle.

The effect of the English system, then, is to displace the focus of public attention from the processes of punishment to the processes of gathering and interpreting evidence. Many criminal trials—undoubtedly the vast majority—were perfunctory or uninteresting, just as they are today. Moreover, justice was often an extremely hasty affair: a routine capital case tried at the quarterly assize sessions could take under an hour. But given the right situation, the English public trial could and did become an arena in which urgent questions of interpretation—questions with implications for a wide variety of social and intellectual practices—had to be addressed in practical terms before a large and curious audience. A guilty secret is "discovered"; a previously hidden criminal fact is brought into view; hermeneutic uncertainty is followed by resolution. The specific question posed by Ralegh and answered by Warburton, the particular demand made by Othello and met by Iago, resonate powerfully with the general concerns of this book.

What was the jury's "finding of fact" supposed to involve? From its earliest origins, the English common law tradition emphasized the importance of clarity and obviousness: what was called the "overt fact" in a period where "fact" often meant "deed." This is not to deny, of course, that people were often convicted upon inadequate evidence. Rather, in theory, the law was imagined to punish socially ob-

6. Thomas Andrew Green provides not only a helpful discussion of the significance of the distinction between finding fact and finding law in the English criminal trial, but an illuminating account of the way the distinction is reimagined in the course of the sixteenth and seventeenth centuries.

7. Foucault, *Discipline and Punish*, p. 43.

served or observable phenomena. Someone who has malicious notions about a neighbor does not commit slander until she voices
them. Someone who contemplates stealing his master's silverware is
not guilty of theft until he actually pockets a spoon or a fork. Richard
Hooker writes:

> Laws politic, ordained for external order and regiment amongst men,
> are never framed as they should be, unless presuming the will of man
> to be inwardly obstinate, rebellious, and averse from all obedience
> unto the sacred laws of his nature. . . . They do accordingly provide
> notwithstanding so to frame his outward actions, that there be no hin-
> drance unto the common good for which societies are instituted.
> (1.1.2–30)

In other words, law ignores unacted desires not because wicked secrets are rare, but rather because they are universal. The courtroom
does not attempt to regenerate individuals, but merely to restrain
them from acting out their inherent obstinacy, rebelliousness, and
disobedience in ways that injure other people.

In a Christian scheme, temporal judgment differs importantly in
this respect from divine judgment. What matters to the truly devout
ought to be not what other human beings see, but what God sees:
"Beware of practicing your piety before men in order to be seen by
them," Christ warns his disciples (Matthew 6.1). The New Testament
is continually declaring the insufficiency of a mere "external" compliance with the Law, insisting upon the significance of socially unavailable material like unspoken intentions and unacted desires. Lasci-
vious thoughts, declares Christ, are as much an evil as outright
fornication: "I say to you that every one who looks at a woman lust-
fully has already committed adultery with her in his heart" (Matthew
5.28). Nonetheless, human beings, who have no access to other
people's thoughts, fantasies, or inchoate intentions, must leave the
chastisement of such transgressions to the all-seeing deity who alone
can detect them. If purely "inward" matters could be made subject to
legal prosecution, every member of a community would be vulnerable to the misconstructions of their neighbors. We have already seen
how heresy, a form of thought-crime usually prosecuted in the ecclesiastical courts rather than at common law, presents stubborn problems of detection and enforcement. Surely sensible people would prefer not to multiply the occasions to adjudicate, or be suspected of,
such crimes.

So the law, in Hooker's words, is "not . . . unjust, but unperfect" (5.9.3). Unlike the religious polemicist, who, as we have already seen, is prone recklessly to lay claim to infallibility and omniscience, the lawyer must respect the distinction between omniscient and limited vision, and between inside and outside, that we have already seen elaborated in many other Renaissance contexts. In Anglo-Saxon times, in fact, the perpetrator's intention was not considered at all: manslaughter was considered the same action as premeditated murder, and elicited the same punishment, a heavy fine paid by the slayer's family to the victim's kin. Even before the Norman conquest, however, different degrees of culpability began to be elaborated, based upon evidence of the perpetrator's intent. By the thirteenth century, Bracton would write that a criminal must not only perform an "overt fact" or "open deed" condemned by statute, legal precedent, or custom, but must possess *mens rea*, or a guilty mind. A person who caused injuries accidentally, while insane, or while a minor, had therefore not committed a crime.

Nonetheless, the focus of the court remained naturally upon the prohibited action, which was, of course, the reason the defendant was being tried in the first place. Until the time of Henry VIII, manslaughter or accidental death was not statutorily separated from premeditated murder; rather, a person who had caused a death accidentally was charged with homicide and then routinely pardoned or acquitted, while deliberate killers were considered "unpardonable."[8] Moreover, although the court was allowed to treat unwitting offenses leniently, the requirement of *mens rea* did not ordinarily lead to elaborate speculation about the defendant's state of mind. The insanity

8. For the slow development of the distinction between manslaughter and murder, see Theodore Plunkett, *A Concise History of the Common Law* (Boston: Little, Brown, 1956), pp. 444–46; Frederick Pollock and Frederic William Maitland, *A History of English Law before the Time of Edward I*, 2:470–79; and Thomas Green, *Verdict According to Conscience*, pp. 29–58. In the thirteenth century the accidental slayer had to obtain a royal pardon *de cursu*; by the end of the fourteenth century he was simply acquitted. Green also cites evidence that medieval juries distinguished between "truly premeditated" and "opportunistic" theft. Complicating the tracing of such conceptual changes, as Green argues, is not only the very flexible medieval pardon system, but the fact that the institution of the jury trial delayed statutory reform. For instance, throughout the Middle Ages and Renaissance the legal definition of justifiable self-defense was much stricter than community standards; but because jurors tended simply to acquit defendants whom they considered to have acted reasonably, even if they did not meet the legal criteria, there was little motivation to alter the statute.

defense, often criticized today for its reliance upon dubious conjectures about motive and responsibility, was apparently restricted to persons so unequivocally demented that it did not generate controversy. *Mens rea*, insofar as it became an issue in the courtroom at all, was conceived to be an additional criterion for or component of a criminal offense; not, as in the New Testament, its essential nature.

The decision in *Hales v. Pettit*, an important case in property law, succinctly recounts the usual rule in Elizabethan law-French:

> *Car imagination de ment de faire tort sans le act fait, n'est punishable en nostre ley, ne le resolution de faire ceo tort, que il ne fait, n'est punishable, mes le feasons del act est le sole point que nostre ley respect.*
>
> [The imagination of the mind to do wrong without the act done, is not punishable in our law; nor is the resolution to do that wrong, which one does not do, punishable, but the doing of the act is the only point which the law considers.][9]

Two kinds of felony, however, complicate the usual, rather straightforward relationship between act and *mens rea*, and confuse the clear distinction between external and internal "facts." Crimes of witchcraft and treason—crimes with which *Othello* is explicitly concerned[10]—are conceived so as often to require the discovery of the defendant's inward truth. Prosecutions for both offenses rise sharply in the Tudor and early Stuart years, forcing the courts to deal with just the kind of entity with which the temporal law usually declines to concern itself.

Elizabethan and Jacobean statutes leave it unclear whether witchcraft is essentially a mental, inward crime—consisting in the secret allegiance to evil powers—or whether it is prosecuted because, like

---

9. *Les commentaries, ou les reportes de Edmund Plowden* (London, 1599), p. 260. I thank W. Nicholas Knight for drawing my attention to this case in his manuscript, *Shakespeare and Equity.*

10. Neither of these crimes was new to the English Renaissance, but both were prosecuted with a zeal unknown in previous ages, and in both cases the definition of the crime was significantly expanded. For an account of the sudden upsurge in witchcraft prosecution in the sixteenth and early seventeenth centuries, see Keith Thomas, *Religion and the Decline of Magic* (New York: Scribner, 1971), pp. 435–583, and Alan Macfarlane, *Witchcraft in Tudor and Stuart England* (New York: Harper and Row, 1970), esp. pp. 200–207. For the expanded prosecution of treason in the sixteenth century, see John Bellamy, *The Tudor Law of Treason: An Introduction* (Toronto: University of Toronto Press, 1979).

murder or theft, it ruins the lives and properties of others.[11] Contemporary commentators call this the problem of "pact or act"; generally they argue that the pact constitutes the crime and that the social harms that result constitute the evidence for the crime. For what might witchcraft be, but a particularly virulent intention to do evil, a mind so thoroughly guilty that its inward imaginings spill over into the visible, tangible outer world? English juries were notoriously reluctant to convict in the absence of material damages, but strictly speaking the blasted livestock, the wasted children, the possessed neighbors, the milk that refused to become butter were merely the effects or symptoms of witchcraft and not its essence. Reginald Scot points out some of the problems of prosecuting a crime defined in this way in his skeptical treatise *The Discovery of Witchcraft*. Scrutiny of motives, Scot claims, is simply inappropriate for criminal prosecution:

> By which reason everyone should be executed, that wisheth evil to his neighbor. . . . But if the will should be punished by man, according to the offense against God, we should be driven by thousands at once to the slaughterhouse or butchery.[12]

In other words, Scot complains that witchcraft prosecutions trample the ordinary scruple against attempting to ascertain another's unmanifested thoughts, presumptuously erasing the difference between God and man.

The problem is easy for Scot, however, only because he does not believe in witchcraft. Those who do, and who insist that the Biblical injunction against witches must be enforced, find themselves in an awkward dilemma. On one hand they realize that witchcraft can only be discovered by the effects it wreaks in the world—effects which, admittedly, can stem from a variety of causes. "The true marks of a witch, or mental characters, are not easy to be discerned," writes John Gaule, insisting that because of the unusually high possibility of error

---

11. Keith Thomas, *Religion and the Decline of Magic*, pp. 435–68, plausibly ascribes the ambiguity of English conceptions of witchcraft to their double origin in indigenous popular belief, which emphasized *maleficium*, and an intellectual tradition that emphasized allegiance to the devil. (Contemporaries do not, however, make a clear distinction between the two traditions.)

12. Reginald Scot, *The Discoverie of Witchcraft* (1584), ed. Brinsley Nicholson (Totowa, N.J.: Rowman and Littlefield, 1973), ix.

in such cases, the evidence for conviction ought to be absolutely compelling. At the same time, the crime is by nature secret, a form of malevolent wishing, and the diabolical forces it employs invisible. The witch does not need to be present at the scene of the crime (so alibis cannot avail her) nor, since she does not employ ordinary weapons, are investigators likely to find unmistakable physical signs of her involvement. So Gaule later concedes:

> Neither is it requisite that so palpable evidence for conviction should here come in, as in more sensible matters. It is enough if there be but so much circumstantial proof or evidence, as the substance, matter, and nature of such an abstruse mystery of iniquity will well admit.[13]

The standards of proof, in other words, should be both more stringent and more lenient than they are in other cases. "Circumstantial proof" seems by its nature dubious, likely to amount to no more than a collection of fortuities. But in witchcraft cases it is normally all that is available.

It is easy to see how this problem arises again and again. Even if juries tend to regard seriously only those cases of alleged witchcraft in which harm has befallen persons or property, they still need to convince themselves that the defendant has indeed produced the catastrophe in question by some occult means. Their task, therefore, is essentially an inductive one. They have to trace the observable evidence, such as it is, back to its supposed origin in the witch's inscrutable inward perversity. The lack of "palpable" evidence in witchcraft cases is thus intrinsically connected with the unusual importance to such cases of the defendant's "guilty mind."

The crime of treason presents related conceptual and practical problems. According to medieval statute, treason is the crime of "compassing or imagining the death of the king," and this language persists through all the many Tudor and Stuart extensions and reformulations of the law. Originally, apparently, the definition was merely meant to permit the prosecution of accessories to a treasonable conspiracy, or to those intercepted before they had had occasion to do any serious harm. (For of course, as John Harington famously remarks, treason always fails, since "if it succeeds then none dare call

13. John Gaule, *Select cases of conscience touching witches and witchcraft* (London, 1646), pp. 91, 194.

[112]

it treason.")[14] By the sixteenth century, however, the statutory language had produced a tradition of interpretation that emphasizes the essentially *internal* nature of the crime. The legal commentator Fernando Pulton explains:

> [the law of treason] doth not only restrain all persons from laying violent hands upon the person of the King, but also by prevention it doth inhibit them so much as to compass, or imagine, or to devise and think in their hearts to cut off by violent or untimely death, the life of the King.

Treason, in other words, may occur in the imagination before and even in the absence of any manifestly treasonous activity. But how is the jury to know what a man has devised or thought in his heart? Pulton continues:

> Seeing compassing and imagination is a secret thing hidden in the breast of man, and cannot be known but by an open fact or deed, it is requisite to have some thing or means to notify the same to others before it can be discovered and punished.[15]

For treason as for witchcraft, then, the "overt act" is not the crime itself—as it would be, say, in a case of theft or murder—but a *symptom* of an offense that has actually already been committed. The difference is subtle but important. For all classes of crimes English courts require both a "guilty mind" and an "overt fact"; but whereas for most crimes the guilty mind is conceived as a kind of supplement to the overt fact, the reverse is true in treason or witchcraft cases.

Thus treason trials throughout the sixteenth and early seventeenth centuries feature arguments over what counts as proof, as what Pulton would call "notification," that traitorous imaginings have occurred. At his trial Henry Neville, one of Essex's friends, protests that he has not taken part in Essex's insurrection itself, but merely partici-

14. *The Epigrams of Sir John Harington*, ed. Norman McClure (Philadelphia: University of Pennsylvania Press, 1926), 4.259.

15. Fernando Pulton, *De pace regis et regnis, viz. A treatise declaring which be the great and generall offences of the realme* (London, 1610), p. 108. In *The Third Part of the Institutes of the Laws of England, Concerning high treason, and other pleas of the crown, and criminall courts* . . . (London, 1644), the important Jacobean jurist Edward Coke reviews the question of evidence in treason cases in similar terms, stressing that the insistence upon an "overt act" protects the defendant against random or spiteful prosecutions.

pated in one of the conferences planning the rebellion: this, he maintains, "was no more treason than the child in the mother's belly is a child." In his view, treason still in the planning stages, because hidden and undeveloped, is therefore not yet a crime at all. But the judges reply that "the compassing of the Kings destruction ... implied in that consultation, was treason, in the very thought and cogitation."[16] For the judges, treason by statutory definition consists in "thought and cogitation," so the consultation with the leaders of the coup suffices as the "overt act," the public manifestation, needed to render such thoughts liable to prosecution. Much more difficult is the case of Thomas More, who refuses to take the Oath of Supremacy and declines as well to specify his reasons.[17] His silence seems to present to observers a smooth and impenetrable surface. When the Attorney General, Christopher Hales, claims that "your silence . . . is an evident sign of the malice of your heart," More reminds the court that silence is ordinarily construed under common law to signify not malice but consent. Where was the "evident sign" that declared to the world More's inward disaffection? Desperate, the prosecutors had finally to resort to a dubious report of a conversation in which More was supposed to have denied Henry's authority in ecclesiastical matters. The conversation, not the silence, could then provide grounds for conviction. Shortly thereafter, a new statute classed refusal and silence themselves as "overt acts"—as circumstantial proof of what Pulton calls the "secret thing hidden in the breast of man."

∂ TREASON AND WITCHCRAFT, conceived as crimes that occur in the mind alone prior to any outward manifestation, pose in especially acute form the skeptical problem of making connections between overt and covert, between visible effect and invisible cause. When the jury goes about trying to "find fact" in such cases, what does it expect to discover? In *The Trial of Witch-craft*, John Cotta writes:

> Many offenses . . . there are, neither manifest to sense, nor evident to reason, against which only likelihood and presumptions do arise in judgment: whereby notwithstanding, through narrow search and strict examination, circumspect and curious view of every circumstance . . .

16. Francis Bacon, *A declaration of the practises and treasons attempted and committed by Robert late earle of Essex and his complices* (London, 1601), K2ʳ.
17. More's trial is described in *State Trials* 1:386–95.

unto the depth and bottom by subtle disquisition fathomed, the learned, prudent, and discerning judge doth oft detect and bring to light many hidden, intestine, and secret mischiefs.[18]

In trials for witchcraft, the accused is stripped and her whole body shaved in an attempt to find a "witch's mark," a hidden nipple in her "secret parts" at which she is supposed to suckle her familiar. This abnormality at a liminal area where inwardness and outwardness meet seems to provide a satisfactory basis for inferring horrible motives and desires further within.

The jury's process of discovery in other cases, too, is usually represented as an unveiling of something which nonetheless remains invisible, beyond sight. This visible invisibility is called the "prodigious," the "unnatural," the "unspeakable," the "monstrous." ("How much more than too too monstrous shall all Christian hearts judge the horror of this treason?" asks the Earl of Northumberland, rhetorically, at the trial of one of the Gunpowder Conspirators.)[19] Thus as we have already seen, Judge Warburton rationalizes the looseness of English evidentiary law, when Ralegh challenges it, in terms of a story about a monstrous interior space, an unnatural crime committed in the privy chamber. The language of monstrosity is characteristically vague, equally applicable to murder, theft, treason, witchcraft, heresy, sodomy, or whatever, so that an accusation of one particular crime tends to slide easily into an accusation of generalized criminality. And the monstrous is a slippery category in other respects as well. It is something the speaker or beholder desperately wants to differentiate himself from, define himself against. But the discovery of monstrosity is put into the hands of a jury of peers, chosen by their apparent resemblance to the defendant. They discover what seems absolutely alien, but they are equipped for this discovery by their similarity to what they investigate.

In order to discover criminal monstrosity the jury examines tokens, traces of a truth imagined as concealed inside the defendant. The purpose of the judicial inquiry is to make that truth publicly available. Early modern England's singular lack of articulated evidentiary standards, in what was in many respects a highly formal judicial system, is consistent with its equally idiosyncratic reliance upon the

18. John Cotta, *The triall of witch-craft, shewing the true methode of their discovery* (London, 1616), p. 18.
19. *State Trials* 2:254.

jury trial: the assumption is that the jury's process of decision making, however difficult it sometimes becomes, involves interpretive skills so fundamental to everyday social existence that codified rules and specialized legal expertise are hardly requisite. Unfortunately, the social judgments the jurors are imagined as practicing constantly in their own lives, and that equip them for their role in the trial, are notoriously subject to error. The connection between outward, public symptom and inward, private cause is universally acknowledged to be tenuous and falsifiable.

The juryman needs, then, to know how much he can presume to know. But the practical difficulties of specifying what constitutes such knowledge are so enormous that the criminal courts of the Tudor and Jacobean period prefer merely to sidestep or ignore the entire problem. Under such circumstances, although a flexible attitude toward evidence may in fact more often produce just verdicts than a stricter procedure, it cannot provide the same basis for theoretical confidence that a more systematic approach could. It does not allow prosecutors, judges, or juries to content themselves in the knowledge that the formalities, at least, are being observed.

How might the jury's performance be made more reliable in the life-and-death matter of common-law felony prosecutions? The prisoner in the dock, asked how he or she would plead, had to answer, "I put myself upon God and my country." The formula both announces and obscures the difference between divine and human vision, the difference so crucial to Renaissance conceptions of inwardness, and so routinely invoked by scholars of the law. Are God and the "country" invoked separately because they are not imagined as working together? Or are they rather supposed to collaborate? Edmund Campion, on trial for treason in 1581, told the jurors that his trial ought to be a "mirror" of "the dreadful Day of Judgment."[20] More than two decades later, Sir John Croke similarly describes the trial of Henry Garnet in the language of *Revelations:*

> This person and prisoner here at the bar, this place, and this present occasion and action, do prove that true, which the author of all truth hath told us; that . . . there is nothing hid that shall not be made manifest, there is nothing secret that shall not be revealed and come in public.[21]

20. *State Trials* 1.1070.
21. *State Trials* 2.217.

The jury trial is supposed to bring human vision in line with divine vision—like God, the jury is supposed to see into the heart of the accused and discern the truth there. But how is it to perform this feat? Justices and defendants alike frequently express the hope that God will "instruct" the jurors so that they will reach the correct verdict. But the jury trial is itself a replacement for the medieval trial by ordeal, which had been discredited by God's apparent reluctance to interfere with human juridical procedures. No one could be sanguine about an automatic correlation between God's verdict and the jury's.

In fact, the best the jury can do in witchcraft and many treason trials is to approach certainty in an asymptotic curve, evaluating the available tokens, traces, and effects of a guilt that cannot be perceived directly. Interestingly, under such circumstances the *sincerity* of the jury's decision—the fact that it reaches a "verdict according to conscience"—becomes crucially significant. It is as if the invisible inwardness of the defendant is rendered accessible, or at least as accessible as it can ever become, by the jurors' resort to their own inwardness, as they look within their hearts and find a verdict there. The same word, "conviction," stands both for the jurors' state of mind and for the imputation of a set of actions to the accused. The procedure tellingly resembles that which we have earlier seen Ralegh describe in *Skeptic, or Speculation:* he claims that the animal's mind is unknowable from our perspective, but at the same time tries to reproduce its "inward discourse" by rubbing his own eye to make his perceptions more closely approximate the goat's or the fox's. The potential dangers in this procedure are recognized by those who, like John Cotta, exhort the jury scrupulously to maintain "a true difference between that which our imagination doth represent to us, from within the brain, and that which we see without by the outward sense."[22] The trial both exacerbates a sense of the inconclusive character of circumstantial evidence, and by its pressure toward a verdict, forces a certain repression of the hermeneutic difficulties involved in obtaining "conviction."

English witchcraft and treason trials, then, frame themselves as rituals of discovery that attempt to perform the highly desirable but technically impossible feat of rendering publicly available a truth conceived of as initially—and perhaps inescapably—inward, secret, and

22. Cotta, *The triall of witch-craft*, p. 83.

[117]

invisible to mortal sight. In this sense such a trial may serve as a paradigm of all social relations that seem to rely upon a more or less highly developed capacity for accurate surmise. It exploits abilities that are supposed to be widely dispersed among the populace, as other skills of governance are certainly not imagined to be during this period. On the other hand, these "easy," normal, everyday skills are almost impossible to codify, or to employ with any absolute certainty of success. Inference, empathetic projection, the careful weighing of probability, an openness to divine guidance: all are supposed to help the jury reach a verdict, but nothing can provide a sure means of escaping the limitations set upon even the most scrupulous human observation.

❧ II ❧

OTHELLO, set in Venice and Cyprus, does not stage in any literal way the procedures of English justice. But the plot replicates the difficulties with which the English criminal courtroom often had to deal. Iago's temptation of Othello, as I have already mentioned, centers upon a discussion of what would constitute adequate proof of Iago's suggestion that Desdemona is unchaste. Although Othello initially insists upon "ocular proof"—the strongest kind of evidence in both English and Continental courts—he almost immediately modifies his demand:

> Make me to see't; or at the least so prove it
> That the probation bear no hinge nor loop
> To hang a doubt on.
>
> (3.3.36–71)

With this revision he allows Iago to begin eroding his original evidentiary scruples, extending the category of acceptable proof to include mere "imputation, and strong circumstances."

Illicit sex could be, and often was, prosecuted as a crime in early modern England, not in the common-law courts that would try felony charges, but in the ecclesiastical courts responsible for spiritual supervision (of which more in the following chapter). People often have something to gain by complaining in court of another party's fornication—a husband might wish to obtain "separation from bed and board" on grounds of his wife's infidelity, for instance, or the next in line to an estate might hope to displace a widow whose control over her late husband's property lasts only so long as she remains "chaste and sole." Unlike witchcraft or treason, however, adultery is not considered to be what I have called a "crime of intention." Jesus might teach that adultery in the heart is as bad as adultery in the act, but Jacobean ecclesiastical courts do not consider sexual fantasy their province, and take considerable care to ensure that the act has in fact taken place. Their evidentiary rules, moreover, are derived from Roman canon law and not from the looser common-law tradition. The courts can convict when they have "vehement presumptions" of adultery—as when a man has set up housekeeping with a woman not his wife, or when a woman has produced a child during her husband's protracted absence. However, they strongly prefer eyewitness evidence.[23] To be sure of winning their suit, plaintiffs need to present two witnesses to the adulterous activity, neither of whom can be the spouse or lover of the accused. Consequently many court cases feature, as Martin Ingram notes,

> churchwardens or other local officers, neighbours or even fellow-servants [who] actively spied on other people's sexual misdoings through window panes or chinks in walls or doors, often taking turns to peer, calling others to look too, and sometimes ending up by bursting in to confront the couple with their 'lewdness.'[24]

Ingram argues plausibly that "these spying cases did not represent normal, spontaneous, neighbourly behaviour but carefully planned, *legally purposeful* activity": an attempt to comply with the court's evidentiary rules and create a watertight case against the defendant. "Legally purposeful" evidence-gathering of the kind prescribed by the ecclesiastical courts is presumably what Othello has in mind when he asks for "ocular proof." He has behind him not only the requirements of canon law but a long dramatic tradition of husbands, lovers, and would-be lovers drawn, for their own complex reasons, to such scenes of discovery and exposure. In *The Spanish Tragedy* Balthazar and Lorenzo hover over the balcony; in *Much Ado about Nothing* Claudio

23. For ecclesiastical court procedure, see Henry Consett, *The Practice of the Spiritual and Ecclesiastical Courts* (London, 1685). Consett explains these safeguards as meant to protect a man who might be unjustly suspected because of "the nude and sole accusation of some naughty woman" (186); they might also protect women like Desdemona. Although the vigor and effectiveness of the ecclesiastical courts declined in the course of the seventeenth century, their procedure was not much altered, so Consett is a reliable guide to the rules of the courts in an earlier era.

24. Martin Ingram, *Church Courts, Sex and Marriage in England, 1570–1640* (Cambridge: Cambridge University Press, 1987), pp. 244–45.

and his prince conceal themselves below it. Prince Edward looks into a magic mirror in *Friar Bacon and Friar Bungay;* Hortensio disguises himself to spy on Bianca in *The Taming of the Shrew.* Attempts at surveillance are the way the cuckold ritually defines himself, inside and outside the playhouse.[25]

Iago, however, rather like Warburton at Ralegh's trial, insists that it is unrealistic to expect ocular proof of adultery. "In Venice they do let God see the pranks / They dare not show their husbands," he tells Othello. "It is impossible you should see this" (3.3.206–7, 407). In other words, he pretends that the merely practical difficulty of surprising an illicit couple in bed represents a real epistemological limitation. Thus Iago encourages Othello to displace adultery into the category of such essentially invisible crimes as treason or witchcraft, fully displayed only before the omniscient eye of God. In this scheme, Othello's apparently unexceptionable demand for ocular proof comes to represent an impossible aspiration to the absolute knowledge of another person.

> OTHELLO: By heaven, I'll know thy thought!
> IAGO: You cannot, if my heart were in your hand.
>   (3.3.166–67)

Iago tantalizes Othello by reminding him of the limitations of his "mortal eyes," and then, by pretending to satisfy his longing, encourages him to imagine those limitations as overcome. Othello lives out the epistemological dilemma of the English juryman to whom everything is supposed to be manifest, but who is nonetheless forced to depend upon clues and surmises, who must treat as clearly visible that which is inevitably beyond sight. He supposes he is pursuing the kind of insight he attributes to his mother's friend, the Egyptian charmer who "could almost read / The thoughts of people" (3.4.57–58). But what he actually relies upon is circumstantial evidence—Iago's flag and sign of love; Desdemona's "token," a handkerchief misleadingly mislaid. Either Othello must accept a degree of uncertainty in his relation to Desdemona, or he must repress his awareness of his own limitations as an observer.

Why does he choose the latter course? An alien in a place where the

25. For a rather different perspective on the issue of sexual jealousy and "ocular proof" in English Renaissance drama, see Katharine Eisaman Maus, "Horns of Dilemma: Jealousy, Gender, and Spectatorship in English Renaissance Drama," *ELH* 54 (1987): 561–83.

natives cultivate a sophisticated awareness of the difference between spurious surface and inward truth, Othello represents himself as incapable even of innocent hypocrisy. "My parts, my title, and my perfect soul / Shall manifest me rightly," he declares when he hears of Brabantio's opposition to his marriage (1.2.31–32); he assumes that the soul is as visible as parts and title to anyone who cares to look. Even late in the play, after he has killed Desdemona, Othello imagines the supremely precious object as a world made "of one entire and perfect chrysolite"—that is, flawlessly perspicuous. Othello is thus, as Stephen Greenblatt notes, deeply attracted to the notion of confession, to a discourse of absolutely sincere revelation to religious or legal authorities.[26] But whereas confession is ordinarily an admission of guilt, for Othello it constitutes a theatrical display of innocence. He has, he claims, nothing to hide. In a play in which, as Patricia Parker demonstrates, problems of narrative unfolding are foregrounded, Othello insists that he is always already unfolded. He does not so much tell his story to the Venetian court as he recounts having told it to Desdemona—and that telling is itself a repetition of a narrative previously offered to Brabantio, who now (ironically enough) accuses him of secret practices. This energetic guilelessness is perhaps compensatory, involving as it does a denial or avoidance of potential discrepancies between surface and interior: a counterstrategy to the Venetian racism that, in one of its more benign but still humiliating forms, imagines Othello as a white man unaccountably lodged inside a black body.

Since Othello initially either lacks or repudiates Hamlet's sense of that within which passes show, it may seem curious that he proves so susceptible to Iago, the character who articulates most fully and cynically the difference between compliment extern and the native act and figure of the heart. Othello capitulates to Iago's slanders because they seem to allow him to preserve one version of his fantasy of perfect transparency: the fantasy that others are absolutely transparent to him. He grants that Desdemona's innocent looks may conceal a corrupt inward truth, but they do not successfully conceal anything from *him:* he imagines her deceptive surface penetrated by his omniscient gaze. Between them Othello and Iago develop a way of comprehending Desdemona that corresponds closely with the judi-

26. Stephen Greenblatt, *Renaissance Self-Fashioning* (Chicago: University of Chicago Press, 1981), pp. 220–54.

[121]

cial models provided in such abundance throughout the play: an inquiry that defines inwardness as guilty secrecy. Once Desdemona becomes a "cause" to be investigated, what is discovered, almost inevitably, is monstrosity. For just as it did in actual legal proceedings, an intuition of invisible monstrosity provokes most of the legal proceedings in the play: the inquiry into what Brabantio claims is Othello's foul and secret sorcery; Othello's investigation into what he describes as the "monstrous" behavior of the revelers and which Cassio attributes to "the invisible spirit of wine"; and finally, the discovery of the "monstrous act" of murder when Desdemona cries out behind the closed curtains of the marriage bed. In this environment Iago functions as a sort of poet of monstrosity, lovingly dwelling on the beast with two backs, the gross issue, the monstrous birth, the unnatural thought, the palace into which foul things intrude.

When Othello comes under the spell of Iago's rhetoric of monstrosity he unknowingly makes serious compromises.

> It was my hint to speak—such was the process:
> And of the cannibals that each other eat,
> The Anthropophagi, and men whose heads
> Do grow beneath their shoulders.
>
> (1.3.141–44)

Othello's courtship of Desdemona suggests that monstrosity has a positive valence—the allure of the marvelous or the exceptional. Desdemona loves him not because he is a wealthy curléd darling of her nation, but because he and his story are "passing strange." Othello's acceptance of conventional notions of criminal monstrosity is an aspect of the tormented racial self-hatred that eventually results in both murder and suicide. For his white colleagues define miscegenation in the same terms they use for adultery, as a monstrous union potentially productive of "gross issue."

> Foh! one may smell in such a will most rank,
> Foul disproportion, thoughts unnatural!
>
> (3.3.237–38)

Iago exploits the slipperiness of the language of monstrosity to especially perverse effect in this passage, entrapping Othello in a bizarre logic which makes Desdemona's "unnatural" devotion to her black husband evidence for her "monstrous" infidelities.

Desdemona, protesting that she has not offended Othello "either in discourse of thought or actual deed" (4.2.185), invokes the standard of guilt applied to thought-crimes like treason or witchcraft, in order to deny the validity of the charge. Complexities in the way her virtue is defined, however, leave her vulnerable. For a discrepancy between surface and interior is one of the hallmarks of female modesty: Iago himself praises the woman who "could think and ne'er disclose her mind" (2.1.157). The judicial imagination is likely to construe this reserve or hiddenness as duplicity. Moreover, although Desdemona protests that the difference between interior and exterior is not significant in her relationship to Othello, she is unable to bring her invisible conscience into court, and equally unable to force her judge to acknowledge the cogency of the unseen. For Othello imagines he can see everything, that there is no difference between the way one knows oneself and the way one knows other people. But chastity is as invisible as Iago claims infidelity to be—Desdemona's "honor is an essence that's not seen" (3.4.16). Stanley Cavell has therefore argued brilliantly that the mere fact that Desdemona possesses a "discourse of thought" to which her husband is not privy terrifies Othello.[27] Cavell diagnoses the hero's skeptical problem as an inability to empathize, to grant to Desdemona the privileges of subjectivity he grants to himself. I would argue, on the contrary, that Othello suffers from a kind of empathetic excess, fatally accepting a European outlook when it is least in his interests, inappropriately applying to Desdemona the conditions by which he defines himself. This is indeed a form of skepticism, but it is the kind that we have seen Ralegh practicing in *Skeptic, or Speculation,* in which the inaccessibility of the other produces not solipsism but a dubious attempt to reconstruct an alien point of view from the inside.

For loving not wisely but too well means making the beloved comprehensible as a version of oneself: fair warrior, captain's captain, general's general. Othello realizes himself in a narrative mode, in confession or storytelling—even in his last moments, as T. S. Eliot complains, he is imagining his career as it will be retold in the letters of the Venetian ambassadors.[28] Desdemona's susceptibility to Othello's story, on the other hand, is the consequence of her own relative inexperience. The apparent eventlessness of Desdemona's life, confined within her father's household, makes her as exotic to a man

27. Stanley Cavell, *The Claim of Reason: Wittgenstein, Skepticism, Morality, and Tragedy* (Oxford: Clarendon, 1979), pp. 491ff.

28. T. S. Eliot, "Shakespeare and the Stoicism of Seneca," *Elizabethan Essays* (New York: Haskell House, 1964), pp. 110–11.

like Othello as he is to her. What kind of narrative can be constructed for the female subject, the greedy ear that devours up discourse? Othello's image suggests a sort of narrative black (or white) hole; as woman and as listener Desdemona is both perfect counterpart and absolute negation, a possibility both intensely desirable and intensely alarming to the phallic narrator. He does not know how to imagine Desdemona apart from her history, but in the world of the play, for a beautiful young woman to have a history can mean only one thing. Insofar as she is a person, Othello imagines, she must have something to narrate; but if she has something to narrate, she is no longer innocent.

"O curse of marriage, / That we can call these delicate creatures ours / And not their appetites!" (3.3.272–74). Othello laments his wife's separateness, even while puzzling over the sense in which she is his own. Unaware of, or unwilling to acknowledge, the difference between one's knowledge of oneself and one's knowledge of other people, he is easily led by Iago to confuse the third-person narration he constructs for and imputes to Desdemona with a first-person narration imagined as self-evidently authentic. Thus as the play proceeds, he becomes unable to distinguish between what is proper to him and what to Desdemona. "Nature would not invest herself in such shadowing passion without some instruction," he tells himself (3.4.38–40), confusing the possible origins of passion, projecting onto Desdemona his own fears and anxieties. In a striking and characteristic passage Othello tells Desdemona, immediately before he smothers her, not to plead innocence, because she cannot "choke the strong conception / That I do groan withal" (5.2.60–61). By this point in the play he has entirely reversed their roles in the tragic drama: the fertile young woman lying in what will become her deathbed is a strangler, the strangler a fertile woman crying out in labor. Discovering, he thinks, Desdemona's monstrosity, he wishes it upon, creates it for, himself: as Emilia says, jealous souls

> are not ever jealous for the cause,
> But jealous for they're jealous. It is a monstēr
> Begot upon itself, born on itself.
>
> (3.4.157–59)

Like the jury that looks within itself to discover the polluted conscience of the criminal, a pollution otherwise inaccessible, Othello looks within himself and finds a corruption he attributes to Desdemona. He is wrong, of course, but wrong in a way that the interpretive process, so defined, seems to invite, because the activities of evidence-gathering and of interpreting others are intimately tied up with a process of projection.

> By heaven, thou echo'st me
> As if there were some monster in thy thought
> Too hideous to be shown!"
>
> (3.3.110–12)

Othello's monster *is* an echo, a reverberation of the self ascribed to the other.

The insidiousness of the quasijudicial inquisitory procedures Othello employs lies in their seductive resemblance to the ordinary processes of romantic love. Desdemona's first thought, when Othello tells her the story of his life, is that "she wished / That heaven had made her such a man" (1.3.161–62). To marry Othello, in other words, is the next best thing to being there. "I saw Othello's visage in his mind," Desdemona declares triumphantly to the Venetian senators (1.3.214), imagining that the relation between lovers looks beyond the obvious in order to discover the hidden, erasing the boundary between public and private, outward and inward, the way one sees and the way one is seen. It does not occur to her to submit Othello's story to the skeptical criteria Iago invokes when he characterizes the traveler's tales of marvels as "fantastical lies." Collaborating in Othello's fantasy that his autobiographical narration is self-evidently true, Desdemona imaginatively leaps the gap between self-knowledge and the normally more limited and conditional knowledge of another.

Iago and Othello likewise erase such boundaries, or imagine themselves erasing them, by reading themselves into others. To Iago, the idea of crime is easy; his cynicism a villain's self-knowledge. Othello's own anxieties produce his suspicion of Desdemona. Evidence is in the eye of the beholder: just as when a suspected witch is stripped and scrutinized, a freakish nipple—freakish because supposedly so exceptional, so misplaced, so unsuspected—almost invariably betrays itself to view. This perspectivism sounds akin to what Ralegh offers in *Skeptic, or Speculation:* what the perceiver sees is determined by his own perceptual idiosyncrasies, not by what is "out there." But Ralegh's treatise allows a luxury of deferred judgment which Shakespeare's play, like the criminal trial, does not finally permit. This is not a tragedy that sidesteps moral absolutes. When Othello discerns that Iago has a horrible conceit shut up in his brain, he is quite correct, in a way he does not yet understand. The problem is not just that people create their own monsters, but also that monsters are really out there, though hard to find: the authorized means for detecting them are both deeply, inescapably unreliable, and at the same time, impossible to abandon.

The fundamental doubts cast on evidentiary procedure in *Othello* put its audience in an uncomfortable position. In *Richard III*, as we have already seen, Shakespeare allows the audience's oversight of the stage action to approximate divine omniscience: we know what is happening, we know what will happen, we approve the design of providence. In *Othello*, this is emphatically not the case. We see more than Othello sees because we hear Iago's soliloquies, see Emilia give him the napkin, but not because we occupy a different order of perceptual reality. The inquiries in the play involve a series of events unseen by us: a courtship and a wedding that occur before the play begins; the mysterious movements of a Turkish fleet; an offstage quarrel between Cassio and Roderigo; Desdemona's nonexistent affair with Cassio. Throughout the first two acts we are constantly asked to imagine Othello and Desdemona in the sexual act, an act which takes place offstage if, indeed, it ever takes place at all. Although favored with Iago's confidence, the audience never gets a satisfactory account of his motives: his final utterance in the play is a defiant vow of silence. The hidden, inward realm remains, in other words, incompletely revealed in the theater: like Othello, we must depend upon circumstantial evidence when we might have expected all to be made manifest.

In *Othello* the capacity, or incapacity, to know another is as pertinent to the relation between spectator and character as it is between character and character. Perhaps this is why *Othello* has struck a number of critics as a play in which "aesthetic distance" is unusually difficult to maintain. The impulse to interrupt, to tell Othello that he is wrong about Desdemona, seems so overpowering because there is a minimal epistemological boundary between characters and audience. At the same time, even while the play encourages an intense identification with the suffering characters, the nature of their suffering suggests that such identification is highly problematic in its motives and often in its consequences. The same mechanisms which seem to break down the boundaries between self and other simultaneously reinforce boundaries that can never really be eliminated. The process of making the invisible manifest inevitably entails falsification. By insisting that the truth always exceeds public methods of representation, *Othello* implies that the theater is as problematic as the jury trial, or as social life itself.

ঌঁ 5 ছ২

PROSECUTION AND SEXUAL
SECRECY: JONSON AND
SHAKESPEARE

ঌঁ I. Impotence and the Satirist's Vocation ছ২

IN THE FOURTH ACT of Ben Jonson's *Volpone*, Celia and Bonario complain in court of Corvino's attempts to prostitute Celia to Volpone, and of Volpone's attempted rape. Initially the *avocatori* empaneled to judge the case are inclined to believe their tale despite its strangeness, since they are both "of unprovéd name" while Corbaccio and Corvino are more dubiously regarded. As the scene proceeds, however, the lawyer Voltore skillfully demolishes their credibility. To their accusations of secret sexual sin he opposes a counteraccusation: Celia and Bonario are adulterous lovers, guilty of the outrages they wish to fasten upon others.

To support his claim, Voltore produces several witnesses. Corvino testifies to Celia's lasciviousness in lurid detail. She is, he announces, "a whore / Of most hot exercise, more than a partridge" who "neighs like a jennet" (4.5.116–18). Although the judges express shock at Corvino's graphic language, his vividness strengthens the plausibility of Voltore's claims, as does Lady Politic's apparently spontaneous deposition immediately following. Then Voltore submits his most telling piece of evidence.

> *Volpone is brought in, as impotent.*
> VOLTORE: Here, here,
>   The testimony comes that will convince,
>   And put to utter dumbness their bold tongues!
>   See here, grave fathers, here's the ravisher,
>   The rider on men's wives, the great imposter,
>   The grand voluptuary. Do you not think
>   These limbs should affect venery? Or these eyes
>   Covet a concubine? pray you mark these hands;
>   Are they not fit to stroke a lady's breasts?
>   Perhaps he doth dissemble!
> BONARIO: So he does.

VOLTORE: Would you have him tortured?
BONARIO: I would have him proved.
(*Volpone* 4.6.23–30)

Volpone's invalid body, Voltore insists, constitutes evidence to which Bonario and Celia cannot possibly reply. In this drama of accusation and counteraccusation, something finally seems decisively to favor one side over the other. The fact that Volpone himself does not speak enhances the credibility of his testimony, which seems to transcend or precede mere rhetoric in its physical factuality and obviousness. The judges, who have become increasingly impatient with Celia and Bonario in the course of the trial, are thoroughly won over. Without further delay they commit Celia and Bonario to custody and request that "the old gentleman be returned with care" (4.6.60).

The trial scene sets up a rhetorically competitive situation conventionally imagined in terms of phallic rivalry. In *Volpone*, however, triumph is ironically achieved by a move that seems to overturn the implicit terms upon which antagonism takes place: by ceding the very grounds that would normally be in question. When a reputation for sexual mastery is relinquished to Bonario, he loses his case rather than winning it. The audience knows, of course, that the outcome of the trial is wrong, and that the "testimonies" Voltore offers are fraudulent. But Jonson has gone to some trouble to emphasize the coherence and plausibility of Voltore's arguments. When Corvino confesses himself a cuckold, or Volpone presents himself to the court as impotent, they enact an abdication of masculine power and privilege so astonishing that unless they are telling the truth their behavior seems inexplicable.

Not surprisingly, the *avocatori* fail to realize that they are witnessing a bizarre charade. Instead they believe that they have been provided what Othello would call "ocular proof" of Volpone's decrepitude. Actually, however, as in *Othello*, the apparent abandonment of crafty and indefinite rhetoric for brute physical fact is a sham. Not the sight of Volpone's body but Voltore's accompanying speech, with its rhetorical questions and leaden ironies, creates an appearance of irrefutability. Bonario attempts to bring the case back into the domain of the arguable by answering one of Voltore's sarcastic rhetorical questions in the affirmative.

Perhaps he doth dissemble!
BONARIO: So he does.

> VOLTORE: Would you have him tortured?
> BONARIO: I would have him proved.

As we have seen in earlier chapters, the surfaces of the body are always capable of being theatricalized, so that while they can be made to seem absolutely trustworthy, they are never actually so. Unlike, say, Anne in *Richard III*, Bonario remains aware of, and continues to insist upon, the possibility of fakery.

Since torture could not be applied to those presumed crippled or infirm, Voltore risks a sarcastic rhetorical question, designed to make Bonario's zeal for truth appear sadistic. In fact, Bonario replies, he wishes only that Volpone be "proved." Yet Voltore has succeeded in discrediting Bonario, and the judges ignore his request. Thus it might seem pointless to dwell upon what Bonario's "proof" might involve, were it not that similar scenarios recur in Jonson's later plays. The entire last act of *Epicoene* is a mock divorce proceeding in which Morose, like Volpone, finds it in his interests to admit the inadmissible.

> MOROSE: I am no man, ladies.
> ALL: How!
> MOROSE: Utterly unabled in nature, by reason of
>   frigidity, to perform the duties or any of the least
>   office of a husband.
>
> (5.4.38–41)

Like Bonario, Epicoene insists that Morose's confession is an act of language, and therefore falsifiable, rather than the "manifest frigidity" he pretends.

> EPICOENE: Tut, a device, a device, this! It smells rankly,
>   ladies. A mere comment of his own.
> TRUEWIT: Why, if you suspect that, ladies, you may
>   have him searched.
>
> (5.4.46–48)

Finally, at the climax of *Bartholomew Fair*, Dionysius Puppet seems triumphantly to provide undeniable evidence of the deficiency to which Volpone and Morose had laid claim.

> BUSY: . . . my main argument against you is that you are
>   an abomination, for the male among you putteth on
>   the apparel of the female, and the female of the male.
>   . . . .
> PUPPET DIONYSIUS: It is your old stale argument

against the players, but it will not hold against the
puppets, for we have neither male nor female
amongst us. And that thou may'st see, if thou wilt,
like a malicious purblind zeal as thou art!
The puppet takes up his garment.
EDGEWORTH: By my faith, there he has answered you,
friend, by plain demonstration.

(5.5.101–14)

It seems worthwhile to ask, therefore, what is at stake when Bonario
asks that Volpone be "proved": what would constitute the proof of
Voltore's assertion, and how that proof would be obtained.

In fact, Bonario is requesting, in vain, a regular procedure for ascertaining impotence in court cases. Although an individual's impotence might well become an issue in a rape trial, like Volpone's, in
early modern Europe sexual dysfunction more commonly came under official scrutiny in the context of a divorce proceeding. Such proceedings were under the purview of the ecclesiastical court system,
which dealt with all kinds of sexual and marital irregularities:[1] action-

1. The strict regulation of the marriage bond is the more striking because of the
apparent indifference of Renaissance courts to deviations that to a modern sensibility
might seem more flagrant. Sodomy, for instance, made a capital crime under common
law in 1533, was almost never prosecuted in Elizabethan and Jacobean England. The
most common view is that this infrequency suggests "a probable low incidence of sodomy" (Richard Wunderli, *London Church Courts and Society on the Eve of the Reformation* (Cambridge, Mass.: Medieval Academy of America, 1981), p. 84. More recently,
gay-affirmative critics have claimed just the opposite, that sex between men was so
frequent and ordinary that it went unnoticed and unclassified as "sodomy" unless
some other social taboo was simultaneously breached: see Alan Bray, "Homosexuality
and the Signs of Male Friendship in Elizabethan England," *History Workshop Journal*
19 (1990): 1–19; and Jonathan Goldberg, *Sodometries* (Stanford: Stanford University
Press, 1992). Bray and Goldberg, following Foucault, have tended to be suspicious of
identifying the domain of the sexual with the domain of the private in the early modern
period, regarding such an identification as an anachronistic application of post-
Enlightenment categories. I shall argue, however, that in both Jonson and Shakespeare
sexual experience becomes a *topos* of unknowable inwardness.

The argument about the frequency of male/male sex correlates with an older disagreement among historians about the effectiveness of the ecclesiastical courts: how
widely their strictures were flouted, what the relation was between moral and legal
strictures on behavior, and so forth. For an account of the argument, see Martin Ingram, *Church Courts, Sex and Marriage in England, 1570–1640* (Cambridge: Cambridge University Press, 1987), pp. 6–17. Ingram himself argues that the ecclesiastical
courts' regulation of sexual conduct was quite effective and was widely supported by
the populace. Of course this debate, replacing the stymied ecclesiastical court judge
with the baffled historian, participates in the same difficulties about the unknowability

able offenses included conceiving a child in advance of a wedding ceremony, indulging in sex outside of marriage, choosing to live apart from one's spouse even for the most pressing economic reasons, and impugning another person's sexual reputation. Incurable sexual incapacity that predated the wedding concerned the ecclesiastical court because the impotent individual could provide his or her partner neither with "solace," defined as penetrative sex, nor with the children that would result from that penetration. Since these two goods were imagined to be the main benefits of marriage, the unimpaired partner could bring suit claiming that an agreement he or she had entered into in good faith could not be performed.

In England, impotence was the only ground upon which a validly contracted marriage might be annulled. Thus the policing of the marriage bond required the development of a definition of impotence, and ways of confirming it in particular cases. According to canon law, "impotence" in women meant neither the inability to experience sexual pleasure, nor infertility, but a physical abnormality that rendered penetration impossible. Jonson attributes this kind of impotence to Queen Elizabeth when he tells William Drummond that "she had a membrana on her that made her incapable of man, though for her delight she tried many."[2] In men, "impotence" could refer either to a genital malformation or to an inability, even in the absence of obvious deformity, to sustain an erection, vaginally penetrate a woman, and emit semen. One consequence of these definitions was that impotence was charged far more commonly against men than against women. The condition was presumed to be permanent if married persons had cohabited for three years without being able to consummate their union.

Claims of impotence were often contested, since the party accused of the disability was normally prohibited from remarrying, and often became a subject of ridicule. When the assertion was undisputed, on the other hand, judges might suspect collusion—an effort between two warring spouses to uncouple themselves by any means possible. In either case, some evidence was required to establish the truth or falsity of the charge. The nature of the proof varied. In France, where

---

of sexual "facts" that I shall be addressing in this essay. I am less interested in whether ecclesiastical court procedures were efficient and fair than in what their professed aims reveal.

2. *Conversations with Drummond of Hawthornden,* lines 342–44.

accusations of, and anxiety about, impotence seem to have become extremely common in the sixteenth and seventeenth centuries, the courts evolved ever more baroque procedures, the most notorious of which was the "trial by congress."[3] This test required husband and wife to lie in a curtained bed together for an hour or two, while court officers waited in an adjoining room. Afterwards the curtains were opened and the couple investigated for signs that sexual intercourse had taken place. Unsurprisingly, few men successfully proved their virility under such circumstances, especially since their partners had no reason to cooperate and often actively resisted their advances.

In England, trials by congress, or any other procedure to make a man demonstrate his potency in the courtroom, were considered uncanonical and obscene.[4] Usually English ecclesiastical courts relied upon "compurgation": the accused might clear himself by bringing seven "oath-helpers"—friends, relatives, or neighbors—to swear to the truth of his deposition. Since the English procedure, unlike the French one, threw the burden of proof heavily upon the plaintiff, English impotence cases were extremely rare. Both in England and on the Continent, however, judges could insist that both a man accused of impotence and his wife undergo physical examinations by qualified physicians or midwives: to assess whether and to what degree the man was impaired, and to ascertain the woman's continued virginity.

This, then, is what Bonario means when he asks that Volpone be "proved." Although Bonario and Voltore are opponents in the courtroom, Bonario's request participates in the same assumptions about the nature of evidence that Voltore uses to persuade the judges. Both

3. For a lively discussion of the French situation, see Pierre Darmon, *Damning the Innocent: A History of the Persecution of the Impotent in pre-Revolutionary France*, trans. Paul Keegan (New York: Viking, 1986). The same book was published in England under the title *Trial by Impotence: Virility and Marriage in pre-Revolutionary France* (London: Chatto and Windus, 1985).

4. George Abbott, the Archbishop of Canterbury who resisted granting Frances Howard a divorce from the third Earl of Essex, discusses the differences between English and French practice in William Cobbett and Thomas Howell, *Cobbett's Complete Collection of State Trials* (London, 1809), 2.851–53. In *Marriage Litigation in Medieval England* (Cambridge: Cambridge University Press, 1974), pp. 88–90, R. H. Helmholz discusses a medieval English case in which an allegedly impotent man was "tested" by a group of women who attempted to give him an erection, but there are no records of this procedure being employed after 1450.

men maintain that there is an undeniable fact-of-the-body that can somehow be made publicly manifest, and that the discovery of this fact will provide the resolution of the case. The difference between what Voltore offers the court, the display of Volpone's limp body, and what Bonario demands, the display of Volpone's limp penis, is only a difference of procedural stringency, not a logical difference or a disagreement about what "truth" might entail.

In practice, however, supposedly irrefutable bodily facts were exceedingly difficult to establish. Tests of impotence were notoriously liable to error. The physical examination of supposedly deficient men usually yielded ambiguous results, except in cases of gross abnormality. Even then, they could be untrustworthy. Jonson may well have known about "Bury's case," which generated a minor scandal and a number of ribald jokes at the end of the sixteenth century. In 1561, a John Bury of Devon had been accused of impotence by his wife, Willmott. Prior to the marriage a horse had kicked Bury in the testicles, so that "nothing but a little one of them remained . . . of the size of a small bean."[5] Later both parties remarried—in Bury's case, apparently despite the terms of the annulment, since impotent people were supposed to be debarred from marrying again. Bury's second wife then gave birth to a son, while his original wife was still alive. In 1599, the son's right to his father's estate was challenged by one Webber, next in line to Bury's inheritance. Webber did not argue that the second wife must have conceived the son with someone other than Bury, for English common law customarily considered all children born during a marriage to be the offspring of their mothers' husbands. Instead he claimed that the production of issue showed that "the holy church was deceived in its first judgment."[6] Since the sentence of divorce was based on spurious evidence, Webber maintained, Bury actually remained wedded to Willmott, and the later marriages of both Bury and Willmott were invalid. In consequence, Bury's son was a bastard, excluded from the line of inheritance. Webber's conundrum occasioned "many arguments and great deliberations." Eventually Bury *fils* won the case on appeal, on the grounds that although his father's second marriage was "voidable"—that is, it could have been

5. *State Trials* 2.850.
6. James Dyer, *Reports of Cases in the Reigns of Henry VIII, Edward VI, Queen Mary, and Queen Elizabeth* (Dublin, 1794), pp. 179–80.

declared invalid during Bury's lifetime—it had not actually been annulled, and "remaineth a marriage until it be dissolved."[7]

If these kinds of complications could ensue even when the defendant was virtually a eunuch, they were all the more likely in the more common situation, where the man was apparently *aptus ad generandum* but seemed incapable of intercourse with his wife. The evidence in the case of women was just as questionable. Wives who claimed that their marriages had never been consummated needed to verify their virginity. Renaissance physicians disagreed, however, over whether that fact could be discovered by physical examination. Some authorities claimed that in virgins, the hymen was always intact. But other influential experts pointed out that all kinds of accidents short of sexual intercourse—including the physical examination itself—could rupture a delicate membrane. A few physicians, notably the important obstetricians Ambroise Paré and Jacques Guillemeau, insisted that the hymen was a mere fiction, declaring that they had never encountered one in the course of dissecting thousands of female corpses.[8]

This rather desperate search for unequivocal physical evidence when none seems likely to be forthcoming is reminiscent of the similarly problematic attempt to specify criminal intention in the kinds of trial discussed in the last chapter. In fact, the Church of England marriage service makes quite explicit the analogy between secret sexual defects and secret criminal intention:

> I require and charge you (as you will answer at the dreadful day of judgment, when the secrets of all hearts shall be disclosed) that if

---

7. *The Reports of Sir Edward Coke* V.98.b second edition (London, 1680), p. 344. The common-law judges supported their opinion by the novel suggestion that Bury might have been impotent during his first marriage but not during his second, a possibility at odds with the ecclesiastical requirement of permanent incapacity. Bury's precedent became important in the Essex divorce case, where the Earl admitted a specific but not a general disability.

8. The phenomenon of the hymen is much discussed in sixteenth- and early seventeenth-century France. Writers who consider the presence of the hymen a sign of virginity include Jacques Duval, *Traité des hermaphrodits, parties, génitales, accouchements des femmes* (Rouen, 1612) and Séverin Pineau, *De integritatis et corruptionis virginum notis* (Paris, 1598); doubters include Ambroise Paré, published in England as *The Anatomy of Mans Body*, in *The Workes of that famous chirurgeon Ambrose Parey*, trans. Thomas Johnson (London, 1649); and Jacques Guillemeau, trans. as *Child-birth, or, the happy deliverie of women* (London, 1612).

either of you do know any impediment why ye may not be lawfully joined together in matrimony, that ye confess it.

The marriage ceremony, like the jury trial, looks forward to and takes as its model the irresistible opening up of secrets that will occur at "the dreadful day of judgment," when the visible will finally be conflated with the true and further debate will become impossible. Like the jury trial, the marriage ceremony hopes to enact that opening-up in the present moment even while, in the very articulation of its hope, admitting that it does not actually possess those powers of disclosure and cannot, therefore, lay claim to such certitude.

Certainly the inquiries that accompany annulment proceedings compare, in their indignity and invasiveness, with the bodily searches commonly conducted in the witchcraft trial. In both cases, the crucial events are unwitnessed or unwitnessable, known with certainty only by the accused and by supernatural agencies that cannot participate in court.

> AVOCATORE 1: What witnesses have you, to make good
> your report?
> BONARIO: Our consciences.
> CELIA: And heaven, that never fails the innocent.
> AVOCATORE 4: These are no testimonies.
> (*Volpone* 4.6.15–19)

As a way out of this dilemma, physical evidence is sought with the idea that it will provide clear, conclusive answers to difficult questions. In both cases, the accused's secrets are supposed to have stamped themselves unequivocally on the material of his or her body: silently proclaiming themselves in a misplaced nipple, a flaccid member, a torn or missing hymen. In both cases, that definitiveness turns out to be illusory, as supposedly stolid flesh evanesces and transmutes before the investigators' very eyes.

Nonetheless, the relationship between the material proof and the question being investigated differs significantly in the two kinds of case. In the witchcraft trial, the "witch's mark" is itself, as we have already seen, merely a sign that refers to a wicked intention hidden further within. In the impotence trial, by contrast, the body is a subject of inquiry for its own sake. The less the mind is likely to have involved itself in the body's vagaries, the better the "proof." In the 1613 Essex divorce case, for instance, the Earl claimed that he was unable to consummate his union with Frances Howard, although he "hath oftentimes felt motions and provocations of the flesh, tending to copulation" with women other than his wife.[9] When asked why he thought he suffered so specific a disability, he ascribed it to his dislike of Frances.

> when they were alone, she reviled him, and miscalled him, terming him cow, and coward, and beast; and he added, that she was as bitter a woman as any in the world: which things so cooled his courage, that he was far from knowing, or endeavoring to know her.[10]

Because such remarks suggested that *"vitium animi non corporis* [the defect was of the spirit, not of the body],"[11] the ecclesiastical authorities balked at granting an annulment. The undoubted fact that Essex and his wife loathed one another was irrelevant to the question of whether they ought to be allowed to dissolve the marital bond. Only King James I's aggressive interference secured the divorce, over the strenuous objections of George Abbott, Archbishop of Canterbury.

The popular nickname for the ecclesiastical tribunal, the "bawdy court," resentfully captures what was seen as the habitual prurience of its procedures. In *The Court and Character of King James*, Anthony Weldon complains that the Essex trial generated "a learned discourse in the science of bawdry . . . wherein were so many beastly expressions, as for modesty sake I will not recite them."[12] Weldon's delicacy seems rather disingenuous, given the scurrilous details he lavishly proffers in the paragraphs immediately following. Yet his curious combination of voyeurism with compunctions about privacy and decorum is in fact entirely characteristic of the proceedings he describes. The scopophilia of the annulment trial was carefully circumscribed. Even in France, the warring couple was sequestered in a curtained bed. In the Essex trial, Weldon reports, when Frances Howard needed to prove a long-lost virginity, she claimed to be overwhelmed by feminine modesty. This demureness seemed only natural to the court, which permitted her to veil her face during the examination: a subterfuge that enabled her to send a substitute to endure the examination in her place. A similar squeamishness is suggested by the English courts' reliance upon compurgation in cases in which the

9. *State Trials* 2.787.
10. *State Trials* 2.819.
11. *State Trials* 2.814.
12. Anthony Weldon, *The Court and Character of King James* (London, 1651).

seven oath-helpers—usually male friends and neighbors of the accused husband—were patently unqualified to testify.

Thus impotence proceedings restrict their territory in two controversial respects. Their first self-limitation is to define sexual inadequacy in a purely physical way, despite the acknowledged tendency in these matters for the state of one's mind to impinge upon the state of one's body. Their second self-limitation is a refusal fully to display even this restricted "truth." They gesture toward, but at the same time recoil from, a public revelation of the "privates," failing to follow through upon the initial voyeuristic impulse although the inquiry is thereby hindered.

This halfhearted inquisitiveness, and the insurmountable impracticalities of obtaining clear-cut confirmation, compels a dependence upon hearsay that is made to seem more blatant by the initial insistence upon decisive material evidence. Obscurely motivated by loyalty, hope of gain, or desire for revenge, servants offer the court their inferences about their masters and mistresses:

> she and the lady's chamber-maid turned down the bed-clothes, and there they saw the places where the earl and lady had lain, but . . . there was such a distance between the two places, and such a hill between them, that this deponent is persuaded that they did not touch one another that night. (*State Trials* 2.791)

Siblings and cousins likewise take their turns speculating about the sex lives of their kin, even while plainly acknowledging their ignorance of the facts. In the Essex divorce trial, George Abbott worries over a report he hears from "a good friend" outside the courtroom

> that my lord of Essex, on that Sunday morning, having five or six captains and gentlemen of worth in his chamber, and speech being made of his inability, rose out of his bed, and taking up his shirt, did shew them all so able and extraordinarily sufficient matter, that they all cried out shame on his lady. (*State Trials* 2.822)

Essex brandishes his "extraordinarily sufficient matter," but not where its display will count as evidence, so that for Abbott, "matter" is frustratingly displaced into the elusiveness of an anecdote overheard.

The impotence trial thus begins to resolve itself into a structure that will be familiar from treason and witchcraft inquisitions: there is an accusation abroad, but the hidden location in which responsibility actually lodges seems frustratingly difficult to specify. In the ecclesias-

PROSECUTION AND SEXUAL SECRECY

tical courts, accusations of sexual misbehavior typically attract count-
ersuits of "defamation," a word that significantly could refer either to
the formal charge of misconduct itself—the court's indictment—or
to a malicious slur irresponsibly cast upon a neighbor. In the sixteenth and early seventeenth centuries the number of defamation
suits skyrocket both in the ecclesiastical and the common-law courts,
as innocent parties pursue cases, sometimes at considerable cost, as a
way of publicly clearing their names. The hypersensitivity of early
modern Englishmen and women to social perceptions was exacerbated not only by the practical importance of a good reputation for
transacting business or living in peace with one's neighbors, but by
an acute sense of how easy and at times how expedient it could be to
accuse others of secret sexual sin. In *Volpone*, as we have already seen,
the only way for the guilty to evade punishment is to slander Celia
and Bonario. Likewise in *Epicoene*, Morose's desperate desire to be
rid of his wife encourages the groundless degradation of Epicoene's
character by Daw and LaFoole.

On the one hand, then, reputation seems dangerously detachable
from fact, as Jonson had reason to know from personal experience.
"Every accusation doth not condemn," he writes from prison in 1605,
in trouble for his collaboration on *Eastward Ho*. "And there must go
much more to the making of a guilty man, than rumor."[13] On the
other hand, despite every precaution, the ecclesiastical courts often
had nothing but "public fame" to rely upon in assessing the guilt of
the parties that came before it; moreover, public fame is essential to
their usual punishments, shaming rituals of the kind Corvino is eventually sentenced to undergo at the end of *Volpone*. If Jonson is more
interested in a relatively uncommon annulment proceeding than in
the much more frequent prosecutions of bigamy and bastardy, it is
perhaps because the evidentiary problems intrinsic to the "discovery"
of sexual secrets are especially acute here, far more so than in cases
where two living wives or an infant bastard might be presented in the
courtroom. In the impotence proceeding, what advertises itself as a
straightforward inquiry into hidden truths, insisting upon the most
definite material evidence, almost inevitably becomes an exercise in
the construction of reputation. What advertises itself as a discovery
of what is not externally perceptible turns out actually merely to

13. C. H. Herford and Percy Simpson, eds., *Ben Jonson* (London: Oxford University Press, 1925), 1:197.

depend upon and elaborate conjecture and surmise. In such cases the difference between fact and reputation is obscure, so that fact can seem nothing more than a particularly convincing form of reputation.

Both the procedures for ascertaining impotence and the dilemmas posed by those procedures are, in their general form, of persistent interest to Ben Jonson. To an unusual degree, Jonson's authorial tactics are closely concerned with the way reputation—his own and other people's—may be controlled and manipulated. Ambitious for personal fame, desirous of associating his own eminence with the unquestioned "fact" of his literary merit, Jonson simultaneously recognizes and excoriates the sordid, contingent means by which reputation may be established: by flattering the powerful, by pandering to the taste of undiscerning audiences, by stealing other people's ideas. Like the judges in the ecclesiastical courts, insisting upon the unreliability and the trustworthiness of reputation at the same time, the want of an alternative seems to force him into a self-contradiction.

In the epigrams and in the comedies Jonson favors the conventional image of the satirist as one who "discovers" a hidden truth by peeling off layers of obscurity or deceit. Asper, his mouthpiece in *Every Man out of His Humour*, promises that

> with an arméd and resolvéd hand
> I'll strip the ragged follies of the time
> Naked as at their birth.
>
> (Induction, 16–18)

The purpose is not always to shame the person or thing thus denuded: in his prefatory letter to *Volpone* Jonson promises to "raise the despised head of poetry again, and stripping her out of those rotten and base rags wherewith the times have adulterated her form, restore her to her primitive habit, feature, and majesty." But all such passages offer the uncovered body, whether degraded or glorious, as a model of truth, just as it is in the Renaissance divorce court. The satirist, in other words, is a literary equivalent of the judicial examiner, expertly stripping the body of the accused. At the same time, the nature of this revelation, in the playhouse as in the courtroom, is uncertain. In the final lines of *Volpone*, the hero announces to the stymied judges that "the fox shall here uncase," removes his disguise, and flatly informs them of his own and his associates' wrongdoing (5.12.85). On the one hand, this resolution seems to provide the kind of "proof" Bonario had originally demanded and Voltore had pretended to offer, an unanswerably veracious exposure of the criminal body.

> AVOCATORE 1: The knot is now undone by miracle.
> AVOCATORE 2: Nothing can be more clear.
>
> (5.12.95–96)

On the other hand, Volpone's divestiture is a metaphor for confession, not a replacement for it: he reveals a plot that does not primarily reside in the material of the body and that could not have been discovered without his cooperation.

Considered as striptease, moreover, Volpone's unmasking hardly satisfies. Early in his career, Jonson virtually invents ways to translate satire from a nondramatic to a dramatic form: he *stages* satiric exposure. But this exposure is performed in a medium associated not with undressing but with an amplification of the importance of attire, the covering of the actor's body with the costume that indicates his dramatic identity. Moreover, Jonson cannot literally strip and exhibit the bodies of fools and knaves, because English Renaissance standards of theatrical decorum, more stringent than our own, did not permit genitalia to be displayed on the public stage. The recognition scenes at the end of *Epicoene* and of *Bartholomew Fair*, and perhaps at the end of *Volpone* as well, jokily conflate satiric revelation with obscene exhibition, but at the same time they shy away from that exhibition, metonymically removing a jacket or a wig, hoisting a garment only when there is nothing to see. The self-limiting voyeurism of Jonson's satiric comedy resembles and shares its rationale with that of the ecclesiastical courts, simultaneously violating and insisting upon the boundary between public and private domains, displaying and concealing secrets by the same theatrical gestures.

As in the impotence trial, the body cannot be fully shown, and even if it could be, what that display could "prove" would be open to dispute. Thus the physical model of revelation-by-making-naked seems inadequate even at the moment at which it is melodramatically evoked. On other grounds as well its very irresistibility continues to raise troubling questions. Throughout his career Jonson is deeply interested in the way human beings helplessly reveal themselves in their bodily demeanor. "Do we not see, if the mind languish, the members are dull?" Jonson writes in *Discoveries*. "Look upon an effeminate person: his very gait confesseth him" (950–53). The word "confess" suggests that the sissy's body, like the body of the impotent, testifies involuntarily and therefore utterly reliably to its shameful secrets. Yet the relation between the "confession" and the "secret" is, typically, peculiar. Since the man's gait is what attracts Jonson's contemptuous attention, allowing him to classify the man as effeminate in the first place, it is logically circular to see that gait as *revelatory* of anything. Rather the man's gait *constitutes* his effeminacy, which does not need to be discovered because it is already on display. The effeminate person is so, that is, "all the way down": there is no discrepancy between surface and depth. In the world Jonson provisionally imagines here, in fact, inwardness as we have seen it elaborated in other writers would not exist. There would be no difference between what is true about a person and what is socially discernible through the material of the body: through manifest tics, gestures, tones of voice, unconscious habits.

In this wholly transparent or legible social world, deception would seem to be an impossibility. But of course Jonson's comedies exhibit worlds in which deception is not only feasible but rampant, worlds inhabited by men and women who have learned to profit from the fissure between truth and what is thought to be true. How can this be the case? Often Jonson reconciles his ideal of transparency with the fact of opacity by attributing the success of his frauds to the greed, egoism, or stupidity of their victims. Thus Mosca and Volpone wonder at the success of their endeavor:

> Too much light blinds 'em, I think. Each of them
> Is so possessed and stuffed with his own hopes,
> That anything unto the contrary,
> Never so true, or never so apparent,
> Never so palpable, they will resist it.
>
> (5.2.23–27)

In *The Alchemist* the creakiness of the scheme is even more blatant: the "venter tripartite" succeeds by so efficiently colluding with the gulls' wishful narcissism that they are willing to ignore its flagrant implausibilities. The responsibility for deception, then, partly shifts from the machiavellian deceiver to the persons he swindles, whose desperate collusion with their own victimization becomes an important subject of Jonsonian satire.

Even while the satirist claims to be stripping the targets of his scorn, then, he simultaneously insists that, like Hans Christian Andersen's emperor, they were always wholly visible. What the satirist effects is less an actual exposure than an adjustment in interpretive perspective. If the nakedness of the satiric object is located in the eye of the beholder, its "uncasing" is a kind of optical illusion. But so too, then, may be the apparent truthfulness thus achieved. Jonson is continually accused of libel, of maliciously defaming rather than guilelessly divesting his satiric objects. When Dekker, for instance, replies to Jonson's *Poetaster* in *Satiro-mastix*, he does so by mocking Jonson's outlook and motives. What Jonson represents as self-evident and impartial, Dekker represents as self-promoting and tendentious. Dekker strips Jonson of his pretensions just as Jonson had tried to strip Dekker: the subtitle of Dekker's counterblast is *The Untrussing of the Humourous Poet.*

In his combination of truculent authorial self-assertiveness with a scarcely concealed nervousness about the sources of his authority, Jonson resembles the religious polemicists I earlier associated with the development of the stage machiavel. He claims to be uncovering brute material facts, but discoverer and discovered, prestigious examiner and denuded examinee, always seem perilously close to switching places. In such a world, all the normal appurtenances of respectability, simply because they are inevitably mere appurtenances, have the potential suddenly to convert into their opposites.

> AVOCATORE 2: The young man's fame was ever fair and
>   honest.
> VOLTORE: So much more full of danger is his vice,
>   That can beguile so, under shade of virtue.
>   (*Volpone* 4.5.60–62)

Certainly Jonson's manipulative protagonists participate in the same complex of epistemological uncertainties that other "machiavels," like Richard III or Hieronimo, learn to exploit and must endure.

What distinguishes Jonson from Kyd, or from the Shakespeare of *Richard III* (though not, perhaps, from the Marlowe of *Jew of Malta*), is his interest in the economic conditions that enable such uncertainties; in particular, in the relationship between material prosperity and the possibility of bodily secretiveness. Acquisitiveness, unlike other forms of self-assertion, does not necessarily demand an audience; nor do the sensuous pleasures of consumption need to be witnessed in order to be actual. Kyd imagines worthy underlings challenging a decadent ruling class for the right to various forms of publicly acknowledged power and prestige. Shakespeare's Richard struggles for, and wins, England's preeminent public role. By contrast, Jonson imagines people of various class origins recognizing that, if they are rich enough, they may live a life of carnal pleasure that could remain entirely apart from public acknowledgment. The courtroom scam in *Volpone* works because the *avocatori* rely, probably without fully realizing it, upon the intuition that it is normally in one's interest to protect one's reputation, even while Volpone's scheme ingeniously ruptures the connection between social status and personal gratification, both for himself and for his gulls.

In fact, the distinction Volpone makes between a private bodily truth and a publicly accepted version of bodily truth is so counterintuitive that he cannot himself keep it securely in mind. When he attempts to seduce Celia, his phallic pride erupts incongruously and disastrously. He assaults her at the moment when he becomes convinced that she will "Think me cold, / Frozen and impotent, *and so report me*" (3.7.259–60; my italics). He forgets at this heated juncture that his entire charade depends upon presenting himself as frozen and impotent, and that if Celia were to inform Corvino or anyone else of his sexual prowess, his profitable game would be up. Volpone cannot bear to think of others condescending to his bodily incapacity, even though that incapacity works to his advantage. He cannot help but attempt to dazzle a real or imagined onlooker: Mosca, Celia, "the great Valois," even when bidding for their admiration works against his own best interests. His theatrical gifts are rooted as much in a love of self-display as in a penchant for deception, and thus his very triumphs bear the seeds of his eventual downfall.

Nonetheless, the possibility of a life of cloistered self-indulgence, a possibility upon which Volpone inconsistently capitalizes, interests Jonson deeply.

> What should I do,
> But cocker up my genius, and live free
> To all delights my fortune calls me to?
> (*Volpone* 1.1.70–72)

Almost alone among his contemporaries, Jonson considers how the possession of wealth provides not merely competitive, novel ways to impress others (what Jonson in *To Penshurst* calls "envious show"), but the means to "live free," to opt out of the activities of a community altogether. Against this kind of threat to social cohesion, even the most pointless forms of conspicuous consumption seem almost reassuring: reassuring because conspicuous, because therefore socially available and responsive to the opinions of other people. Egotistical and fundamentally gregarious, Volpone cannot finally bear the disgraceful solitude to which his own acquisitive logic condemns him. His impotence may not be "true," bodily impotence, but it is its social equivalent. At the same time, the very gratuitousness of Volpone's self-betrayal suggests that another person of different temperament—more shameless, more misanthropic, or more insensitive—might succeed where he fails: *Sejanus*'s sinister Tiberius, perhaps, or *Epicoene*'s chilly Dauphine.[14]

Perhaps such entirely private characters, able to indulge themselves in nameless unsupervised pleasures, fascinate Jonson so persistently because they are so deeply subversive of his literary endeavor. To the extent that someone might wholly rebuff another's scrutiny, wholly disregard another's censure, satire becomes impossible. The effectiveness of satiric excoriation, like the effectiveness of the ecclesiastical courts, depends upon a consensus about what is shameful, and a collective fear of being publicly humiliated. Ideally, in fact, this consensus should be so unquestioned, so automatic, that it seems not to be a social artifact at all, but a natural truth or brute fact about human beings. A shameless person, defying such unanimity or even devising ways to exploit it for gain, challenges the inevitability of consensus, insinuating the contingency and fragility of a given social arrangement.

Thus it is not surprising that *Epicoene*, a play about a recluse, should become Jonson's fullest treatment of the implicit, troubled analogy between the satirist's revelatory theater and the ecclesiastical judge's revelatory courtroom. I shall argue that Jonson makes the conundrum of Morose's marital fitness a kind of metonymy for far more general problems of sexual identity and theatrical representation in Jacobean London. The setting and plot of the play encourages Jonson to confront not merely the relatively limited epistemological problems attendant upon the impotence trial, but the difficulty of establishing any kind of ground for sexual supervision or discipline, and hence for the satirist's endeavor, in a heterogeneous urban world.

Epicoene stages a conflict between two ways of imagining the marriage bond and by extension of imagining sexuality generally, each of

14. Jonson's truest dramatic heir in this vein might thus be William Wycherley, in whose *Country Wife* the brazen Horner puts into practice a scheme more thoroughgoing and more successful than what Volpone finds himself able to accomplish.

which receives some institutional support from early modern English marriage customs. Morose's assumption that marriage is compatible with seclusion was theoretically endorsed both by canon and common law, which required for a valid marriage merely a promise passed between a couple, followed by sexual consummation. No public ceremony, no consent of kin, and no witnesses were necessary. At variance with this private conception of the marital relationship, both in *Epicoene* and in early modern England generally, is a conception of marriage as a social institution of interest to, and subject to regulation by, the larger community.[15] Ian Donaldson has suggested that the middle acts of *Epicoene* stage one such method of social regulation: the influx of noisy wedding "guests" constitutes, he claims, a *charivari* or social expression of comic outrage at an ill-suited match.[16] Of course, the parodic ecclesiastical proceedings with which the play concludes invoke another, more elaborately ceremonious, way in which the community systematically exercises its authority over the marital household.[17]

These two conceptions of marriage, at odds with one another throughout the play, are also occultly related. Anne Barton has remarked that it is strange that Morose, who affects to hate noise and people, should live in the bustling commercial center of Europe's biggest city. But where else would Morose live? Early seventeenth-century London, as Jonson recognizes, provides at least for the well-to-do not merely the possibility of manipulating one's social *persona*, but of simply dispensing with it altogether. Morose's possession of a modest fortune enables him to indulge peculiarities unthinkable in the limited confines of a village. The labor pool is large enough, for instance, that for the right price one might conceivably obtain a silent barber, a servant willing to converse in sign language and wear tennis-court socks, construction workers capable of building a room with double walls and treble ceilings. At the same time, for a person of Morose's independent means, the city diminishes pressures for social

15. Lawrence Stone charts the legal instability of these two conceptions of marriage in *The Road to Divorce: England 1530–1987* (Oxford: Oxford University Press, 1990).

16. Donaldson, *The World Upside-Down: From Jonson to Fielding* (Oxford: Clarendon, 1970), pp. 38–41.

17. Martin Ingram points out the similarities between the informal sanctions of the *charivari* and the formal ones of the ecclesiastical courts in "Ridings, Rough Music, and Mocking Rhymes in Early Modern England," *Past and Present* 105 (Nov. 1984), p. 92, 111.

participation and conformity. In a large, heterogeneous community, the opinions of one's neighbors are likely to be far less intimidatingly uniform than in a small village. Thus in seventeenth-century London, social historians have found, *charivari* was a distinctly rustic survival: when urbanites became the butt of such humor, they were more likely to file suit for defamation than blushingly to reform their ways. For similar reasons, the effectiveness of the ecclesiastical courts' regulation of sexual behavior varied inversely with the size of the communities over which the courts attempted surveillance.[18] Procedures and sanctions dependent upon "common fame" fail when the community grows so large that nothing is common to all of it. The rituals of compurgation, which depend upon people's unwillingness to risk manifestly perjuring themselves before their friends and neighbors, break down in London: dubious personages lurk outide the courtroom, offering to serve as oath-helpers on any matter whatsoever, for a price. Ecclesiastical punishments, shaming rituals designed to be intensely humiliating in the intimate context of village life, are less vividly experienced in the looser urban setting, not to mention easier to evade altogether.

Morose's constantly frustrated desire for silence and solitude is hardly shared by the rest of the cast of *Epicoene*, who form overlapping, interconnected pairs or groups: the Collegiate Ladies, the Otters, the wits, Daw and LaFoole. Nonetheless, his particular form of absurdity constitutes both an opportunity and a caution for his sometimes obsessively sociable colleagues.[19] *Epicoene* concerns itself, as P. K. Ayers notes, with members of an urban gentry class deracinated from their original rural power base and responsibilities, whose moral code "owe[s] little to traditional social patterns or sources of value."[20] Like Morose, profoundly dependent upon the community from which he withdraws, "polite society" requires the resources of the large indiscriminate and undiscriminating population against

18. In *London Church Courts and Society on the Eve of the Reformation* (Cambridge, Mass.: Medieval Academy of America, 1981), pp. 137–39, Richard Wunderli traces dissatisfaction with the enforcement capacity of London ecclesiastical courts back to the 1490s.

19. As is recognized by Anne Barton, who complains about *Epicoene*'s "scrupulously maintained distance between people," and the lack of "an honest, genuinely significant relationship with anyone else." *Ben Jonson: Dramatist* (Cambridge: Cambridge University Press, 1984), p. 128.

20. P. K. Ayers, "Dreams of the City: The Urban and the Urbane in Jonson's *Epicoene*," *Philological Quarterly* 66 (1987): 75.

which it may then define itself. The same breakdown of public discipline that permits Morose's idiosyncratic withdrawal likewise allows the flowering of contingent, voluntarily assumed statuses and social affiliations, which prove at least as significant as formal, publicly ascertainable institutions for the production of the characters' various identities. Affection and loyalty seem to have become unmoored from the ties of kinship; spinsterhood is no guarantee of virginity; marriage fails to indicate who cohabits with, sleeps with, or dominates whom.

This failure, of course—this chasm between private experience and public institution—is just what the traditional regimen of the ecclesiastical courts was meant forcibly to close: censuring shrewishness in women, prohibiting spouses from residing apart from one another, punishing fornication, ensuring that husbands controlled their households and properly penetrated their wives. But even as the urban world enables Morose's eccentric repudiation of normal social intercourse, it disables the traditional public means of inhibiting eccentricity. In the absence of community consensus, any punishment of the individual eccentric must itself be egregious. When Truewit invades Morose's house, a stranger who purports to be "careful after your soul's health," his phrasing recalls the rationale of the ecclesiastical courtroom. But Morose exclaims indignantly:

> Have I ever cozened any friends of yours of their land? Bought their possessions? Taken forfeit of their mortgage? Begged a reversion from 'em? Bastarded their issue? What have I done that may deserve this? (2.2.37–40)

Even as Morose spurns Truewit's meddling, his language clarifies how peculiar Truewit's mission actually is: an attempt at enforcement warranted neither by comprehensible family allegiances nor by recognized governmental function. The inclination to discipline has become a private whim, merely a new form of eccentricity: the illegitimate, self-promoting churlishness of which Dekker accuses Jonson in *Satiro-Mastix*.

Rather like Volpone, Morose often seems to resist his own supposed objectives. While he pretends to concern himself with no one but himself, he is in fact obsessed with his nephew's every minor misstep; by idiosyncratically withdrawing from the world, he makes himself a public laughingstock. Nonetheless, in Morose as in Volpone Jonson plays with the tantalizing possibility of keeping oneself, or at least aspects of oneself, wholly unknown. Critical private facts about

Morose remain obscure. By marrying, he threatens to belie the presumption of sexual quiescence implied by his age, oddity, and reclusiveness. In the early part of the play, Morose's phallic fantasies seem merely foolish: he is sublimely unaware of his unprepossessing demeanor when asking Epicoene whether she feels love "suddenly shot into you, from any part you see in me" (2.5.24–25). Likewise when Truewit pretends to ascribe Morose's omission of wedding festivities to the pressure of exorbitant sexual desire, the joke depends upon Truewit's knowledge, and ours, that lust is hardly a credible motive. When Morose assures himself that "this night I will get an heir" he seems likely to be deluding himself or cheering himself up, or both. On the other hand, if Morose really were impotent, and known to be so, then Dauphine's elaborate plot would be virtually beside the point. And as the play proceeds, moments of comic exorbitance as well as of deficiency accumulate around Morose. In act 2, scene 1, he is introduced with a "trunk" or long speaking tube; in act 4, scene 3, Mistress Otter complains that "he came down with a huge, long, naked weapon in both his hands"; in act 4, scene 7, he enters bearing the two "naked weapons" confiscated from Daw and LaFoole in a ceremony of symbolic castration. Morose seems simultaneously insufficient and excessive, judged rather like Essex to be lacking despite "extraordinarily sufficient matter." Clermont characterizes old men by their "gray heads and weak hams, moist eyes and shrunk members" (1.1.38–39); but Morose's example seems to jeopardize this casual extrapolation from visible head and eyes to unseen hams and members.

Neither we, the theater audience, nor any of the characters swirling about the stage know, as Jack Daw puts it, "what's what" with Morose. As an interpretive conundrum, Morose suggests the slipperiness of the conventional signifiers of sexual prowess. For the virility of all the male characters, not merely of Morose, is constantly at issue in this play,[21] requiring us to wonder how one is supposed to assess that capacity. The more a man talks about his conquests, the less likely he is

21. Comments on the "epicene" quality of the various male characters are endemic to the criticism of this play: "Even these apparently normal men [the gallants] are somewhat ambiguous, sexually" writes Partridge in *The Broken Compass* (London: Chatto and Windus, 1958), p. 170. Barbara Millard in "An Acceptable Violence: Sexual Contest in Jonson's *Epicoene*," *Medieval and Renaissance Drama in English* 1 (1984): 153, likewise claims that "if the implied norms are valid, there is not a normal male in the play except Epicene in his/her silent period."

to have had them, as Daw and LaFoole demonstrate; but silence could as well indicate inexperience as propriety. Thus oblique forms of "proof" must be made to serve: skill in physical, verbal, or wit combat substitute for the proscribed public display of "extraordinarily sufficient matter." The sheer stupidity of Daw and LaFoole seems to convict them of a corresponding sexual ineptitude; certainly when the Collegiate Ladies are brought to believe that Dauphine has engineered their humiliation, they incontinently abandon the losers for the victor. At the same time, an ability to write clever poems, or to play aggressive practical jokes, or to skewer an opponent in a duel is obviously only remotely related to the ability the Collegiate Ladies most desire to assess. It is as if the men in this play were all on trial for impotence, required to marshal "proofs" that never seem entirely adequate or convincing.

The social construction of femininity is at least as remote from bodily fact as is masculinity. The most conventionally "feminine" individual in the play, shy virgin and assiduous housewife, is not genitally a woman at all. Moreover, the urban breakdown of institutional consensus affects women's social representation even more than men's. Women's social and moral status is traditionally established in reference to their marital status, but in the world of *Epicoene* marriage indicates nothing about the hidden truths of sexual conduct or of gender identity. In the absence of a uniform, obvious standard of assessment, women must establish a *persona* by an improvisatory assembly of incongruous elements. Clerimont deplores Lady Haughty's "pieced beauty"; and Tom Otter announces of his wife that "all her teeth were made i' the Blackfriars, both her eyebrows i' the Strand, and her hair in Silver Street" (4.2.81–83). Conventionally the signifiers of prostitution—"Every part of the town owns a piece of her," the apparently cuckolded Otter equivocally complains—cosmetics might seem dependably to reveal interesting facts about sexual availability even as they conceal blemishes of the bodily surface. But as the traditional distinctions between wife and whore are blurred, so the marks of the professional harlot lose their stigma, and become everywoman's property. The debate about cosmetics in *Epicoene* exploits, as a number of critics have pointed out, common misogynist *topoi;*[22]

22. Barbara Baines and Mary C. Williams, "The Contemporary and Classical Antifeminist Tradition in Jonson's *Epicoene,*" *Renaissance Papers* 1977, pp. 43–58; Karen Newman, "City Talk: Women and Commodification in Jonson's *Epicoene,*" *ELH* 56 (1989): 503–41.

but *Epicoene*'s variety of misogyny hardly lets men off the hook, since they perforce participate in the same epistemologically troubled social arena as the women do.

When the surfaces of the body conceal rather than reveal—when the signs of gender difference are externally applied, rather than an emanation from or a guide to a hidden truth—all heterosocial interaction contains the potential for trickery. Morose's *error personae* instantiates risks everyone runs. On the other hand, the intelligent can attempt to minimize those risks, remaining mindful of the chasm between visible exterior and invisible interior. The need to guard against sexual duplicity puts a premium upon *knowingness*. Secrets thus become a supremely valuable commodity. The silly Otter attempts to curry favor with his drinking companions by advertising what he claims to be the mysteries of his wife's dressing table. (Who knows whether he is telling the truth?) Daw and LaFoole, even more desperately, invent and ascribe secret improprieties to Epicoene, resorting to sheer defamation. The garrulity of these informants is not merely amusing but useful to the wits, who cultivate their company even while condemning their inability to keep their mouths shut. The wit's intelligence, in the sense of sagacity, requires intelligence, in the sense of information.

The individual who would be knowing, therefore, tends to find himself in a partially compromised position, like the canon lawyers spying on the secrets of the marriage bed even while veiling their eyes and disclaiming their voyeurism. Truewit, for instance, insists highmindedly that men ought not inquire what women do in their dressing rooms: "Is it for us to see their perukes put on, their false teeth, their complexion, their eyebrows, their nails?" (1.1.104–5). But having "followed a rude fellow into a chamber" where a woman was dressing, he is nonetheless able to provide an authoritative account of the counterfeiting he labels as privy and inscrutable: separating himself, typically, both from importunity and naiveté.

In *Gender Trouble*, the feminist theorist Judith Butler writes of the transvestite Divine:

> His/her performance destabilizes the very distinctions between the natural and the artificial, depth and surface, inner and outer through which discourse about genders almost always operates. Is drag the imitation of gender, or does it dramatize the signifying gestures through which gender itself is established? Does being female constitute a "natural fact" or a cultural performance, or is "naturalness" constituted

through discursively constrained performative acts that produce the body through and within the categories of sex?[23]

In *Epicoene* Jonson formulates remarkably similar questions, toying with the possibility that virility is a facade and with the corresponding possibility that femininity is merely a matter of *appliqué*.

At the same time, he cannot quite accept the morally corrosive implications of the radical conception that there is nothing "real" underneath, no *substance* to the illusions of masculine or feminine identity. A thoroughgoing constructivist like Butler, who thinks there is no alternative to the theatrical production of gender identity, is in some ways in a more comfortable position than Jonson, the framer of theatrical fictions who nonetheless requires real or natural gender difference to provide the satiric standard by which all his characters may be judged and found lacking. Both the obsolescence and the residual power of that standard are suggested in the final scene, in Otter's broken Latin.

> OTTER: . . . So your *omnipotentes*—
> TRUEWIT: Your *impotentes*, your whoreson lobster!
> OTTER: Your *impotentes*, I should say, are *minime apti
> ad contrahenda matrimonium.*
> TRUEWIT: *Matrimonium?* we shall have most
> unmatrimonial Latin with you. *Matrimonia*, and be
> hanged!
> DAUPHINE: You put them out, man.
>
> (5.3.164–70)

Confusing omnipotence with impotence, Otter rehearses the conflation of exorbitance and inadequacy associated throughout the play with Morose, who after all is the individual whose plight is under discussion here. Significantly Otter stumbles, too, over the gender of his Latin words, making the feminine *matrimonia*, marriage, into a neuter noun. The wits, characteristically, recognize Otter's incompetence in comprehending and manipulating gender categories, but cannot afford simply to disown his ineptitude: Truewit's indignant insistence upon "correctness" merely threatens to derail an improvisatory *tour de force*. Rather like Jonson himself, Truewit fuses a proficiency in colorful colloquial idiom—"whoreson lobster"—with a commitment to decorum almost too punctilious for his own good.

23. Judith Butler, *Gender Trouble* (New York: Routledge, 1990), viii.

The Latin language is surprisingly prominent in *Epicoene:* the wits and would-be wits effortlessly quote Juvenal, Ovid, Horace, Catullus, and Seneca, and even a lowborn drunkard and a barber are able to manage a fractured approximation of an academic debate. In Latin, gender is often obvious from the terminations of nouns and adjectives. Even here, of course, the category of the neuter disturbs a binarism of masculine and feminine, and words designated as *epicoene* are ambiguously gendered. But the unclarities pale in contrast to the vernacular, in which, Jonson claims in *The English Grammar,* there are six genders, none of which can be discerned from the configuration of the words themselves. In his attempt to describe the structure of English Jonson does not, significantly, merely dispense with gender as a grammatical category, as modern linguists do.[24] Rather he insists upon assigning gender to nouns and adjectives despite their lack of distinguishing characteristics. In *The English Grammar,* as in *Epicoene,* the effect is both to imply a certain defectiveness in the material to which the laws of gender so imperfectly apply, *and* to call into question the appropriateness of the laws being invoked. The standard of the silent woman permits Jonson's satiric critique upon actual chatterers and gossips, who break the rule enjoining female silence. At the same time, the fact that silent women do not exist in Jacobean London suggests that the rule is moot; therefore, Morose's insistence upon a silent wife is likewise a butt of satire.

In *Epicoene*—the title itself simultaneously designates an ambiguity of bodily sex and a grammatical uncertainty[25]—Latin stands in the same relation to English that normatively gendered behavior stands in relation to the behavior of seventeenth-century Londoners. In the archaic language, most words indicated their gender plainly. Once upon a time, Jonson imagines, men's and women's socially obvious features—their marital status, valor, wit, freshness of complexion—were likewise dependable guides to their truth. In the contemporary world, however, those indicators are no longer reliable, and

24. The criticism of Jonson's Latinism is at least as old as the late seventeenth century. Herford and Simpson, *Ben Jonson,* vol. 1, p. 358, quote William Wotten commenting on Jonson's *Grammar:* "For want of reflecting upon the grounds of a language which he understood as well as any man of his age, he drew it by violence to a dead language that was of a quite different make."

25. Jonson was apparently the first to use the word *epicoene* to refer to human gender. See Philip Mirabelli, "Silence, Wit, and Wisdom in *The Silent Woman,*" *SEL* 29 (1989): 309–36, and Steve Brown, "The Boyhood of Shakespeare's Heroines: Notes on Gender Ambiguity in the Sixteenth Century," *SEL* 30 (1990): 243–63.

gender becomes invisible, just as it is in the vernacular tongue. Like knowing Latin, understanding the disregarded decorum of sexual difference is at once superfluous, the mastery of an obsolete signifying system, and prestigious, a sign of the knowingness to which everyone aspires. But the prestige thus attained is of a problematic kind. As we have already seen, the outrageousness with which *Epicoene*'s characters all violate what are supposed to be the "natural" rules of sexual conduct necessarily reflects not only upon them but upon the adequacy of the rules themselves. Similarly a satirist finds it easier to chastise individual offenders against a commonly accepted standard than to reform an entire society in which that standard is nowhere instantiated.

As Jonson becomes less interested in individually grotesque humours characters, and more interested in the shared failings of large groups, the increasing ambitiousness of his satiric project inevitably endangers his authority. For increasingly his effectiveness, like the effectiveness of the ecclesiastical court judge, seems to depend not upon the sheer conspicuousness of vices, shortcomings, and anomalies, but upon an agreement by the larger society to regard them as vices, shortcomings, and anomalies in the first place. Moral policing thus appears to be less the discovery of material facts it pretends to be than a way of manipulating opinion, an attempt to force others into an attitude of disapproval. Jonson finds both threatening and irresistible the possibility that neither satire nor the impotence trial really displays self-evident material facts, but rather constitutes occluded forms of persuasion that depend, like all persuasion, upon highly fluid standards of plausibility and obviousness. Jonson's satire, in other words, relies upon its claims to a factual material basis even while persistently undermining those claims.

The critical debate about *Epicoene* has turned largely on whether the wits are meant to be surrogates for the author-satirist, or satiric targets themselves.[26] Critics on both sides of this discussion have as-

26. For the first option, see the influential discussion of *Epicoene* in C. H. Herford and Percy Simpson's edition of Ben Jonson's collected works, and Alan Dessen, *Jonson's Moral Comedy* (Evanston: Northwestern University Press, 1971), p. 107 ff. For the second, see Edward Partridge's Introduction to *Epicoene* in the Yale edition: "That Jonson sees [the wits'] plots against Daw, La Foole, and Morose as at least partly judicial, does not mean that he places himself on their side" (p. 19). John Enck, in *Ben Jonson and the Comic Truth* (Madison: University of Wisconsin Press, 1957), and Jonas Barish, *Ben Jonson and the Language of Prose Comedy* (Cambridge, Mass.: Harvard University Press, 1960), believe Jonson cannot make up his mind about how to portray these characters.

sumed that if the wits are in some measure self-portraits, Jonson must have intended them to be viewed in a positive light; and that therefore, to whatever extent he was able to see them as cruel or exploitative, he must have desired to distance himself from them. But perhaps Jonson is not so self-protective. Clerimont's suspicion that "all is not sweet, all is not sound" with Lady Haughty does not assuage his sexual hunger for her, and Dauphine's contempt for the pretensions of the Collegiates does not prevent him from falling "in love" with all of them at once. The wits fully comprehend how they are implicated in and tainted by the rules of the game, but they do not for that reason opt out of the game. If Jonson eventually comes to view his own satiric activity as compromised or epistemologically insecure, as dependent upon the exorbitance it attacks, and as unable to achieve a fixed and absolute perspective, then he may think of his authorial endeavor in *Epicoene* in a similarly bleak, clear light. Certainly this disillusion or sense of limitation would help account for what many critics have noticed in the plays between *Volpone* and *Bartholomew Fair:* a progressive easing of the unself-conscious disciplinary zeal that pervades the earlier comical satires.[27]

And if Jonson does not let himself off the hook, neither does he reassure his audience about their motives or their capacity to judge. *Epicoene* opens upon "Clerimont, making himself ready": a liminal scene that hovers between a private nakedness that cannot be exhibited onstage and the fully public self-presentation that Clerimont seems to prepare himself for here, but that, of course, he is already undergoing in the eyes of the theater audience. We are allowed to congratulate ourselves that we are "privy" to these characters' secrets, that they bare themselves to us. For after all, as spectators since Aristotle have reassured themselves, theatrical maskings are paradoxically undertaken to the end of revelation; deception is put in the service of making truth visible. Actually, even in other Jonson plays there are limits upon what we know about his characters: who can tell whether Volpone is actually "as hot, and high, and in as jovial plight" as he claims to be in his interview with Celia? The end of *Epicoene*, how-

27. See, for instance, Harry Levin, "Jonson's Metempsychosis," *Philological Quarterly* 22 (1943): 231–39; John Enck, *Ben Jonson and the Comic Truth* (Madison: University of Wisconsin Press, 1957); Jonas Barish, "Feasting and Judgment in Jonsonian Comedy," *Renaissance Drama* new series 5 (1972): 3–51; Katharine Eisaman Maus, *Ben Jonson and the Roman Frame of Mind* (Princeton: Princeton University Press, 1985), pp. 126–34.

ever, in a move unprecedented and rarely imitated in English Renaissance theater, roughly and unmistakably disabuses the spectators of
any complacent assumption of omniscience. Epicoene's male identity
is at least as much a surprise to us as to his fellow characters: probably
more of a surprise, since we have justifiably imagined that the playwright would let us in on such a secret earlier. At the same time, we
recognize with some chagrin that we knew all along that Epicoene,
like every female character on the Renaissance stage, was played by a
boy. Like the typical Jonson gull, we have collaborated in our own deception.

What sort of pleasure or interests has our wilful forgetting served?
The Silent Woman was, of course, written for a company of boy
actors, and the play's skeptical qualms converge on the highly ambiguous body of the cross-dressed adolescent boy.[28] Boys are not mar-
riageable, we learn from Tom Otter, because they are *"impotentes,"*
incapable of "rendering the debt." But the boys on Jonson's stage,
hovering on the edge of puberty, beg precisely that question. Clerimont wonders in the opening scene over the reasons for his page's
popularity at Lady Haughty's house; Truewit suggests that the boy
serves as Clerimont's "ingle" or homosexual pet; Dauphine claims
that the "metamorphosed" Epicoene "is almost of years, and will
make a good visitant within this twelvemonth." Are these boys pre-
sexual or sexual beings? Phallic subjects or nonphallic objects? In a
binary sexual system, are such liminal creatures classified with men,
because they will be so eventually, or with women, because they apparently lack the potency which is the male's defining trait? Much as
Othello encourages the audience to imagine Desdemona in bed with
Othello, but leaves unclear what if anything is happening offstage,
Epicoene eroticizes its epistemological quandaries, and in so doing
makes qualms a site of pleasure. Pedophilia—captivation by what is
not yet visible or clear-cut, by what straddles or evades the lines of
gender difference—seems a sexual analogue to the intellectual vertigo

28. For general accounts of the erotic charge of the transvestite boy, see Lisa Jardine, "'As boys and women are for the most part cattle of this colour': Female Roles
and Elizabethan Eroticism," *Still Harping on Daughters: Women and Drama in the Age
of Shakespeare* (Totowa, N.J.: Barnes and Noble, 1983); Stephen Greenblatt, "Fiction
and Friction," *Shakespearean Negotiations* (Berkeley: University of California Press,
1988), pp. 66–93; Stephen Orgel, "Nobody's Perfect: Or, Why Did the English Stage
Take Boys for Women," *South Atlantic Quarterly* 88 (1989): 7–29; Bruce R. Smith, *Homosexual Desire in Shakespeare's England* (Chicago: University of Chicago Press, 1991),
pp. 145–56; Marjorie Garber, *Vested Interests* (New York: Routledge, 1992), pp. 165–85.

induced by the vagaries of the impotence trial. The titillating equivocations of boy theater make it an ideal vehicle for exploring the *apo-
riae* of Jonsonian satire.

ꙮ II. Sexual Secrecy in *Measure for Measure* ꙮ

LIKE *EPICOENE*, *Measure for Measure* treats of the public regulation of sexual behavior in a disorderly urban world. Shakespeare's
Vienna, like Jonson's London, defies traditional forms of policing,
because an enforceable consensus on sexual morality no longer seems
possible to attain. Like *Epicoene*, too, *Measure for Measure* reflects
contemporary misgivings over the functioning of the ecclesiastical
courts. In the early seventeenth century an increasingly influential
group of Puritans, disgusted by what they considered the courts' leniency and their preference for mediation over retribution, recommend stiffening punishments imposed for sexual transgressions. Angelo seems zealously to subscribe to the arguments that forty years
later, in the Cromwell regime, eventuate in a statute making adultery
a capital crime. And Angelo's special animus against Claudio reflects
a perennial complaint about the ecclesiastical courts' misplaced priorities, since the courts often fail to deter serious offenders, but come
down hard on less insolent sinners who are often easier to locate and
to embarrass.[29]

These marks of current controversies do not necessarily mean,
however, that *Measure for Measure* constitutes an explicit policy rec-
ommendation. As Margaret Scott points out, "The law of *Measure for
Measure* is . . . story-book law"; and it is not at all clear that English
customs with regard to the marital precontract, for instance, are
imagined to hold in Roman Catholic Vienna.[30] In fact, I would argue
that like Jonson's, Shakespeare's concerns are more general, more

29. The problems of selective enforcement, and of difficulty controlling the professional sex trade, were not new: see Richard Wunderli, *London Church Courts and Society on the Eve of the Reformation*, pp. 49–53 and 81–102, for an account of the early
sixteenth-century situation.

30. Margaret Scott, "'Our City's Institutions': Some Further Reflections on the
Marriage Contract in *Measure for Measure*," *ELH* 49 (1982): 794. For a variety of views
of the problems of precontract in *Measure for Measure*, see Ernest Schanzer, "The Marriage Contracts in *Measure for Measure*," *Shakespeare Survey* 13 (1960): 81–89; J. Birje-
Patil, "Marriage Contracts in *Measure for Measure*," *Shakespeare Studies* 5 (1969):
106–11; Harriet Hawkins, "What Kind of Pre-Contract Had Angelo? A Note on Some
Non-Problems in Elizabethan Drama," *College English* 36 (1974): 173–79. For the claim

profound, and more closely wedded to his theatrical medium. As we have already seen in the case of *Epicoene*, the ecclesiastical courts' supervision of sexual conduct poses difficult problems about the relationship between truth and public knowledge, between individuals and communities, and between precepts and behavior. These issues matter to Shakespeare, too; but his notion of what is at stake is substantially different from Jonson's.

While Jonson's fascination with the impotence trial recurs in play after play, Shakespeare's emphasis on explicit sanctions in *Measure for Measure* is quite atypical. In Shakespeare's earlier comedies, although the connection between sexual desire and its "fulfilment" in marriage often seems less than automatic, marriage remains a recognizable *telos* as it never is in Jonson's plays. In *As You Like It* Touchstone succinctly describes the alternatives:

> Come, sweet Audrey,
> We must be married, or we must live in bawdry.
> (3.3.95–96)

In *As You Like It* living in bawdry is not a genuine option, so Audrey and Touchstone march to the altar with the rest of the young couples, despite the implausibility of their union. In *Measure for Measure*, however, any link between desire and marriage seems to have snapped. No one, with the possible and problematic exception of the Duke, weds unless and until compelled to do so. Elbow is the only husband in the play, and his wife, "whom I detest before heaven," risks being debauched in Mistress Overdone's brothel. Once desire comes unhinged from the institution that is meant to contain and direct it, to make it publicly useful, it begins to seem scandalously subversive of personal and social order. Even Claudio, the would-be bridegroom, speaks the language of destructive compulsion:

> As surfeit is the father of much fast,
> So every scope by the immoderate use
> Turns to restraint. Our natures do pursue,

---

that Shakespeare wished to influence James's policy toward sex offenders, see Donald McGin, "'The Precise Angelo,'" *Joseph Quincy Adams Memorial Studies*, ed. James McManaway, Giles Dawson, and Edwin Willoughby (Washington: Folger Shakespeare Library, 1948), pp. 125–39, and Catharine F. Siegel, "Hands Off the Hothouses: Shakespeare's Advice to the King," *Journal of Popular Culture* 20 (1986): 81–88.

Like rats that ravin down their proper bane,
A thirsty evil, and when we drink we die.

(1.2.126–30)

It is difficult to imagine Lysander or Orlando censuring his own passion so savagely.

When sexual indulgence is imagined to bring with it turmoil, animalism, even suicide, celibacy can seem a positive relief, certainly the only way to maintain self-respect and to retain the respect of others.[31] The three morally ambitious characters in *Measure for Measure*—Isabella, Angelo, and the Duke—differ from the retrospectively self-reproachful Claudio not in their outlook, but in the energy and consistency with which they translate their principles into action. All three take it for granted that sexuality is dangerous, that their virtue demands sexual continence, and that such continence in turn sanctions their social power. In *Measure for Measure*, as Barbara Baines writes, "chastity authorizes authority."[32] Even those characters whose behavior strays farthest from the ideal of chaste virtue admire that ideal: Lucio, for instance, tells Isabella that her vow of perpetual virginity renders her "a thing enskied and sainted / By your renouncement an immortal spirit" (1.4.34–35). Julietta, pregnant under indefinite circumstances, admits that her sin is "of heavier kind" than Claudio's, and "take[s] the shame with joy" instead of attempting to make a case for herself (2.3.28, 30). Even Pompey Bum admits that his trade "does stink in some sort, sir" (3.2.28). It occurs to no one in *Measure for Measure* to argue for the social utility of sexual enjoyment. Only Lucio's brief analogy between Julietta's pregnancy and agricultural fecundity even approaches a celebratory tone.

> Your brother and his lover have embraced.
> As those that feed grow full, as blossoming time
> That from the seedness the bare fallow brings

---

31. Richard Wheeler makes a similar point in *Shakespeare's Development in the Problem Comedies: Turn and Counter-Turn* (Berkeley: University of California Press, 1981), p. 102, when he describes the "attitudes that imply an ineradicable tension between moral aspiration and an inherently debasing sexual nature."

32. Barbara Baines, in "Assaying the Power of Chastity in *Measure for Measure*," *SEL* 30 (1990): 284–98, points out that the social prestige that attaches to chastity in Vienna leads the morally self-conscious characters—Isabella, Angelo, and the Duke— to make a virtue out of sexual renunciation and to value a reputation for celibacy.

CHAPTER FIVE

To teeming foison, even so her plenteous womb
Expresseth his full tilth and husbandry.

(1.4.40–44)

In Lucio's formulation, Claudio's desperate "surfeit" becomes the "fullness" of innocent gratification, and appetite not a "ravening down" but a natural impulse that regenerates the abundance upon which it feeds. Attempting to enlist Isabella's support for her brother, Lucio emphasizes the connections between Claudio's behavior and the innocent cycle of bloom and harvest, momentarily recovering the morally less tense and conflicted view of the earlier comedies. Just as a spark intensifies darkness, the effect of these radiant lines in their grim setting is to underscore the prevailing distrust of sexuality by providing a glimpse of a less troubled alternative.

The prevailing idealization of "purity" in Vienna far exceeds communal need. With the important exception of Angelo's harassment of Isabella, the sexual "crimes" the Duke wishes to root out of Vienna are victimless and the city, however seedy, in no real danger of revolution or collapse. Jonathan Dollimore has plausibly argued that the sense of sexual crisis in Vienna, as in Jacobean London, is an ideological screen for an anxiety of a different nature: the real targets of repression are members of the lower classes who might foment rebellion against their "betters."[33] But sexual surveillance in Vienna does not merely oppress the proletariat while letting the elite off scot-free. If anything, rather like its English counterpart, it has more severe consequences for better-off people concerned to protect their "good fame." I would suggest that concepts of restraint and transgression, discipline and capitulation, seem indispensable to the upper-class characters not primarily because they provide an excuse to oppress others (although they may indeed provide that excuse) but rather because those terms so profoundly structure the experience of desire in Measure for Measure that in some cases they can come to seem indistinguishable from personality itself.

Once sexual desire is regarded as intrinsically, disgracefully errant, and therefore as subject to public punishment, it becomes by reflex something to hide. The play's numerous enclosures—convent, private study, locked garden, moated grange—are sites congested with

33. Jonathan Dollimore, "Transgression and Surveillance in Measure for Measure," Political Shakespeare: New Essays in Cultural Materialism (Manchester: Manchester University Press, 1985), pp. 72–87.

sexual desire, actual or rumored, frustrated or enacted. Even the prison is populated by fornicators. Consequently, when Lucio calls Vincentio a duke of dark corners, we recognize instantly that the dark corner metonymizes sexual voracity. Prohibition and concealment, surveillance and inwardness, mutually produce and necessitate one another, in a dialectic that by now ought to seem familiar.

As in *Epicoene*, then, sexuality seems a particularly troublesome issue because it is double-faced, both importantly public and intensely private. We have already seen how the law of early modern England acknowledges this doubleness: on the one hand making marriage the basis of weighty familial and social obligations, and on the other hand permitting valid marriages between two people by verbal promise only, without presence of witnesses or consent of parents. In *Measure for Measure* Claudio and Julietta founder in this legal quagmire.

> Thus stands it with me: upon a true contract
> I got possession of Julietta's bed.
> You know the lady, she is fast my wife
> Save that we do the denunciation lack
> Of outward order.
>
> (1.2.145–49)

What is Claudio claiming here? He might be arguing that the contract is "true" only in the sense that it was faithfully undertaken, or he might be claiming, in the stronger sense, that it ought to be acknowledged as valid. His equivocal word "fast" nicely captures the ambiguity of the lovers' situation. If "fast" means "very nearly," Claudio implies that he and Julietta do not consider themselves married until they have undergone a public ceremony. If "fast" means "securely," Claudio is asserting the binding force of the private contract, beside which "the denunciation . . . of outward order" is a formality that only ratifies what is already the case.

In either case Claudio and Julietta, in "the stealth of our most mutual entertainment," have attempted rather like Jonson's Volpone or Morose to create for themselves an unseen life of bodily pleasure, a life that dispenses with the consent and collaboration of the community. Unlike Jonson's protagonists, however, these lovers do not anticipate keeping their secret indefinitely; they wish only to defer their public commitment until Julietta's kin have come to favor the match. The entirely provisional quality of their clandestine arrangement allows them to remain thoughtless to its implications. Since they have apparently never bothered to justify their conduct to themselves, they are easily brought to repent of their "error" once their union is accidentally made public. Neither Claudio nor Julietta attempts to argue that the existence of a private contract, however "true" or "fast," means that they are innocent of fornication after all.

Angelo's internalization of Vienna's disciplinary regimen is far more complex than Claudio's simple avoidance strategy. Angelo's initial qualification for judicial office is that he possesses, as the Duke says, "a kind of character in thy life, / That to th'observer doth thy history / Fully unfold" (1.1.28–29). "Character" here refers to legible writing, the self made publicly available. Angelo denies himself a private life, apparently everting his entire person to the public gaze. This ambition for transparency seems wholly compatible with the Christian tradition of asceticism. For "we owe to asceticism," as Geoffrey Galt Harpham writes, "the notion that the exemplary self is observable."[34] The ascetic everts his inwardness, holding his self-mortification up for display: even when his struggles, his agonies, his triumphs are undertaken in rigorous isolation, they acquire meaning insofar as they are narrated to or witnessed by others, rendered into patterns for others to emulate.

Nonetheless, Angelo's legalistic identification of the true with the publicly available turns out not to be merely impossible, but morally dangerous. It allows him to muddle the relationship between the realm of intention—acts merely contemplated but not executed—and the realm of the secret, which might include deeds as well as intentions. When Escalus, seeking clemency for Claudio, asks Angelo whether he is not himself subject to the same unruly desires, Angelo replies:

> Tis one thing to be tempted, Escalus,
> Another thing to fall. I not deny,
> The jury passing on the prisoner's life
> May in the sworn twelve have a thief or two
> Guiltier than him they try; what's open made to justice,
> That justice seizes.
>
> (2.1.17–22)

34. Geoffrey Galt Harpham, *The Ascetic Imperative in Culture and Criticism* (Chicago: University of Chicago Press, 1987), p. 27.

Angelo begins by drawing a distinction between being tempted and actually committing a crime, but his example cuts in another direction, differentiating the known thief in the dock from the unknown thief on the jury. Whereas logic requires him to supply an example of a successfully resisted temptation, Angelo cites a person who really has acted on his temptation, but who merely happens not to have been apprehended. This unintentional but revealing blunder foreshadows the slippage that permits Angelo's sexual harassment of Isabella. His equation of truth with publicity means that the secret act, which is not "open made to justice," may as well never have occurred.

Thus Angelo's pretension to complete visibility turns out to have an escape hatch, as it were, into a hidden room in which he may conceal everything he does not wish to acknowledge to the world. Moreover the secrecy of this hidden place itself arouses Angelo's appetite.

> these black masks
> Proclaim an enshield beauty ten times louder
> Than beauty could, displayed.
>
> (2.4.79–81)

In his imagination, in other words, the ignominious pleasures of sexual abandon require and are abetted by interdiction and concealment. Angelo's yearning for a clandestine union is simply the flip side of his equally intense yearning for rigid containment. Whereas Claudio desires a woman that happens to be denied him, and sleeps with her in the expectation that their relationship will eventually be legitimized, Angelo desires a woman because she is forbidden, choosing as the object of his passion the most ostentatiously pristine woman in Vienna.

Angelo's behavior is exactly what one would expect of someone who assumes that all sexual expression is tantamount to moral ruin. "I have begun," he tells Isabella, "And now I give my sensual race the run." Once embarked upon such a "race," he imagines, there is no stopping, no limit, no brake. Angelo's phrase recalls an earlier locution of the Duke's, who speaks of "strict statutes and most biting laws / The needful bits and curbs to headstrong jades." In Plato's ancient metaphor, the appetitive part of the soul is a strong but recalcitrant horse which requires, but often escapes, a rider's firm management. Paradoxically but necessarily, the Duke's emphasis on the importance of control mutates easily into Angelo's excuse for capitulation: for if sexuality is essentially antisocial, it cannot be expected to contain and direct itself any more than a horse could be expected to govern itself without bit or bridle. At the same time, Angelo needs constantly to remind himself that Isabella is taboo, that he is defiling her, that his proposition flagrantly violates the rules he has been entrusted to administer.

> Is this her fault, or mine?
> The tempter or the tempted, who sins most, ha?
> Not she; nor doth she tempt; but it is I
> That, lying by the violet in the sun,
> Do, as the carrion does, not as the flower,
> Corrupt with virtuous season.
>
> (2.2.162–67)

Angelo quite accurately recognizes that the very awareness of merit that ought to foster his excellence in fact precipitates his disintegration. He struggles to remember, even to exaggerate, the prohibition against which he determines to act, because for him prohibition is aphrodisiac. If he were to rationalize his behavior, or blame it on Isabella, the novice of St. Clare would interest him no more than the devoted, licit Mariana. Therefore Angelo's extraordinarily lucid self-condemnation functions not as an impediment but as a spur, and leads not to penitence but to an increasing moral recklessness. The importance of what Angelo thinks of as "external" controls can hardly be overestimated, both for the rigidity of his principles and for the peculiar liberties he takes with them.

Isabella's asceticism is more rigorous and consistent than Angelo's, for she does not confuse God's unlimited knowledge with the limited perspective of the courtroom. She possesses the subjectively constitutive sense of divine supervision that, as we have seen, so many Renaissance clerics try to cultivate in themselves and in their followers. A number of consequences follow from this vivid conviction of omniscient witness. The first is that in Isabella's case, the bar against sexual transgression must be absolute. There is no nook or cranny undetectable by God within which she might permit herself release. Nor could she acquiesce to Angelo merely in body, retaining the purity of her mind intact: for the purity of her mind is constituted precisely by her refusal to allow space for anything clandestine. In fact, the clandestine is an almost impossible category for Isabella, since worldly reputation, in relationship to which secrecy acquires its meaning, is insignificant to her compared to what God thinks. As she considers Angelo's proposition, it never even seems to occur to her that she might return to her nunnery after a wild night in the locked garden with her good fame unscathed. For good fame, in this sense, is no concern of hers unless it happens to match up with the truth. Similarly, Isabella cannot countenance compromising her primary supernatural allegiance for the sake of secondary, natural ones. Although, of course, it is Claudio's life rather than her own that she proposes to jettison, it is not entirely absurd that Isabella thinks of herself as a kind of martyr, like those saints who renounce spouses, siblings, offspring in order to be burned at the stake, torn on the wheel, or devoured by savage beasts. Like martyrs in the first century or in the sixteenth, she refuses to define herself in terms of her affection for or duty toward her kin.

Yet Isabella's way of coming to terms with Vienna's disciplinary regimen entangles her, too; and the debate about her among *Measure for Measure* critics reveals how the trap works. Critics who approve of her, like G. Wilson Knight and Muriel Bradbrook, tend to read the play as an allegory in which the function of the characters is iconic. In this scheme Isabella "stands for sainted purity," or "represents both Truth and Mercy."[35] For such critics, Isabella has no "inward truth" at variance from her superficies, for that kind of inwardness would violate what they understand to be the play's generic conventions. They apprehend Isabella much as she would like to apprehend herself, as a woman with nothing to hide whose very limpidity allows her to reflect a truth outside of, and greater than, herself. Critics who disparage Isabella presume that she is a psychologically complex character, and use that presumption of complexity to attack her. Anne Barton chastises Isabella for an "irrational terror of sex which she has never admitted to herself"; Carolyn Brown and Harriet Hawkins for "her subliminal attraction to sexual abuse"; J. W. Lever for her "psychic confusion"; Arthur Kirsch for her "unconscious sexual provoca-

35. G. Wilson Knight, "*Measure for Measure* and the Gospels," *The Wheel of Fire: Essays in Interpretation of Shakespeare's Sombre Tragedies* (London: Oxford University Press, 1930), p. 81; Muriel C. Bradbrook, "Authority and Justice in *Measure for Measure*," *Review of English Studies* 17 (1984): 386.

tion"; Harold Goddard for her "unplumbed sensual element"; Barbara Baines for her ignorance "of how she, as a subject, is constituted and subjected by her chastity."[36]

All these critics believe they can detect something about Isabella that she does not, or will not know. If even guilty intentions, according to the New Testament, are culpable, then one way to escape culpability is scrupulously to renounce those intentions. In Isabella's case this disavowal seems to require, however, a massive screening of herself from herself. It is hard to second-guess Angelo, because in his soliloquies he freely admits what he is. Isabella's more stringent version of the ascetic project, by contrast, seems to demand not merely self-denial, or careful conduct before others, but a repression-into-unconscious. Then her conscience can indeed be clear, but only because it is partial. Many Renaissance Christians, especially those of ascetic leanings, devoted themselves to various forms of introspective discipline designed to protect them from committing this error:[37] which is, in fact, a more subtle, less witting version of Angelo's mistake. If Angelo might be said to construct a hidden garret behind his public facade, Isabella might be said first to devise one and then contrive to forget where the door is, so that she seems to be mere facade even to herself. For many modern critics, psychoanalytic techniques of undoing this disavowal have seemed called for, because Isabella's

36. Anne Barton, Introduction to *Measure for Measure* in *The Riverside Shakespeare* (Boston: Houghton Mifflin, 1974), p. 546; Carolyn Brown, "Erotic Religious Flagellation and Shakespeare's *Measure for Measure*," *ELR* 16 (1986): 162 (Harriet Hawkins makes a similar argument in "'The Devil's Party: Virtues and Vices in *Measure for Measure*," *Shakespeare Survey* 31 (1978): 104–14); J. W. Lever, Introduction to the Arden *Measure for Measure* (London: Methuen, 1965), p. lxxix; Arthur Kirsch, "The Integrity of *Measure for Measure*," *Shakespeare Survey* 28 (1975): 96; Harold C. Goddard, "Power in *Measure for Measure*," in *The Meaning of Shakespeare* (Chicago: Chicago University Press, 1951); Barbara Baines, "Assaying the Power of Chastity," p. 288.

37. Ignatius Loyola, William Perkins, Thomas Cooper, and many others provide members of the various Christian confessions with methods of meditation designed to ferret out and acknowledge recesses of the self the fallen, self-loving individual would prefer not to acknowledge. The most complete discussion I have encountered on this problem, however, is Daniel Dyke's now relatively little-known *Mystery of self deceiving*, first published in London in 1614. Dyke is interested not only in how and why people can be mistaken about one another, but in why even one's apparently unmediated self-knowledge can be incomplete or uncertain: "Man knoweth his inward thoughts, purposes, and desires, but the frame and disposition of his heart he knows not, nor yet always the qualities of those thoughts, whether they tend, what secret deceit lies, and lurks in them" (p. 312).

denial of her own complexity seems precisely the kind of psychic mechanism that psychoanalysis is designed to expose and reverse. The unexamined assumption of the "therapeutic" view, in sixteenth-century writers like William Perkins or Daniel Dyke as much as in Freud, is that self-knowledge despite its painfulness is invariably ameliorative.

Possibly, however, Isabella's dilemma challenges this notion. A favorite term for her in the criticism is "hysterical,"[38] a term for a psychological malady that originally referred to a bodily disorder. A "hyster" is a womb, the secret inner place that, as we shall see in the following chapter, becomes a corporeal analogy for psychological inwardness in the minds of many male writers in the English Renaissance. Perhaps it is possible to see Isabella's furious resistance to Angelo as a way of protecting her mental virginity, refusing to touch the seal upon her inwardness, in which case her critics' attempts to penetrate beyond or behind her "face value" or "virtuous facade" recapitulates Angelo's scandalous importunity. Of course, however, we *cannot help* but see that Isabella, insofar as she can be perceived as more than an allegorical abstraction, is victimized by her own principles. In *Measure for Measure*, then, the ascetic impulse to complete self-display before God or before others ironically but inevitably invites accusations of hypocrisy—not merely, as in *Richard III*, because the appearance of guilelessness can itself be a studied tactic, but because the residue of anarchic secrecy that attaches to sexual desire can never successfully be exorcised.

⚶ LIKE *EPICOENE, MEASURE FOR MEASURE* depicts a world in which traditional means of socially specifying what sexual relations take place, and between whom, are no longer trustworthy. At the same time, no other way of indicating the secret life of individuals or couples has taken its place. Thus in both plays, sexuality somehow exceeds the publicly ascertainable. Yet the nature of this excess or evasion is conceived very differently by Jonson and by Shakespeare. In the impotence trial the erect penis serves theoretically as the "absolute insignia of manhood" even while its invisibility and evanescence call that absoluteness into question. Similarly in *Volpone* and *Epicoene*, the genitals that cannot be shown in public become "that within which

38. See, for instance, J. W. Lever, Introduction to the Arden *Measure for Measure*, p. lxxx; Kirsch, "The Integrity of *Measure for Measure*," p. 97; Hugh Richmond, *Shakespeare's Sexual Comedy: A Mirror for Lovers* (New York: Bobbs Merrill, 1971), p. 155.

passeth show." They are a metonymy for a private truth constituted not as an individual essence or an inalienable right, but as the unstable limit beyond which an intense, imperfect scrutiny, whether theatrical or juridical, cannot proceed. The obscene materiality of Jonsonian subjectivity is entirely consistent with the practices of the ecclesiastical courts, which deliberately restricted their definition of marital incompatibility to bodily defectiveness. Jonson is, as we have seen, acutely aware of the difficulties of naive materialism both in the courtroom and the playhouse, but he cannot or does not choose to elaborate an alternative to a material standard of truth.

Measure for Measure occasionally makes reference to sheerly corporeal secrets; for instance, in Lucio's speculations that Angelo is an "ungenitured agent" who pisses ice. But significantly, Lucio's speculations are facetious; and the kind of defamation he practices, however it infuriates the Duke, never poses the kind of practical danger it does in Jonson's plays. In general, bodies in *Measure for Measure* are not secretive: they unequivocally publicize sexual behavior. The furtive dalliance between Claudio and Julietta is exposed by pregnancy, which offers exactly the kind of uncontestable proof that Bonario, in *Volpone*, had found so frustratingly elusive.

> The stealth of our most mutual entertainment
> With character too gross is writ on Juliet.
>
> (1.2.154–55)

As in the Duke's praise of Angelo, the word "character" refers to a publicly legible inscription which betrays any attempt at "stealth." While Jonson's dramatic purposes lead him to the impotence trial, troubled as it is by the difficulty of obtaining material evidence, Shakespeare's lead him to the inquiry into fornication, in which the woman's belly physically obtrudes her culpability. And the paternity of extramaritally conceived children, which might have incited a Jonson-style probe into undecidable physical particulars, is never disputed by anyone in *Measure for Measure*; even Lucio admits, despite his earlier courtroom perjury, that he has fathered a child upon his whore.

Nonetheless, the revelatory bodies of *Measure for Measure* do not settle much. The bed trick drives a wedge between corporeal performance and the intention that the law generally assumes attaches to performance, complicating, for the male protagonist, the relationship between the inner domain of intention and subjective awareness and the "external" behavior of the body. This trick merely poses in a dramatically acute form a more general difficulty that plagues attempts at sexual policing throughout the play: the problem that bodily acts fail to have meaning in themselves, but acquire the significance participants and witnesses attach to them. Angelo compares Claudio's offense to murder and counterfeiting; Lucio thinks it "a game of ticktack." The sex act does not mean the same thing to Isabella and to Mistress Overdone, or even to Isabella and Mariana. The loving union of Juliet and Claudio seems importantly different from the commercial relationship of Lucio to his whore, and likewise from the vexed, covertly legitimate connection between Angelo and Mariana. Motives, outcomes, class position, religious conviction, temperamental imperatives, all complicate what Lucio calls "this downright way of creation." The problem is not merely how strictly the authorities ought to regulate particular sexual behaviors, but how that behavior is to be defined and interpreted.

The ecclesiastical courts' inquiry into sexual privacy, then, actually involves not one kind of problem, but two. The first dilemma, with which Jonson is deeply concerned, involves the epistemological puzzles in ascertaining physical facts to which no disinterested party can possibly be a witness. The other problem—Shakespeare's main concern in *Measure for Measure*—is that the material terms in which the ecclesiastical courts construe sexuality may be entirely inadequate to an accurate understanding and evaluation of erotic desires and behaviors.

A radical response to this sense of inadequacy would entail abolishing the external regulation of sexual behavior altogether. In fact John Milton argues for just such an abolition in *The Doctrine and Discipline of Divorce* several decades after the first performances of *Measure for Measure* and *Epicoene*, when the triumph of Milton's own party has made the enactment of severe laws against sexual transgression more likely than they had been in Shakespeare's time.

> How vain therefore is it, and how preposterous in the canon law to have made such careful provision against the impediment of carnal performance, and to have had no care about the unconversing inability of mind, so defective to the purest and most sacred end of matrimony. ... 'Tis read to us in the liturgy, that "we must not marry to satisfy the fleshly appetite, like brute beasts that have no understanding:" but the

canon so runs, as if it dreamt of no other matter than such an appetite to be satisfied.[39]

Milton's conception of the relation between body and mind is, as we shall see in the next chapter, anything but settled; still, he is convinced that restricting the truths of marriage to "the mere instrumental body" improperly inverts the superiority of spirit over matter, and of inwardness over externals.

The position Milton advances in the divorce tracts, characterizable as antinomian or extreme casuist,[40] would have it that sexual and marital dilemmas are impossible for third parties to adjudicate. His argument involves three interrelated assumptions. First, individual circumstances are imagined to be highly variable, and those idiosyncrasies weigh more heavily than any apparent similarities among cases. Secondly, the experience of those circumstances "from the inside" is always radically different from its experience "from the outside." Thirdly, the true, "internal" state of affairs, which Milton believes must serve as the basis for moral decision-making, is a mental, not a bodily condition. The body is, in fact, a positive distraction, because its visibility to others, and its similarity to other human bodies, falsely obscures the variability of inward experience, and deceptively suggests that sexuality might be regulated by external precept. In effect, Milton locates the experience of sexuality in that inward realm, disembodied and unavailable to secular jurisdiction, which some of his contemporaries controversially associate with the domain of religious conviction. He argues that no general law can be formulated to encompass the infinite diversity of individual situations; no evidentiary criteria can possibly be established to prove or disprove essentially invisible mental states; no magistrate can possibly acquire the knowledge required to monitor the sexual conduct of others.

I've devoted some time to describing Milton's position in *Doctrine and Discipline of Divorce* because it is one that Shakespeare could conceivably embrace, but seems deliberately to abjure. *Measure for Mea-*

39. John Milton, *The Doctrine and Discipline of Divorce*, chapter 3, in *The Works of John Milton* (New York: Columbia University Press, 1931), 3.2:393.

40. For a persuasive account of Milton's antinomian politics in another treatise see Stanley Fish, "Driving from the Letter: Truth and Indeterminacy in Milton's *Areopagitica*," in *Re-Membering Milton*, ed. Mary Nyquist and Margaret Ferguson (New York: Methuen, 1987), pp. 234–54.

sure acknowledges the kind of difficulties Milton adduces, but does not subscribe to Milton's radical solutions. While carefully specifying an extraordinary diversity of attitudes toward sexuality—different kinds of asceticism, various degrees of libertinage, and so forth— *Measure for Measure* is fascinated at the same time by the ways in which human beings resemble one another. Again and again in the play, characters are confused, exchanged, or substituted for one another. Isabella's attitudes to sexuality, and to Angelo, are entirely different from Mariana's, but in the dark, Angelo cannot tell them apart. Claudio is the scion of an honorable family, Ragozine a hardened pirate, but their heads are interchangeable.

A fascination with the substitutability of one body for another is recurrent in Shakespeare. In many of his comedies, it reflects a primary irony of sexual desire: that the lover's vivid conviction—or illusion—of the beloved's uniqueness conflicts with a kind of *eros* perhaps best described as depersonalized genital attraction. The history plays and tragedies make a less specifically sexual assertion of bodily community, when kings in moments of despair insist upon their corporeal equivalence with their subjects.

> Mock not flesh and blood
> With solemn reverence, throw away respect,
> Tradition, form, and ceremonious duty,
> For you have but mistook me all this while.
> (*Richard II* 3.2.171–74)

In all these cases, just as in Milton, the ground of human similarity is imagined to be a bodily ground. It may seem curious to conceive of human beings as corporeally indistinguishable: do persons really differ more mentally than they do physically? Do not social and temperamental differences impress themselves upon the body as well as upon the mind? Surely the patent improbability of the bed-trick is part of what constitutes its charm as a "literary" device. In fact, however, one possible effect of the schematic differentiation between inward and outward which this book has been attempting to trace is the fantasy, or romance, or fear of a common, unindividuated corporeality, an embodiment that is both part of the self, and outside of or distinct from it.

It may be helpful to summarize at this point a three-way contrast among the attitudes I have called, almost by shorthand, Jonsonian,

CHAPTER FIVE

Miltonic, and Shakespearean.⁴¹ These writers posit three different ways in which the categories body/spirit, outward/inward, and
communal/individual might be imagined to interact. In the comedies
of Jonson's prime, there is no separate spiritual realm. The routine
and the singular, the visible and the secret, the inward and the external: all are conceived to be material effects (Jonson calls the internal
materials that produce idiosyncrasy "humours"). In this scheme
some facts might be hard to discover, but they are not different in
kind from facts that are easy to know. The Milton of the divorce
tracts, by contrast, associates particularity and privacy with a mental
inwardness qualitatively distinct from the manifest workings of the
body, workings associated by contrast with a degraded publicity and
lack of differentiation. In *Measure for Measure* Shakespeare endorses
Milton's implicitly dualist ontology: whereas in Jonson the body is
the ground of truth, but is hard to "get at," in *Measure for Measure*
the body is relatively easy to get at but truth seems not to be grounded
there. At the same time, Shakespeare does not subscribe to Milton's
ethics; the fact that all human beings are embodied seems to remain
morally momentous to him, rather than an ethical distraction.

What accounts for this difference—and what are its consequences
for *Measure for Measure*? In this play the bed-trick and the sleight-of-
heads are only two instances of a pervasive and complex pattern of
substitutions, deputations, and interchanges by which one person or
thing is "taken for" or made to stand in the place of another.⁴² The

41. I should emphasize that all three writers are more complex than the positions
with which I associate them here. What I am calling "Miltonic" is Milton's position in
the divorce tracts; his attitude to the body is equivocal in the early poetry and changes
fundamentally later in his career, as suggested by the following chapter and as scrupulously charted by James Turner in *One Flesh: Paradisal Marriage and Sexual Relations in
the Age of Milton* (Oxford: Oxford University Press, 1987). Likewise, what I am calling
"Jonsonian" here is characteristic of Jonson's comedies between *Every Man Out of His
Humour* and *Bartholomew Fair*: his attitude in the masques and poems is often quite
different. See my "Satiric and Ideal Economies in the Jonsonian Imagination," *English
Literary Renaissance* 19 (1989): 42–64, for a fuller account of Jonson's work in other
genres. Shakespeare, of course, is an immensely complicated case, and I do not pretend
to account for anything except *Measure for Measure*.
42. Many have pointed out the crucial role substitutions, deputations, and exchanges play in the plot of *Measure for Measure*. See, for example, Richard Wheeler,
Shakespeare's Development in the Problem Comedies, pp. 120–38; Meredith Skura, "New
Interpretations for Interpretation in *Measure for Measure*," *boundary 2* 7, no. 2 (1979):
39–58; Alexander Leggatt, "Substitution in *Measure for Measure*," *Shakespeare Quarterly*
39 (1988): 342–59; Marc Shell, *The End of Kinship: "Measure for Measure," Incest, and*

title of the play itself refers to the principle of talion justice, a principle by which a violation of social order can be undone or wiped out by a *quid pro quo* reversal of the original direction of the transgression: "life for life, eye for eye, tooth for tooth, hand for hand, foot for foot" (Deuteronomy 20.21). Ordinarily a simple restoration of the *status quo ante* is impossible. Because a murderer cannot return his victim's life, an assailant cannot return his victim's damaged limb, he must render up a life, eye, or tooth equivalent to the one he took. "Justice," in other words, involves substitution in kind or in proportion.

It may be less obvious that mercy, the renunciation or apparent opposite of talion justice, likewise operates by a principle of substitution. Shakespeare takes the title of *Measure for Measure* from a passage from the Sermon on the Mount characterized by a rapid alternation of active and passive constructions.

> Judge not, that ye be not judged. For with what judgment ye judge, ye shall be judged: and with what measure ye mete, it shall be measured unto you again. (Matthew 7.1–3)

One refrains from judging because one is capable of imagining oneself as the victim of censure; one is convinced to forbear from punishment by considering that one might, oneself, become the object of such punishment. For a passage often construed as offering hope and renewal, Christ's formulation is remarkably menacing. He reveals that the transcendence of talion law itself turns upon a principle of taliation.

In *Measure for Measure* as in Matthew, appeals for mercy commonly involve similar invitations to occupy, imaginatively, another person's position. Escalus, for instance, attempts to get Angelo to mitigate Claudio's punishment:

> Let but your honor know
> (Whom I believe to be most straight in virtue)
> That, in the working of your own affections,
> Had time cohered with place or place with wishing,
> Or that the resolute acting of your blood
> Could have attained th'effect of your own purpose,

the Idea of Universal Siblinghood (Stanford: Stanford University Press, 1988), pp. 97–136.

Whether you had not sometime in your life
Erred in this point which now you censure him.

(2.1.8–15)

Isabella attempts to make a similar case:

If he had been as you, and you as he,
You would have slipped like him; but he, like you,
Would not have been so stern.

(2.2.64–66)

What is the relation between the kind of imaginary taking-of-another's-place invoked by Escalus and Isabella, and the "cruder," bodily substitutions of Mariana for Isabella, Ragozine for Claudio? Angelo, the slow learner who cannot suppose himself capable of Claudio's "slip," is made physically to reenact it. If he were able to put himself in Claudio's place in the conditional, hypothetical way Isabella and Escalus propose, he would not need to do so in actuality. In other words, vicarious or empathetic identification with the wrongdoer constitutes an alternative to bodily reenactment. So conceived, empathy stands in relation to reenactment much as we have seen persuasion stand in relation to coercion in Marlowe's plays: as the less forceful, more voluntary, and therefore morally more attractive mental analogue to a painful corporeal process. Just as persuasion mimics coercion and depends upon its possibility, even while seeming to evade its brutal physicality, so the capacity for vicarious feeling depends upon the possibility of reenactment, even while that possibility remains in the realm of imagination.

Now the theater audience, insofar as it is instructed by the action of *Measure for Measure*, proves itself capable of the kind of imaginative flexibility that Angelo cannot initially manage; for the theater, according to such defenders as Sidney and Heywood, is a place where spectators are supposed to imagine themselves undergoing the events depicted onstage by the actors, so as to acquire the lessons of another's experience without themselves having actually to suffer it. The conditions of apprehending *Measure for Measure* thus recapitulate in some degree the moral problems raised by it. The spectatorial exercise of self-substitution is, however, as we have already seen in the case of *Othello*, highly undependable, subject to misleading analogies between self and other.

How are we to know which substitutions are right? It is possible to see the history of *Measure for Measure's* reception as a series of debates about what kinds of empathetic substitution are appropriate, about which equivalences and cathexes are and are not suitable. Do Mariana and Angelo recapitulate the crime committed by Julietta and Claudio, or is there a significant difference in the kind of precontract by which they are bound?[43] When Isabella recruits Mariana to take her place in bed with Angelo, does she, as David Lloyd Stevenson argues, preserve her chastity only by becoming a bawd, foisting her quandary onto another? Or is it more important to remember, with Bernice Kliman, the "difference in the sex act as an expression of mutual love . . . and the sex act as a humiliating act of violence?"[44] Does the Duke's arrangement of the bed-trick reduce him to the level of the panderer Pompey, as Richard Wheeler believes?[45] Does commercial prostitution seem "comparatively harmless," as Harriet Hawkins argues, "when set beside the diseases of the soul?"[46] Is Angelo, as Marc Shell claims, the Duke's substitute in a sexual as well as a governmental sense, so that his proposition to Isabella acts out the Duke's disowned or repressed desire for her, as eventually revealed in his marriage proposal?[47]

The importance of evaluating comparatively the propriety of various substitutions in *Measure for Measure* has made certain strategies of reading seem especially fruitful or plausible. Allegorical readings, for instance, like G. Wilson Knight's, M. C. Bradbrook's, or Roy Battenhouse's, involve a symbolic transfer of meaning from an original to a substitute object.[48] Similarly psychoanalytic readings, like Richard Wheeler's, Meredith Skura's, or Marc Shell's, tend to dissolve the differences among individuals and between actuality and fantasy, freeing them to occupy one another's places. ("Whereas the Duke is

43. For the claim that there is a significant difference, see Ernest Schanzer; for the claim that there is not, see Harriet Hawkins, "What Kind of Pre-Contract Had Angelo?"
44. David Lloyd Stevenson, "Design and Structure in *Measure for Measure*," *ELH* 23 (1956): 256–78; Bernice Kliman, "Isabella in *Measure for Measure*," *Shakespeare Studies* 15 (1982): 137–48.
45. Wheeler, *Shakespeare's Development in the Problem Comedies*, p. 122.
46. Harriet Hawkins, "The Devil's Party," *Shakespeare Survey* 31 (1978): 112. See also Harold C. Goddard, in "Power in *Measure for Measure*," p. 450: "The vices of the two ends of 'society' turn out under examination to be much alike."
47. Shell, *The End of Kinship*, pp. 92–93.
48. G. Wilson Knight, "*Measure for Measure* and the Gospels"; M. C. Bradbrook, "Authority and Justice in *Measure for Measure*," *Review of English Studies* 17 (1941): 385–99; Roy Battenhouse, "*Measure for Measure* and the Christian Doctrine of Atonement," *PMLA* 61 (1946): 1029–59.

Angelo's surrogate and Mariana Isabella's surrogate," claims Rupin Desai, for instance, in *The Psychoanalytic Review,* "the definite marriage of Angelo and Mariana and the probable marriage of the Duke and Isabella are, in fact, a marriage between Angelo and Isabella by double proxy."[49]) Recent new historicist readings like Jonathan Dollimore's or Barbara Baines', with their emphasis upon ideological "displacement," likewise register the strange *mobility* of meaning in the play, the difficulty of fixing or specifying significance, priority, or proportion in a world where everything could conceivably be replaced by something else. Vicariousness is raised from a moral axiom (the exercise of mercy), or a fact about audience response, to a principle of semiotic indeterminacy.

For knowing what lessons the viewing of *Measure for Measure* is supposed to convey is difficult, not merely because members of any audience inevitably vary, but because the play provides them so little guidance. Assessing "damages" requires some consensually-acceptable standard of adequacy, of "fairness." Penalties must "fit" crimes; and even if they are excused in an act of forgiveness, the possibility of punishment must still be adumbrated in order for mercy to register as such. But in the world of *Measure for Measure,* there is little such consensus, no standard of appropriateness. We have already seen how the play's generally jaundiced view of sexuality does not much ease the task of judging sexual "offenses": sexual acts seem to have no natural or plausible valence but can be evaluated in wildly different ways, depending upon one's frame of reference.

The commitment of several characters to a Christian religious vocation further complicates the possibility of establishing some kind of commensurability. Isabella, especially, assumes that spiritual goods like honor and purity are infinitely more important than secular, visible possessions. In her system of values, a promise of ardent prayer constitutes the most potent bribe she can offer Angelo, beside which gold is barren and trivial. The counterintuitive otherworldliness of Isabella's concept of commensurability is central to Christianity, a religion founded upon the spectacularly lopsided substitution of the

49. Rupin Desai, "Freudian Undertones in *Measure for Measure," Psychoanalytic Review* 64 (1977): 487–94. A similar claim is made by W. L. Godshalk, *"Measure for Measure:* Freedom and Restraint," *Shakespeare Studies* 6 (1970): 137–73: "Although they remain physically pure, both the duke and Isabella symbolically share the sin of Angelo and Mariana in the illicit bed, as they recapitulate the act of Claudio and Juliet" (p. 146).

blameless Christ for sinful humanity in the system of God's justice. But since such religious convictions are not subject to the verification of the senses, they are open to challenge by those more firmly attached to the things of this world—like Claudio, for whom any fate seems better than death. His hierarchy of priorities is different from Isabella's, and so therefore are his conceptions of commensurability.

Measure for Measure seems, then, to make two incompatible assertions. First, human beings differ radically from one another, so that one person's meat is another person's poison, one person's truth another person's falsehood, one person's propriety another person's scandal. Second, human beings are not all that different from one another, and can exchange themselves, or be exchanged for one another, quite freely. Shakespeare is not the first Renaissance dramatist to make these contradictory claims simultaneously: as we have already seen, they also inform the theater of Kyd and Marlowe. On the one hand, the lack of transcendent guarantees in the secular theater of the Renaissance seems to open up the prospect of untrammeled individualism, typically figured as "inward" or "unseen." Members of audiences, like characters, can generate an infinite variety of interpretive options. On the other hand, social life seems to demand, despite this individualism, a fund of consensually accepted principles and a sense of shared human lot. In *Measure for Measure* as in *The Spanish Tragedy* the capacity for vicariousness, which holds communities together and which gives theater its purpose, originates in the publicly obvious, universally shared fact of human embodiment. The *mechanism* of empathy, in other words, is aligned with the spectacularly externalized aspects of theatrical performance, and with the conception of an audience as a consensual community. At the same time, in Shakespeare as in Kyd or Marlowe, no particular empathetic attachment can be counted upon to work. So the *consequence* of empathy— the interpretation that a spectator makes of the play—is aligned with invisibility, inwardness, and incalculable idiosyncrasy.

So Shakespeare resembles Jonson in the way he flirts with the possibility of an entirely privatized existence but finds it impossible to do away with the "external" realm. His art is bound up, however uncomfortably, with the values of public exposure and group experience. (Perhaps Milton's indifference to this latter possibility, by contrast, accompanies his preference for nondramatic forms, relatively unaffected by the corporeal exigencies of performance.) For both playwrights, the exterior, interpersonal domain is indispensable despite its manifest inadequacy, or the inadequacy of its manifestation. Thus, too, the ambiguously interiorized domain of sexual experience figures for Jonson and Shakespeare as both threat and promise, fraught with many of the same contradictions as theater itself.

The end of *Measure for Measure*, which so many have found troubling or unsatisfactory, registers strongly the conflicts of the tradition of which it is a part. Since the play cannot reach closure if its contradictions are simply left radically unreconciled, the drastic discrepancies between the various characters' moral and social outlooks are provisionally adjusted by Duke Vincentio, a concealed authority who learns everybody's secrets in the course of the play. As we have seen in chapter 2, English Renaissance writers associate power that takes the form of invisible omniscience not only with God but also with the machiavel who denies God even while appropriating his attributes. Both characterizations have been accorded the Duke by different critics, and each receives some support in the play, which opens with a scene of deputation familiar to readers of *The Prince*, and concludes with Angelo's comparison of Vincentio to "providence divine." Given the structural similarity between machiavel and deity, these alternatives may not be as starkly opposed as they seem.[50]

Perhaps, given the dilemmas in which *Measure for Measure* implicates itself, the Duke ought to be seen as Shakespeare's rather desperate contrivance to mediate between the characters' secret, subjective worlds and the external domain of publicly administered law. By act 3, the play's problems can only be solved by someone who can obtain access to motives and intentions, a privilege usually reserved for a confessor. At the same time, unlike a clergyman, he must retain the secular ruler's ability to mandate changes in behavior in order to bring matters to a satisfactory conclusion. In the real world such a combination would approach tyranny. Thus even in Shakespeare's England, in which the functions of church and state were closely in-

50. Certainly some of the complaints about the Duke—usually mounted as objections to a "providentialist" reading of his role—recall traditional skeptical complaints about the Christian God. When Marcia Riefer, in "'The Instruments of Some More Mightier Member': The Constriction of Female Power in *Measure for Measure*," *Shakespeare Quarterly* 35 (1984): 160, criticizes the Duke on the grounds that he "is actually setting up Angelo for a fall while protecting himself," she recapitulates the objection Milton's God must deal with in *Paradise Lost* III, that the whole history of man is a setup by a deity who knows in advance that his puppet will fail him, then punishes him for failing, then expects to be worshipped for "redeeming" him.

tertwined and in which the king called himself the church's Supreme Governor, the sovereign's actual power to interfere in ecclesiastical affairs was quite restricted.[51] In *Measure for Measure,* however, a prince disguised as a friar is able to bridge, however unsteadily, the gap between power and knowledge, outside and inside, in order to enjoin a resolution.

Although the Duke's unusual means of access to his subjects some-times—often—seems creepy and presumptuous, he is no villain: Gyges and his descendants give us some context for the way Vincentio chooses to deploy his unusual privileges. Yet he remains an earthly ruler confronting juridical dilemmas that are framed so as to be insoluble by earthly power. The generic anomaly of *Measure for Measure*— what A. P. Rossiter speaks to when he complains of "the *imposed* quality of the action"[52]—is a direct consequence of the play's contestatory way of imagining the relationship between sexuality and community. For the final marriages, then, can only be achieved by outright coercion, by the enforcement of laws that prevent whoredom, promiscuity, extramarital dalliance, sexual harassment, breach of promise, and the nonsupport of bastard children. Inevit ably in this scheme, marriage is inflicted as a form of discipline—as an alternative to capital punishment, in fact; it no longer seems a conduit of pleasure, or a flowering of mutual commitment. Richard Wheeler complains of *All's Well That Ends Well* that "the play does little to suggest that the bed trick, which allows the comic plot to be completed, significantly alters the psychological conditions that have made it necessary."[53] The same might be said of *Measure for Measure,* because the Duke does not have the capacity to "alter psychological conditions" by decree. He can manipulate, educate, cajole, and punish, in ways not guaranteed to succeed. He can bring the aggressive, devouring, suicidal impulses associated with sexuality throughout the play under the institutional rubric of marriage; but in order for us to

51. For a short account of the limits placed on the royal supremacy by the Parliament of 1559, see A. G. Dickens, *The English Reformation* (New York: Schocken Books, 1964), pp. 294–306; for Elizabeth's ecclesiastical policy, see William Haugaard, *Elizabeth and the English Reformation* (Cambridge: Cambridge University Press, 1968); for a more detailed and technical account of the legal issues involved, see Robert E. Rodes, *Lay Authority and Reformation in the English Church: Edward I to the Civil War* (Notre Dame: University of Notre Dame Press, 1982), pp. 67–243.

52. *Angel with Horns: Fifteen Lectures on Shakespeare,* ed. Graham Storey (London: Longman, 1961), p. 58.

53. Wheeler, *Shakespeare's Development in the Problem Comedies,* p. 55.

experience the ending as "happy," we have to forget the critique of such disciplinary structures mounted in the earlier acts, overlooking the fact that merely institutional arrangements do not address the fundamental unruliness of sexual desire. The Duke's powers, despite his special capacities, are still conceived as "external" to the subjects he coerces into some semblance of harmonious community. The "internal" renovation of human nature presumably remains the prerogative of a God who can at most only be adumbrated in the theater.

One symptom of the Duke's limitation, and the theater's, is the way that the characters' inwardness, apparently so entirely divulged to his (and our) omniscient, managing vision, recedes almost instantly into unknowability in the midst of what is structured as a scene of revelation and pardon. Isabella, arguing that Angelo ought to be pardoned, makes a distinction between intention and behavior that would have been familiar in a Renaissance courtroom, but that her ascetic scruples would not have permitted her earlier in the play:

> Thoughts are no subjects,
> Intents but merely thoughts.
>
> (5.1.553–54)

Whether or not this constitutes a good reason for pardoning Angelo, or merely indicates Isabella's moral confusion, has been much debated by critics since Samuel Johnson. What Isabella certainly does describe here is the constraint Shakespeare places both upon the power of his duke and the power of his audience. Angelo never indicates that he prefers the Duke's mercy, and life with Mariana, to the death he had requested. Lucio frankly announces he prefers capital punishment to wedded life with Kate Keepdown, but it is unclear whether he is "serious." Claudio and Julietta are accorded no lines to celebrate their unexpected reunion. Isabella, so eloquent in her plea for Angelo's life, fails to acknowledge Claudio's restoration or to respond to the Duke's proposal. "Unorthodox" readings of *Measure for Measure* have involved "reading in" defiance where previous critics assumed acquiescence: Isabella flees in horror from the Duke. What seems important is not whether such interpretations are likely, or whether they were played on Shakespeare's stage, but that they are possible. The expected expressions of gratitude, wonder, or acceptance are capable of being withheld, and once they are withheld we cannot take them simply for granted. In the final lines of *Measure for Measure* most of the characters resist, even repudiate, our scrutiny. Shakespeare seems deliberately to puncture the illusion of complete revelation, reasserting the problem of unknowable inward truth just at the moment when it might be supposed to disappear.

A WOMB OF HIS OWN:
MALE RENAISSANCE POETS
IN THE FEMALE BODY

ॐ I ९६

AGAIN AND AGAIN in the foregoing chapters, perplexities about inwardness and its display turn out to overlap with, imply, or have consequences for questions about the relation of body and mind. The problem of how people possess interiors is not simply synonymous with the problem of how they inhabit their flesh; rather, the issues seem, as it were, knotted together, multifariously differentiated even while snarled and entwined. A Renaissance poetic commonplace with surprisingly close affinities to the theatrical dilemmas already discussed provides an opportunity to explore some of these complex interrelationships. At the same time, I hope to address more explicitly another issue that has hovered just below the surface of much of the foregoing analysis: the implications of a skeptical dynamic for the way gender and sexuality can be imagined in the English Renaissance.

In the sixteenth and seventeenth centuries, many writers associate the creative imagination with the female body. In the first sonnet of *Astrophel and Stella* Philip Sidney describes himself as "great with child to speak, and helpless in my throes" (12). In *Poetaster*'s "apologeticall dialogue," Ben Jonson represents his "long-watched labors" as "Things, that were born, when none but the still night, / And his dumb candle saw his pinching throes" (217–19). In the Cary-Morison ode the turn of the infant of Saguntum, "half got out" but already retreating back into a womb that will become its tomb, rehearses the "turns" and "counterturns," the strophes and antistrophes, of a poem generated to commemorate the dead. When Richard Hooker dies just after completing *On the Laws of Ecclesiastical Polity,* John Spenser eulogizes: "Like Rachel he died as it were in the travail of them, and hastened death upon himself, by hastening to give them life."[1] Shakespeare burlesques the figure in *Love's Labor's*

---

1. Quoted in the textual introduction to Richard Hooker, *On the Laws of Ecclesiastical Polity,* ed. P. G. Stanwood (Harvard University Press, 1981), p. xv.

Lost, in which the would-be poet Holofernes boasts that his effu-
sions "are begot in the ventricle of memory, nourished in the womb
of *pia mater*, and delivered upon the mellowing of occasion"
(4.2.68–70).[2]

Nobody in the English Renaissance argues that the analogy between poetic creation and childbirth means that women make better
artists than men. Although recent feminist scholarship has drawn attention to several ambitious women of letters in the early modern
period, the relative scarcity of female writers in this period contrasts
vividly with the unprecedented literary activity of their male contemporaries, with the emergence of important women writers on the
Continent, and with the positive explosion of female talent into the
literary marketplace after the Restoration. Nor would this scarcity
have astonished many Renaissance intellectuals. Sixteenth- and early
seventeenth-century medical authorities explain women's unfitness
for serious intellectual pursuits on physiological grounds. Citing
Galen, they claim that a woman's body in general and her womb in
particular is cold and moist:

> Were it not so, it would fall out impossible, that her monthly course
> should flow, or she have milk to preserve the child nine months in her
> belly, and two years after it is born; but that same would soon waste
> and consume.[3]

By contrast, bodily heat and dryness are qualities associated with, indeed constitutive of, maleness. They are also, hardly coincidentally,
qualities associated with intellectual exertion in general and imaginative creativity in particular:

> To think that a woman can be hot and dry, or endowed with wit and
> ability conformable to these two qualities, is a very great error; because
> if the seed of which she was formed, had been hot and dry in their
> domination, she should have been born a man, and not a woman. . . .

---

2. Elizabeth Sacks discusses Shakespeare's use of this and similar metaphors in
Shakespeare's Images of Pregnancy (New York: St. Martin's Press, 1980), and gives further examples from Nashe, Harvey, Whetstone, Skoleker, Dekker, Lyly, and Daniel; but
despite her title she is less interested in pregnancy specifically than in generative sexuality generally, and tends to ignore differences between male and female reproductive
functions.

3. Juan de Dios Huarte Navarro, *Examen de Ingenios. The Examination of Mens
Wits*, trans. R. C[arew] (London, 1604), p. 270.

She was by God created cold and moist, which temperature, is necessary to make a woman fruitful and apt for childbirth, but an enemy
to knowledge.[4]

What makes women fertile—what makes them *women*—also renders
them stupid. Their bodies disable their minds.

Contemporary feminist literary critics have emphasized the powerful effect this supposed female incapacity, variously justified in various eras, has had both upon men and upon women. Sandra Gilbert
and Susan Gubar begin their groundbreaking book on the Victorian
novel, *The Madwoman in the Attic*, by remarking that literary creativity is generally construed as a masculine attribute.

> The poet's pen is in some sense (even more than figuratively) a penis.
> . . . The patriarchal notion that the writer "fathers" his text just as God
> fathered the world is and has been pervasive in Western literary civili-
> zation.[5]

Writing from a different theoretical standpoint, such French feminists
as Luce Irigaray, Hélène Cixous, and Catherine Clément have emphasized a Lacanian connection between linguistic representation and
the phallus.[6] For feminist critics, then, the preeminent question is
how female artists ought to conceptualize their own activities: "If the
pen is a metaphorical penis," Gilbert and Gubar inquire, "with what
organ can females generate texts?"[7] Irigaray, Cixous, and Clément,
Margaret Homans, Susan Gubar, and others have tried to chart
the literary development of a "woman's language" that eschews or
subverts "male," phallic forms of representation, seeking alternative
terms appropriate to the female body.[8] Even while they dispute an

4. Huarte, *Examen de Ingenios*, p. 274.
5. Sandra M. Gilbert and Susan Gubar, *The Madwoman in the Attic* (New Haven:
Yale University Press, 1979), p. 4. As Gilbert and Gubar indicate, Harold Bloom's powerful Oedipal account of poetic influence and originality in *The Anxiety of Influence: A
Theory of Poetry* (Oxford: Oxford University Press, 1973) is premised upon this "more
than figurative" analogy.
6. Irigaray, *Speculum of the Other Woman* (1974), trans. Gillian C. Gill (Ithaca:
Cornell University Press, 1985); Cixous and Clément, *The Newly Born Woman* (1975),
trans. Betsy Wing, (Minneapolis: University of Minnesota Press, 1986).
7. Gilbert and Gubar, *Madwoman in the Attic*, p. 7.
8. See above, and Margaret Homans, *Bearing the Word: Language and Female
Experience in Nineteenth-Century Women's Writing* (Chicago: University of Chicago
Press, 1986); Susan Gubar, "'The Blank Page' and Issues of Female Creativity," pp.

oppressive connection between virility and good writing, however, these critics share an important premise with their phallocratic opposition. They assume that writers naturally imagine their creativity in terms of their own bodies, their own genders. Such analogies, moreover, are taken to be essentially celebratory or at least positive ones. Men think of their literary creativity as a form of sexual potency because they value both capacities; women, insisting heroically upon the culturally undervalued importance of their own distinctive experiences, must redeem both their bodies and their creative energies for themselves, if they are not to succumb to neurosis or bad faith or both.

English Renaissance poets, however, seem flatly to defy the imperative of a simple, healthy allegiance to one's own bodily structures. Sidney's hectoring Muse is his midwife; Jonson, often described as the most aggressively "masculine" of English Renaissance writers, depicts his creativity as a maternal function; Milton, phallic poet *extraordinaire* in Gilbert and Gubar's account, relies in *Areopagitica* upon extended analogies between "the issue of the brain" and "the issue of the womb." Given the vigor with which the masculine prerogative was asserted in the early modern period, what attracts these writers to such analogies? What leads male writers to imagine their poetic and intellectual endeavors in terms of a sex to whom those endeavors were proscribed—in terms, moreover, of the very organ that is supposed quite literally to chill and dampen the female intellect?[9] The anomaly seems even greater when we recall how exclusively female was the experience of giving birth in the late sixteenth and early seventeenth centuries, when midwives and female "gossips" rather

---

292–313 in *The New Feminist Criticism*, ed. Elaine Showalter (New York: Pantheon, 1985).

9. In her essay "Apostrophe, Animation, and Abortion," Barbara Johnson has claimed that male poets have little difficulty imagining their literary activity in maternal terms: it is rather women who have trouble with the metaphor, because for them the poem substitutes infanticidally for the child (*A World of Difference* [Baltimore: Johns Hopkins University Press, 1987], pp. 184–99). But Johnson's brilliant reading of women poets' deployment of this trope passes over too quickly the strangeness of its male appropriation, especially its appropriation by Renaissance writers. In *Ventriloquized Voices: Feminist Theory and English Renaissance Texts* (New York: Routledge, 1992), pp. 76–115, Elizabeth D. Harvey links seventeenth-century male poets' rhetorical appropriation of women's bodies with the initial attempts by male physicians to displace female midwives in the birthing chamber.

than male physicians attended the woman in travail, and husbands were excluded from the birthing chamber.[10]

The easiest explanation for the poets' counterintuitive claims is that men envy women's ability to give birth. Yet this "explanation" merely raises further questions, even if it is plausible at all in an age in which "the companion of birth [is] travail, the grief whereof being so extreme, and the danger always so great."[11] "Womb envy," if it exists, is surely no more a fact of nature than "penis envy," but rather a cultural construct the mechanism of which begs to be investigated. Moreover, what these poets manifest is not "envy," understood in the normal sense as a consciousness of lack and a search for substitutes. In Freud's account the woman who is supposed to be suffering from "penis envy" eventually resolves her complex by making her child stand proxy, as it were, for the missing penis. But Sidney, Jonson, and Milton do not indicate any sense of inadequacy. Their bland appropriation of what does not seem "appropriate" is not a search for a substitute but a claim that they are already possessed of the real thing.

The prehistory of the Renaissance commonplace gives some clues both to its persistent significance, and to the particular ways in which it becomes especially intensified and elaborated in early modern England. Analogies between mental creativity and bodily fecundity are not new to sixteenth-century England, nor do they require the exaltation of femaleness or of a quasifemale function. In the *Theaetetus*, Socrates informs his interlocutor that his mother was a midwife, and that he has inherited her gift. He does not have ideas himself, but his interrogative technique helps others bring forth theirs:

> So great, then, is the importance of midwives, but their function is less important than mine. . . . Mine differs from theirs in being practised upon men, not women, and in tending their soul in labor, not their bodies. . . . Now I have said all this to you at such length, my dear boy, because I suspect that you, as you yourself believe, are in pain because you are pregnant with something within you. Apply, then, to me, remembering that I am the son of a midwife and have myself a midwife's gifts, and do your best to answer the questions I ask as I ask them. And

10. On this point see Audrey Eccles, *Obstetrics and Gynecology in Tudor and Stuart England* (Kent, Ohio: Kent State University Press, 1982); for some protofeminist implications of such childbirth customs see Adrian Wilson, "The Ceremony of Childbirth and Its Interpretation," in *Women as Mothers in Pre-Industrial England: Essays in Memory of Dorothy McLaren*, ed. Valerie Fildes (London: Routledge, 1990), pp. 68–107.

11. Richard Hooker, *Of the Laws of Ecclesiastical Polity*, 5.74.1.

if, when I have examined any of the things you say, it should prove
that I think it is a mere image and not real, and therefore quietly take
it from you and throw it away, do not be angry as women are when
they are deprived of their first offspring.[12]

Even while deriving his talents from his mother-midwife, Socrates
discards her specific skills and attributes. He not only differentiates
male from female and mind from body in a familiar hierarchical arrangement, but aligns both pairs of terms, making the superiority of
mind over body equivalent to, and a reason for, the superiority of
male over female. By Greek custom, the father of a newborn had the
right to order it killed if it were in some way unsuitable—if it were,
for instance, a deformed child, or a daughter rather than a son. Socrates flatteringly contrasts the young man's sensible readiness to relinquish unsatisfactory ideas with a woman's irrational attachment to
the doomed infant she painfully delivered just hours or days before.
In Socrates's account, the very similarity of thinking and childbirth
sharpens the difference between mind and body, male and female,
excluding women from philosophy by a principle that seems as natural as the principle which precludes men from giving birth.

English Renaissance renditions of apparently similar analogies,
however, typically complicate the neat Socratic distinctions. In retire-
ment at Wilton House, Philip Sidney writes the first version of his
Arcadia, dedicating it to his sister, who was pregnant during the composition of the romance.[13] In the prefatory letter, Sidney alters the
Socratic paradigm even while invoking it:

> For my part, in very truth (as the cruel fathers among the Greeks were
> wont to do to the babes they would not foster) I could well find in my
> heart to cast out in some desert of forgetfulness this child which I am
> loath to father. But you desired me to do it, and your desire to my
> heart is an absolute commandment. Now it is done only for you, only
> to you; if you keep it to yourself, or to such friends who will weigh
> errors in the balance of goodwill, I hope, for the father's sake, it will
> be pardoned, perchance made much of, though in itself it have de-
> formities. ... In sum, a young head not so well stayed as I would it
> were ... having many fancies begotten in it, if it had not been in some

12. Plato, *Theaetetus* 150B–151C, trans. Harold North Fowler (London: Heine-
mann, 1977).

13. Most critics believe that the *Old Arcadia* was largely written in the period
1578–79; John Osborn mentions Mary's pregnancy during this time in *Young Philip
Sidney 1572–1577* (New Haven: Yale University Press, 1972), p. 504.

way delivered, would have grown a monster, and more sorry might I
be that they came in than that they gat out. But his chief safety shall
be the not walking abroad; and his chief protection the bearing the
livery of your name.[14]

Pregnant with his fancies, Sidney produces an issue which, like
Theaetetus's inadequate ideas, would in the Greek scheme of things
deserve a quick death. The birthing is, however, therapeutic, apparently both for parent and for child. The word "grown" in the phrase
"would have grown a monster" could mean "become"—in which
case Sidney's head is threatened with monstrosity—or "generated,"
in which case the work is itself deformed: a monster if it were not
delivered, and monstrous even now that it is.

Fortunately, the fate of the child-work depends here not upon the
authority of the "cruel" father-writer but on that of the compassion-
ate female reader. More has changed between Socrates and Sidney
than intuitions about the morality of infanticide. In Sidney's witty
reformulation, the childbirth metaphor makes the genders cross. The
birthgiving man submits to the woman's will ("Your desire to my
heart is an absolute commandment"), and she in turn provides the
child with shelter and a name. The Countess of Pembroke is compli-
mented on her ability to fill the place of a man: Sidney is the father
of the *Arcadia,* but the Countess is its patron, from the Latin *pater,*
father. This blurring and interchange of gender roles aptly prefaces a
romance in which a prince assumes a transvestite disguise in order to
pursue a heterosexual agenda, thoroughly disrupting the familial and
erotic loyalties of the two women and one man who fall in love with
him. The tone of the prologue is playful; Sidney seems unconcerned
about the authorial masculinity that his deliberate scrambling of maternal and paternal attributes might seem to compromise.

To other writers such reversals can seem more immediately threatening. Milton's description of the birth of Truth in *The Doctrine and
Discipline of Divorce* suggests uneasiness:

> Though this ill hap wait upon her nativity, that she never comes into
> the world, but like a bastard, to the ignominy of him that brought her
> forth: till Time the midwife rather than the mother of Truth, have

14. Sir Philip Sidney, *The Countess of Pembroke's Arcadia (The Old Arcadia),* ed.
Jean Robertson (Oxford: Oxford University Press, 1973), p. 3. The prefatory letter is
published in the first printed edition of the work (that is, "The New Arcadia") in 1590
and in subsequent editions as well.

washed and salted the infant, declared her legitimate, and churched the father of his young Minerva, from the needless causes of his pur-gation.[15]

Truth comes forth from her originator as if from a mother, but like Sidney, the author swiftly regains a specifically male identity: it is as Truth's *father* that he must, scandalously, be "churched." Milton can represent this obligation as preposterous not only because left-wing Protestants considered the ceremonial purification of new mothers a Popish superstition,[16] but because his topsy-turvy version of the ritual outrageously subjects the male writer to the female authority of Time, and moreover identifies the male intellect with an unclean childbear-ing body. The incoherence of Milton's trope originates in an ambiva-lent wish to conflate intellectual originality with childbearing, while simultaneously implying that to identify the two processes is to con-fuse carnal and spiritual in a typically Catholic error. But Socrates's clear-cut, confident separation of male and female, mind and body, seems beyond him.

Why should this be so? Connections between the womb and the imagination, and between completed works, speeches, or actions and babies, do not seem to have been merely the property of poets in early modern England. In an earlier chapter I quoted Henry Neville, one of the Earl of Essex's co-conspirators, maintaining at his treason trial that he had not taken part in Essex's revolt, but merely attended a planning meeting: this, he maintained, "was no more treason than the child in the mother's belly is a child."[17] Neville's defense seems curiously self-defeating: although he claims that the child in the mother's belly is not a child, he calls it a child nonetheless. Clearly, however, he is relying upon the same analogy between thinking and

15. *The Doctrine and Discipline of Divorce*, in *The Works of John Milton*, vol. 3, part 2 (New York: Columbia University Press, 1931), p. 370.

16. For an account of the Puritan hostility toward the "churching" of mothers, see Keith Thomas, *Religion and the Decline of Magic* (New York: Scribners, 1971), pp. 59–61, and Adrian Wilson, "The Ceremony of Childbirth and Its Interpretation," pp. 78–82. In *An Apology Against a Pamphlet Called A Modest Confutation of the Animad-versions upon the Remonstrant Against Smectymnuus* (1642), Milton comments sarcastically upon "errors, tautologies, impertinences" in the ritual (*The Complete Prose Works of John Milton*, volume 1, ed. Don M. Wolfe [New Haven: Yale University Press, 1953]).

17. Francis Bacon, *A Declaration of the Practices and Treasons Attempted and Com-mitted by Robert late Earle of Essex and his Complices* (London, 1601), K2ʳ.

pregnancy, acting and giving birth, that Sidney, Jonson, Shakespeare, and Milton use in much more sophisticated and self-conscious ways. In this respect Neville's analogy is extremely suggestive. He stresses less the womb's fecundity than its hiddenness, or rather a fecundity that seems dependent upon hiddenness. The womb is the private space of thoughts yet unuttered, or actions yet unexecuted. It is a container, itself concealed deep within the body, with something further hidden within it: an enclosed and invisible organ, working by means unseeable by and uncontrolled from the outside. Sixteenth-century anatomists go into great detail upon the stratification of skins and membranes that constitute the womb, "tunicles" and "panicles" layered one inside another like a set of Chinese boxes; some insist, moreover, that the womb is additionally divided into two, five, or seven cells like a honeycomb or labyrinth. Galen had insisted that women's reproductive organs are exactly parallel to men's, but inside out, or rather, outside in:

> All the parts, then, that men have, women have too, the difference between them lying in only one thing . . . namely, that in women the parts are within the body, whereas in men they are outside. . . . Consider first whichever ones you please, turn outward the woman's, turn inward, so to speak, and fold double the man's, and you will find them the same in both in every respect.[18]

Or as the great sixteenth-century French physician Ambroise Paré echoes him, "that which man hath apparent without, that women have hid within."[19] The anatomical reticence of the female body can be a source of embarrassment for Renaissance obstetrical writers, whose writing and diagrams indecorously display what seems to demand concealment. Thus Jacques Guillemeau's English translator assures his readers that "I have endeavoured to be as private and retired, in expressing all the passages in this kind as possibly I could."[20] Both men and women have "secret parts," but women's are genuine secrets.

18. Galen, *On the Usefulness of the Parts of the Body,* trans. and ed. Margaret Tallmadge May (Ithaca: Cornell University Press, 1968), p. 628. The fullest account of these theories is Thomas Laqueur's *Making Sex* (Cambridge, Mass.: Harvard University Press, 1990).

19. *The Anatomy of Mans Body,* in *The workes of that famous chirurgeon Ambrose Parey,* trans. Thomas Johnson (London, 1649), p. 128. Paré's works were first issued in Latin and French in the latter part of the sixteenth century.

20. James Guillemeau, *Child-birth, or, the happy deliverie of women* (London, 1612), p. 3.

The female body imagined in these terms is a variation upon, rather than a departure from, a familiar misogynist *topos*. Antifeminist texts from classical satire to *film noir* complain that the woman's visible body, a fascinating surface further elaborated by cosmetic enhancements, has nothing to do with the essence concealed within, the soul or secret parts—if, indeed, there is anything inside at all. In *The Araignment of Lewd, Idle, Froward, and Unconstant Women* (London, 1616) Joseph Swetnam rehearses this *topos:*

> [Women] are also compared unto a painted ship, which seemeth fair outwardly, and yet nothing but ballast within her; or as the idols in Spain, which are bravely gilt outwardly, and yet nothing but lead within them. (3)

The anonymous author of *A Discourse of the Married and Single Life* (London, 1621), similarly explains:

> Sometimes at marriages walnuts are scattered up and down; which sheweth, that a woman is like unto a walnut, that hath a great shell, but a little kernel; fair without, but rotten within. (96)

The outside is no clue to the inside. A notion of women as deceptive or hollow surfaces produces paranoid complaints about female hypocrisy and vacuity.

At the same time, the disparity between inside and outside can sometimes be exhilarating. Anticipating an invasion by the Spanish Armada, Elizabeth I rouses the courage of her troops at Tilbury by telling them that she has "the body of a weak and feeble woman, but . . . the heart and stomach of a king, and a king of England too."[21] Elizabeth's claim seems to reverse the metaphors I have been considering here, since it involves a woman appropriating male bodily parts, but it relies upon an identical intuition: it can never be obvious what a woman has inside her.

The safe possession of a hidden or unreadable space can also be extremely agreeable, as we have already seen again and again, to those who want to protect some aspect of themselves from public scrutiny or control. The woman's body, in other words, incarnates in risky but compelling ways some of the particular privileges and paradoxes of Renaissance subjectivity. On one hand she is constituted as something preeminently *seen;* the paradigmatic focus, as numerous femi-

21. George P. Rice, ed., *The Public Speaking of Queen Elizabeth: Selections from the Official Addresses* (New York: AMS, 1951), p. 96.

nist writers have pointed out, of the male gaze. At the same time her interior "difference," her lack of visibility, can enable a resistance to scrutiny, since possibly her inner truth is not susceptible to discovery or manipulation from the outside. In *Astrophel and Stella* Sidney gets over his labor pains when he eschews external aids and begins to trust his depths: "Look in thy heart and write." Jonson often associates his claims to a womb with quasi-Stoic assertions of independence: he gives birth to his work in proud solitude, his labors unattended. His expressiveness is not truly the contrary of self-concealment, but rather its corollary. As he writes in *Discoveries,*

> it was excellently said of that philosopher . . . that the rashness of talking should not only be retarded by the guard, and watch of our heart; but be fenced in, and defended by certain strengths, placed in the mouth it self, and within the lips. (333–39)

If brilliant utterance requirs incubation in a silent, carefully policed interior, then it is only apparently paradoxical that Jonson's philosopher should *voice* his contempt for talk, repudiating chatter with an excellent saying.

In *The Revenge of Bussy d'Ambois,* Chapman's Stoic hero Clermont suggests the advantages and disadvantages of a subjectivity formed upon this model:

> The garment or the cover of the mind
> The human soul is; of the soul, the spirit
> The proper robe is; of the spirit, the blood;
> And of the blood, the body is the shroud.
>
> (5.5.170–73)

The mind is elaborately insulated by layers of increasingly material substance—soul, spirit, blood, body—which provide necessary shelter for the true, vulnerable center of human identity, even while precluding any direct communion between the interior subject and exterior objects. Perhaps, then, the womb is another of those small enclosures in which so many seventeenth-century poets discover their poetic identity and freedom; like Donne's little room, Carew's hidden garden, Lovelace's prison cell. The clearly bounded and delimited body is the space of freedom.

While it might seem that the calculated cultivation of a hidden space within would be incompatible with misogynist paranoia, the reverse is in fact the case. The very unreadability that seems so attractive in one's (male) self seems sinister in others; one man's privacy is another woman's unreliability. The female interior encloses experiences unappropriable by an observer: adultery, orgasm, and so forth are both unseeable and possible. This dilemma, essentially a version of the "problem of other minds," produces the paradoxes or oxymorons of antifeminist rhetoric: women conceal their true thoughts but they talk without circumspection; women are inscrutable but they disclose everything. Hamlet boasts to his mother that he has "that within which passes show" but her own unforthcomingness drives him, literally, nearly crazy. In books III and IV of *The Faerie Queene* Spenser's exaltation of Britomart, the armed figure of chastity, militantly closed to penetration, coexists with much more disturbing portraits of female figures who exploit their inscrutability, like Helinore or the false Florimell.

The Renaissance male appropriation of the womb as a figure for the imagination, then, is perfectly consistent with an ideology that strictly limits female sexual freedom, and excludes actual women from literary endeavors. As we have already seen, in *The Doctrine and Discipline of Divorce* Milton's daring mixture of metaphors relies upon an ultimately conservative notion of woman's subjection to man's authority. For men the womb can become a figure for a kind of limited freedom; but the very hiddenness of that freedom can preclude allowing it to the actual possessors of those wombs, whose bodies, unreadable from the male point of view, figure a kind of anarchy.

The appeal of the woman's body, then, for a man who wants a subjective refuge, seems to be the way it is closed in upon itself, the way her interior is protected by opaque bodily perimeters. At the same time, as an emblem of a "closed" subjectivity the female body is defective insofar as it is penetrable, insofar as it is, in fact, a sort of paradigm of penetrability. "To know" something, as we have seen abundantly elsewhere, means to obtain power over it by gaining access to its inside. Thus that favorite King James Bible word "knowledge" has both a carnal and spiritual significance; men "know" their wives but the expression is not reciprocal. When Donne in *Holy Sonnets* 14 asks to be raped by God, takes on a position that seems "feminine" or passive, the point is that his position is already feminine, insofar as God is always already inside him. Ordinarily, however, to be "known"—to suffer or to enjoy penetration—is to be humiliated, to jeopardize one's full humanity by disclosing one's interior secret to another.

Childbirth, moreover, both in reality and as metaphor for rhetorical production, involves permeability in the other direction, a sensational transfer from inside to outside through an orifice that ordinarily, in Jonson's phrase, ought to be "fenced in, and defended by certain strengths." Gail Paster comments upon the persistent satiric representation of women as incontinent in Jacobean city comedy, and Peter Stallybrass remarks upon a concern in early modern England to girdle women's bodies, as if their too fragile defenses required reinforcement.[22] This kind of imagery might seem to rely upon intuitions virtually the reverse of the ones I have been discussing, but in fact both *topoi* depend upon an idealization of the body-as-sanctuary. The recognition that women's bodies are readily violated by various kinds of ingestion and discharge, that liquids and solids wash into and out of them, produces in turn an indignant reaction against the deceptive promise of female intactness. For then that intactness seems not an assurance of inward truth, but itself a form of masquerade.

How might the excellences of the female body be preserved against these threats, its secretiveness sequestered, as it were, from its secretions? Unfortunately, if the mechanics of impregnation are repudiated, then some of the chief attractions of the female body as a metaphor for poetic creativity—its receptivity and fruitfulness—seem endangered too. Sidney and Jonson both identify themselves with a pregnant female body, struggling to "deliver," to "express," an interior fullness. The act of poetic creation seems to require a reference to an inside even as that inside is being externalized; as the difference between inside and outside is transgressed or annihilated. But labor and delivery apparently occur without impregnation. At the end of the first sonnet of *Astrophel and Stella,* Astrophel's pregnancy is revealed to be essentially self-generated: something comes out, but nothing came in. He becomes able to give birth when he recognizes his own self-sufficiency, stops relying upon externals, and looks within his own heart. The Muse gives him advice, but she does not give him the poem: she is a midwife, not an origin or even a co-begetter. Jonson, too, manages simultaneously to employ and disavow the childbirth metaphor in *Timber, or Discoveries,* when he writes that language "springs out of the most retired, and inmost parts of us, and is the image of the parent of it, the mind" (2032–33). He wants to empha-

22. Gail Paster, "Leaky Vessels: The Incontinent Women of City Comedy," *Renaissance Drama* 18 [1987]: 43–65; Peter Stallybrass, "Patriarchal Territories: The Body Enclosed," *Rewriting the Renaissance,* ed. Margaret Ferguson, Maureen Quilligan, and Nancy Vickers (Chicago: University of Chicago Press, 1986), pp. 123–42.

size the interior space in which the creative imagination works, without stipulating how the language got in there in the first place. So the mind, although it functions like a mother, becomes merely a "parent," divested of its gendered specificity. Likewise John Spenser praises Richard Hooker for his self-sacrifice in intellectual travail, dying that his offspring might live, but in the next sentence immediately reverts to calling him the "father," not the mother, of his work.

It would seem that Renaissance poets could avoid these awkwardnesses by imagining themselves in terms of the female body but at the same time making clear—as Socrates had—that the figure was an analogy, that the processes of the mind and the body could not be confused or conflated. But instead, as we have seen, for English Renaissance writers such metaphors become sites of disorientation rather than of clarification. In vernacular sixteenth- and early seventeenth-century speech and writing, the whole interior of the body—heart, liver, womb, bowels, kidneys, gall, blood, lymph—quite often involves itself in the production of the mental interior, of the individual's private experience. Humours psychology is perhaps the most systematic working out of this premise, but often it is invoked more casually. "When I am dead and opened," Mary Tudor puns to her counselors, "you shall find Calais [callous] lying in my heart."[23] Edward Coke, presiding at the trial of the Gunpowder conspirators, describes to the prisoners the rationale behind the punishment that awaits them: the traitor's "bowels and inlaid parts [are] taken out and burnt, who inwardly had conceived and harboured in his heart such horrible treason."[24] The traitor comes to the scaffold quite literally to spill his guts, to have the heart plucked out of his mystery. The corporeal way inwardness is sometimes conceived in the English Renaissance has sometimes misled critics who think of the body as something displayed, something "wholly present" to observation.[25] But only the surface of the body, strictly speaking, is really visible,

23. John Foxe, *Acts and Monuments*, ed. George Townsend (London, 1839), 8:625.

24. William Cobbett and Thomas Howell, *Cobbett's Complete Collection of State Trials* (London, 1809), 2.184. The rationale, like the punishment itself, is traditional; see John Bellamy, *The Law of Treason: England in the Later Middle Ages* (Cambridge: Cambridge University Press, 1970), pp. 39, 47, 52.

25. Francis Barker, *The Tremulous Private Body: Essays in Subjection* (New York: Methuen, 1984), p. 74; see also his comments on "the spectacular visible body," pp. 23–26. In *Renaissance Fictions of Anatomy* (Amherst: University of Massachusetts Press, 1985), Devon Hodges helpfully explores sixteenth- and early seventeenth-century conceptions of the dissected body.

and even that is normally "cloaked," a favorite Renaissance word for hypocrisy. In sixteenth- and early seventeenth-century England the bodily interior is still mysterious in a way perhaps hard to recapture in an age of medical sophistication, and in a way quite precisely analogous to the mysteriousness of human motives and desires.

Of course, none of this language need suggest anything like consistent materialism on the part of early modern Europeans. There is considerable philosophical dispute in the Renaissance among neo-Stoics, neo-Platonists, Galenists, Paracelsans, Aristotelians, and others about the relation of bodily and mental phenomena,[26] but the patterns of speech I am discussing here are largely subphilosophical, suggesting habits of mind rather than carefully articulated systems of thought. Except in the case of philosophers like Descartes, few attempt to sort out the implications of their own linguistic practices, which bring the carnal and the spiritual into frequent but highly unstable intimacy.

Consequently when a sixteenth- or seventeenth-century man lays claim to a womb, the precise character of his assertion is sometimes difficult to assess. Renaissance speech habits can make it difficult to know when what seems to us a bodily analogy is really an analogy; when we are dealing with metaphor and when with a bare statement of fact—and whether, many times, this kind of distinction is even germane. Moreover, even given a general lack of clear distinctions between bodily and mental processes, the womb seems a particularly indefinite organ. Although early sixteenth-century anatomists had disproved Aristotle's claim that the uterus wandered about the body, and discredited Galen's notion that it constituted a separate animal, notions of its errancy and autonomy persisted in the popular imagination and undoubtedly suggested comparisons with the idiosyncratic itineraries of fantasy. The word "pregnant" could refer to spirits

26. This dispute or uncertainty is not merely a matter of competing explanations originating in different schools of thoughts: materialists vs. dualists, for instance. Individual schools of thought, even when they can be isolated in the philosophically syncretic Renaissance, are often internally contradictory. For instance, Plato comes to different conclusions about mind-body problems in different dialogues, and the variety of his thinking is inherited by Renaissance neo-Platonists. Neo-Stoicism likewise inherits from its Roman and Greek sources both a rigorous materialism and a tendency to exempt virtue from the constraints of corporeality, an inconsistency I discuss in *Ben Jonson and the Roman Frame of Mind* (Princeton: Princeton University Press, 1985), pp. 26–29, 153–67.

and wits as well as to wombs, and the word "wit" itself is Elizabethan slang for the genitalia. Rhetorical treatises elaborate the similarities. Thomas Wright claims that hasty and imprudent speakers "commonly are with child with their own conceits, and either they must be delivered of them, or they must die in child-bed."[27] Words like "conception," "issue," and "delivery" imply affinities between childbirth and thinking or speaking. Patricia Parker has discussed many of these punning affinities between the pregnant woman and the text or *corpus:* for instance the pun on *mater,* matter, mother; the connection between the copious, amplified text and the enlarged, fertile female body; the traditional association of women with a loquacity that lacks any "point." In *Still Harping on Daughters* Lisa Jardine has described the implications of the common Renaissance association between sexual promiscuity and female speech.[28]

These half-analogical, half-literal relationships could only have been reinforced by intimate causal connections between the brain, in which Galen had located mental functioning, and the womb. Huarte writes of the uterus: "The member which most partaketh the alterations of the belly, all physicians say, is the brain, though they have not set down the reason whereon they ground this correspondence."[29] Gynecological writers, following Aristotle and Galen, invariably warn that a pregnant woman's mental state affects the physical and psychological disposition of the fetus, that the developing child is likely to be imprinted by the images that come before the mother's eyes or are entertained in her imagination. Conversely, disorders that originate in the womb—hysteria, greensickness—produce and are diagnosable by primarily mental symptoms.

These medical beliefs complicate the neat contrasts Socrates makes in the *Theaetetus.* The most significant difference between the midwife and the philosopher, in Socrates's account, is the ability of the latter to tell true from false, a talent irrelevant to the delivery of babies: "For women do not, like my patients, bring forth at one time real children and at another mere images which it is difficult to distinguish from the real" (150B). For Renaissance gynecologists and obste-

27. Thomas Wright, *The Passions of the Minde in generall* (1604), ed. Thomas O. Sloan (Urbana: University of Illinois Press, 1971), p. 110.
28. Parker, *Literary Fat Ladies: Rhetoric, Gender, Property* (New York: Routledge, 1987), pp. 17–35. Jardine, *Still Harping on Daughters: Women and Drama in the Age of Shakespeare* (Totowa, N.J.: Barnes and Noble, 1983), pp. 103–40.
29. Huarte, *Examen de Ingenios,* p. 273.

tricians, however, the close links between mind and body make malformed children as likely as malformed ideas; the former, in fact, are a consequence of the latter. "Monstrous creatures of sundry forms are also generated in the wombs of women," writes Paré, "somewhiles alone, otherwhiles with a *mola,* and sometimes with a child naturally and well made, as frogs, toads, serpents, lizards."[30] The monstrous birth, transgressing categories, becomes not merely a tragic instance of deformity but an intriguing intellectual puzzle. The fascination with misleading evidence evinced in these treatises seems part of the same pattern: the instructions on how to tell a tumor from a fetus, a genuine conception from a psychosomatic pregnancy, a male from a female child before delivery. The sixteenth-century midwife needs to tell true from false, monster from human, *mola* from embryo, in a way Socrates had reserved for the philosopher. The gynecological writers require of her the talents that writers on political subjects require of statesmen, that judges require of juries, and that the authors of "discovery literature" so proudly and anxiously proffer to their readers: the ability to discern an inward truth, and to seize upon an emerging one just at the moment of its manifestation.

ꙅ II ꙅ

ALL OF THESE COMPLEXITIES surrounding the difference between male and female, mind and body, inside and outside, converge upon the poetry of the young Milton, for whom all three sets of oppositions are crucially important. The association of intellectual creativity with the fecund female body is extremely attractive to him, as we have already seen. But it is also more problematic than it is for Sidney and Jonson, since at this point in his life his poetic gift, he insists, is predicated upon sexual renunciation.

Milton devises a solution which preserves many of the advantages of the trope of the poet-in-childbirth while adapting it to the decorum of his particular situation. As many critics have noted, the author of *Comus,* whose sexual fastidiousness had earlier earned him the nickname "Lady" from his contemporaries at Cambridge, invests himself in the character of the Lady, speaking from the place of

---

30. Paré, *The Anatomy of Mans Body,* p. 763. This passage comes from a treatise on smallpox, measles, and worms; Paré's fascination with anomaly is more fully displayed in another work, *On Monsters and Prodigies,* later in the same collection.

the virgin.[31] In a university rhetorical exercise, written six years before *Comus,* Milton suggests how he may have imagined this investment:

> Have I by killing a snake suffered the fate of Tiresias? Has some Thessalian witch smeared me with magic ointment? ... From some I have lately heard the epithet, "Lady." But why do I seem to those fellows insufficiently masculine? ... Doubtless it was because I was never able to gulp down huge bumpers in pancratic fashion; or because my hand has not become calloused by holding the plow-handle; or because I never lay down on my back under the sun at mid-day, like a seven-year ox-driver; perhaps, in fine, because I never proved myself a man in the same manner as those gluttons [*Ganeones*]. But would that they could as easily lay aside their asshood as I whatever belongs to womanhood.[32]

Here, as in *Comus,* Milton imagines an individual threatened by a metamorphic power, but here the metamorphosis is false—both because, of course, he is not actually the victim of a Thessalian witch, and more importantly because he embraces rather than denies the ascription of effeminacy. The Lady, here as in *Comus,* advertises his/her rejection of indiscriminate sensuality and his/her withdrawal from coarsely physical toil and pleasure. For his adversaries, Milton

31. The first critic I have found making the connection between the Lady in *Comus* and Milton's nickname at Cambridge, "the Lady," is James Holly Hanford, *John Milton, Englishman* (New York: Crown, 1949), pp. 63–64. For an account of Milton's investment in the female body as an Oedipal flight from paternal authority, see William Kerrigan, *The Sacred Complex* (Cambridge, Mass.: Harvard University Press, 1983), pp. 24–56, and Christopher Kendrick, "Milton and Sexuality: A Symptomatic Reading of *Comus,*" in *Re-Membering Milton,* ed. Margaret W. Ferguson and Mary Nyquist (New York: Methuen, 1987), pp. 48–49. James Turner makes the more general point that "most of the special sensibilities that Milton ascribes to the poet were universally construed as 'female' in his day" (*One Flesh: Paradisal Marriage and Sexual Relations in the Age of Milton* [Oxford: Oxford University Press, 1987], p. 187).

32. Milton's original Latin is: "numnam ego percusso angue *Tyresiae* fatum expertu sum? ecqua me *Thessala* saga magico perfudit unguento? ... A quibusdam, audivi nuper Domina. At cur videor illis parum masculus? ... scilicet quia Scyphos capacissimos nunquam valui pancratice haurire; aut quia manus tenenda stiva non occaluit, aut quia nunquam ad meridianum Solem supinus jacui septennis bubulcus; fortasse demum quod nunquam me virum praestiti, eo modo quo illi Ganeones: verum utinam illi possint tam facile exuere asinos, quam ego quicquid est foeminae." Donald Leman Clark, ed., Bromley Smith, trans;, *Prolusiones VI. In feriis aestivis Collegii. The Works of John Milton* vol. 12 (New York: Columbia University Press, 1936), pp. 240–41.

uses the word *Ganeones*—an insult that means not only "gluttons" but "rakes" or "perverts"—turning the homosexual implications of his nickname back upon his hypermasculine opponents and conflating, just as he will in *Comus*, sexual profligacy with dietary intemperance. But Milton also imagines that his own occupation of a feminine position is a matter of choice; that he is free to lay aside whatever belongs to womanhood as one cannot lay aside an immutable characteristic like stupidity. His imaginative identification with the Lady in *Comus* might be seen as the same kind of gesture, an attempt to assume a role that while deeply self-expressive can nonetheless be discarded as soon as it becomes inconvenient.

Milton's identification with a virginal character allows him to enjoy the advantages of the secure interior space associated with the female body without suggesting, even by the studious omissions of Sidney and Jonson, that the interior need be compromised in order to obtain a poetic result. At the same time, of course, he affiliates himself with a rich classical and Christian tradition of thinking about the virgin female body in terms of what Theresa Krier has recently called, in Spenser's case, a fascination with "warmly eloquent surface and protected interior." But as Krier points out, Spenser's "creative impulse . . . is to honor the otherness of feminine bodily life."[33] He maintains a certain distance between his virgin characters and the experience of the male author or reader, who occupies the place of a spectator. Milton, by contrast, follows Sidney and Jonson in *identifying* himself with the woman. He thinks of his poetic vocation in terms of inhabiting the Lady's physical position.

Comus explores the implications of that identification with unprecedented boldness and rigor. Versions of the Lady's body, a perfectly enclosed, strictly delimited interior space, pervade the masque. The Attendant Spirit tells us that the gods live "insphered / In regions mild of calm and serene air" (3–4); Echo, in the Lady's song, is "unseen / Within thy airy shell" (230–31); the lost brothers are imagined to be hidden in a "flow'ry cave" (239); the sheep are "folded flocks penned in their wattled cotes" (344); the Attendant Spirit refers to "the litter of close-curtained sleep" (554). These lovely and reassuring images have their nightmare counterpart in terrifying visions of

33. Theresa Krier, *Gazing on Secret Sights: Spenser, Classical Imitation, and the Decorums of Vision* (Ithaca: Cornell University Press, 1990), pp. 129, 139. Krier's discussion of Spenser makes an argument related to mine about the way the female body's protected interior space can be imagined as a place of privacy and refuge.

involuntary confinement: mortals are, the Attendant Spirit announces, "confined and pestered in this pinfold here" (7); the night
is a "dragon womb of Stygian darkness" (131–32); Comus and
his followers, "within the navel of this hideous wood," perform "ab-
horred rites to Hecate / In their obscured haunts of inmost bowers"
(520, 535–36).[34]

For Comus the invisible space is the place of transgression; if, as
he says, "'Tis only daylight that makes Sin" (126) then he can do anything he likes as long as no one sees him. In his impious conviction
of his own invisibility he resembles Haggard's Gyges or Shakespeare's
Richard. His magical powers seem an effect and a demonstration of
the machiavel's typical alienation from social controls—even though
at the same time, like his theatrical predecessors, Comus inevitably
exaggerates his autonomy. Almost the first thing we learn about him,
after all, is his parentage: the bastard union of Circe and Bacchus
delimits the terms of his transgressiveness, making his claims to bold
independence as predictable as they are dubious.

The machiavel's alienation, as we have already seen, mirrors and
parodies the radical unworldliness of the saint. Milton's masque dramatizes a confrontation between these two uncannily similar opposites. Unlike her antagonist, the Lady thinks of herself as always fully
displayed before an omniscient divine eye, a spectator that both keeps
her safe and evaluates her, that by observing her provides her with
her own capacity of observation. "Eye me blessed Providence," she
prays (329), asking both to be watched and to be given eyes, granted

34. All quotations from *Comus* are taken from *The Poetical Works of John Milton*,
ed. Helen Darbishire (London: Oxford University Press, 1958): spelling has been modernized. The pervasive imagery of enclosure is noted by Roger B. Wilkenfeld, "The Seat
at the Center: An Interpretation of *Comus*," *ELH* 33 (1966): 170–97, as he argues for
the unification of the masque around the emblem of the paralyzed Lady. Stanley Fish
discusses the same imagery in the course of his analysis of what he calls "the double
perspective" of the masque in "Problem Solving in *Comus*," *Illustrious Evidence: Approaches to English Literature of the Early Seventeenth Century*, ed. Earl Miner (Berkeley:
University of California Press, 1975), pp. 115–31. I share Fish's interest in the way
Comus presents its readers with problems: "Questioning is the activity to which *Comus*
moves us," Fish writes, "and therefore it seems reasonable to regard the questions we
are moved to ask as primary data, rather than as loose ends that are to be tied up as
neatly and as quickly as possible" (p. 116). But whereas Fish sees the reader's problem-
solving leading to the adoption of an essentially Augustinian belief in the separability
of spiritual issues from bodily ones, my concentration upon issues of gender identity
leads me to argue that the adequacy of the Augustinian view remains open to question,
and that the competing "Ovidian" possibility is never definitively ruled out.

vision. Similarly the Elder Brother contrasts the transparent interiority of the virtuous with the opacity of the bad:

> He that has light within his own clear breast
> May sit i' th' center, and enjoy bright day,
> But he that holds a dark soul, and foul thoughts,
> Himself is his own dungeon.
>
> (380–84)

Complicating this distinction is the fact that the virtuous individual maintains a well-lit interior only by strictly policing its boundaries, whereas Comus, who exploits the sinful potential of the hidden refuge, does so by insisting upon the necessity of penetrating, violating that space.

Thus not only is the enclosed female body simultaneously fortress and trap, but how one experiences the space inside depends upon one's moral perspective. The virtuous person's freedom exactly resembles the vicious person's confinement, and vice versa. Exchanges between Comus and the Lady elucidate both the resemblance and the crucial distinction.

> COMUS. Nay Lady, sit; if I but wave this wand,
> Your nerves are all chained up in alablaster,
> And you a statue; or as Daphne was
> Root-bound, that fled Apollo.
> LADY. Fool do not boast,
> Thou canst not touch the freedom of my mind
> With all thy charms, although this corporal rind
> Thou hast immanacled, while Heav'n sees good.
>
> (659–65)

This recalls the Ovidian text:

> Hanc quoque Phoebus amat positaeque in stipite dextra
> sentit adhuc trepidare novo sub cortice pectus
> conplexusque suis ramos ut membra lacertis
> oscula dat ligno; refugit tamen oscula lignum.
>
> [Phoebus loved her even now, and his right hand, placed upon the trunk, felt the heart still trembling under the new bark. Embracing the branches as if they were human limbs, he bestowed kisses upon the wood; but the wood shrank from his kisses.]
>
> (*Metamorphoses* I, 553–56; my translation)

Forced to endure Apollo's unwanted caresses, Daphne is nonetheless preserved from rape. The moment contains both threat and promise:

Daphne is paralyzed inside the body from which she is miraculously emancipated. Likewise Comus's attempt to intimidate the Lady becomes the very material of her defiance.

When the Lady asserts that Comus's power over the "corporal rind" cannot extend to "the freedom of her mind," she insists that what is inside her is of a fundamentally different kind than what is on the surface. The Ovidian text is pointedly ambiguous on this issue. On the one hand Daphne's heart still beats under the laurel bark, and the wood cringes from her would-be violator like flesh beneath a garment. On the other hand the wood Apollo kisses (*ligno*) is the same wood that shrinks (*lignum*); so that by the end of the passage, as Daphne's metamorphosis completes itself, the difference between surface and depth seems to collapse.

The exchange between Comus and the Lady thus puts tremendous pressure on the ambiguities I mentioned earlier in Renaissance analogies between body and soul. If the universe of *Comus* is dualist, then the Lady's intuition of the safety of her mind within her body, her "corporal rind," is correct. If it is not, she is not. The rest of the masque gives us little help in deciding the issue. On the one hand Comus can imagine the Lady residing within her body as a person within a house:

> Sure something holy lodges in that breast,
> And with these raptures moves the vocal air
> To testify his hidden residence.
>
> (246–48)

But the emblematic function of the Lady's virginity depends upon the assumption that the body and the mind are of the same substance, or at least that the body is in some intelligible relation to the mind. Moreover, moral issues are persistently figured in corporal terms.

> when lust
> By unchaste looks, loose gestures, and foul talk,
> But most by lewd and lavish act of sin,
> Lets in defilement to the inward parts,
> The soul grows clotted by contagion.
>
> (463–66)

How is mental sin different here from carnal impurity? Throughout *Comus*, Milton combines an Ovidian discourse with Augustinian and Stoic ones that are at odds with it. In Ovid, especially as he was interpreted in the Renaissance, physical transformations represent psychological ones. When Comus's victims drink his potion

> their human countenance,
> Th'express resemblance of the gods, is changed
> Into some brutish form.
>
> (68–70)

The multivalent pun on "express"—external, exact, pushed out—suggests that the body visibly reproduces the form of the soul, which presses upon it from the inside as a stamp presses upon metal: a point the Attendant Spirit makes later when he describes Comus's potion as "unmolding reason's mintage / Charactered in the face" (529–30). The implication here is that the body has no independent configuration, and that it testifies reliably to the nature of the spiritual power that gives it shape. The traditionally allegorical masque form intensifies this tendency to identify the body's condition with the mind's, for the whole point of the genre is to personify abstractions and make them visible, devising ways to present what Ben Jonson had called "more removed mysteries" to the eyes of the spectators.

In such a system the vulnerability of the body to external force becomes a primary philosophical problem, because when the body is raped or wounded its characteristics seem imposed from without, rather than pressing out from a spiritual interior. It is hardly surprising that *The Metamorphoses* is virtually a series of rape stories that constantly raise but never really confront the question of innocent suffering. Opposed to Ovid's deliberate vagueness is the sterner Augustinian claim that the condition of the body is irrelevant to spiritual worth—a claim upon which martyrs and heretics, as we have already seen, stake their lives. It is hardly coincidental that Augustine's most vigorous assertion of this principle occurs in a discussion of rape victims in *The City of God*. Women who have suffered rape, Augustine insists, are in no sense defiled, because they have not consented to the action. Even if in the course of the act their bodies have, against their will, helplessly experienced sexual pleasure, their souls—the only things that finally matter—remain pure. Likewise the "budge doctors of the Stoic fur" (707) derided by Comus and quoted approvingly by the Elder Brother strive to separate inward spiritual worth from the accidents of the body. In this respect the budge doctors resemble the Milton of *The Doctrine and Discipline of Divorce*, who attempts, as we saw in the last chapter, to consign bodily facts to the category of the morally trivial. In this scheme, the body does not necessarily express any moral truth whatsoever: its reliability as a spiritual indicator is practically nil.

By equating the free mind with the impenetrable body, then, Milton makes rape a highly problematic issue. The Elder Brother, describing the unassailability of "true virgins," reassures the Younger Brother of his sister's "hidden strength":

> 'Tis chastity, my brother, chastity:
> She that has that, is clad in complete steel.
>
> . . . .
>
> No goblin, or swart faery of the mine,
> Hath hurtful power o'er true virginity.
>
> (420–21, 436–37)

Our problem in assessing the Elder Brother's claims is that it is unclear whether or not they are meant to be evaluated apart from their generic context. In the magical world of romance, in which aggressors quail from "sacred vehemence" (795) and river goddesses hurry to rescue virtuous young girls, the Lady has nothing to worry about. But in real-world Renaissance Britain, a woman's moral worth was inevitably involved with the fate of her vulnerable body, and the Elder Brother is close to suggesting that since "true virgins" are unassailable, rape victims are responsible for their own fate. In some sense, they must have asked for it.

This would hardly have been an academic issue for the Earl of Bridgewater's family. Their notorious relative, the Earl of Castlehaven, had recently been executed for a variety of sexual crimes, one of which involved encouraging his servant and homosexual lover, Skipwith, to violate his twelve-year-old stepdaughter, Elizabeth Audley, while he watched.[35] Elizabeth—first cousin and agemate of Alice Egerton, who played the Lady in Comus—had been married the year

35. Barbara Breasted provides a good summary of the Castlehaven trial, and its possible influence on Comus, in "Comus and the Castlehaven Scandal," Milton Studies 3 (1971): 201–24, though she is to my mind too willing to accept Skipwith's claim that Elizabeth's participation was voluntary. The brief passages I quote regarding this case are taken from Breasted's essay. Leah Marcus, in "The Milieu of Milton's Comus: Judicial Reform at Ludlow and the Problem of Sexual Assault," Criticism 25 (1983): 293–328, draws attention both to the rumored frequency of rape in the Welsh marches, and in particular to a rape case that the Earl of Bridgewater was investigating in his judicial capacity as Lord President of Wales, in the months before Comus was performed. In this case, the initial response of the authorities was to imprison the raped woman.

before the rape to Castlehaven's seventeen-year-old son, but the marriage had evidently not been consummated; although the Earl provided Skipwith with "oil to open her body" he was at first unable to penetrate her. After Skipwith confessed to the authorities, Elizabeth was convicted of adultery, fornication, and incontinency. Her grandmother, who took in the rest of the Castlehaven children in this time of crisis, refused to provide a refuge for Elizabeth, on the ground that "some sparks of my grandchild Audley's misbehavior remaining . . . might give ill example to the young ones which are with me." Clearly this child, who seems to modern sensibilities a victim of outrageous abuse, was held responsible both by legal authorities and by her own family for the assault committed upon her.

Thus the Lady's body refuses to allow itself to be disregarded. And Milton keeps the pressure on by making it difficult to dematerialize her virginity too completely. One such moment occurs when, surprisingly, she responds to Comus's seductive language with the phrase, "I had not thought to have unlocked my lips"(756). But what seems like capitulation turns out to be resistance: the Lady unlocks her lips in order to refute Comus's argument, not to drink his potion or allow him any other kind of access. Another moment has provoked more critical discomfiture; after the brothers enter, the Lady proves to be stuck to her chair by "gums of glutinous heat" (917). Phrases like these force attention upon the Lady's body as a body, not as an emblem for something else, highlighting the ambiguous metaphoricity of Renaissance mind-body relationships. If the body is expressive of the soul, then line 917 suggests that the Lady is saying no while meaning yes. Hugh Richmond writes that "the Lady's . . . body acknowledges [Comus's] authority"; John Carey that

> there are . . . elements in the masque which suggest some spiritual deficiency [on the Lady's part]. She does, after all, get glued to Comus's chair, and the chair "smeared with glutinous heats" brings to mind the sexual heat for which Comus's enchantments are allegories.[36]

36. Hugh Richmond, *The Christian Revolutionary: John Milton* (Berkeley: University of California Press, 1974), p. 72; John Carey, *Milton* (London: Evans Bros., 1969), p. 46. What, exactly, this phrase represents and from whom the gums originally issue is debated in J. W. Flosdorf, "Gums of Glutinous Heat: A Query," *Milton Quarterly* 7, no. 1 (1973): 4–5; John Shawcross, "Two Comments," *Milton Quarterly* 7, no. 4 (1973): 97–98; Stanley Archer, "'Glutinous Heat': A Note on *Comus* l. 917," *Milton Quarterly* 7, no. 4 (1973): 99; Edward Le Comte, *Milton and Sex* (London: Macmillan, 1978), pp. 1–4.

If the body is distinct from the soul, on the other hand, then it is necessary to insist with Augustine that involuntary physical responses, even sexual ones, are morally inconsequential.

Problems like "the vulnerability of the body" or "the problem of other minds" or "the relation between mind and body" might seem, in other words, to contain no explicit reference to gender. Nonetheless, their solutions are likely to seem different when the minds and bodies are male than when the minds and bodies are female. By explicitly gendering such questions in the confrontation of Comus and the Lady, Milton makes them more acute and troubling, especially given the fact that Milton is imagining himself as *inhabiting* the Lady's body, whatever that may come to mean in a work that calls into question the difference between mind and body. For if mind and body are inseparable, then it is a sheer impossibility for a male poet imaginatively to occupy a position physically designated as female, even while retaining the intellectual qualities associated with masculinity. The fantasy Milton elaborates in *Prolusiones VI* of occupying a feminine position temporarily, like a house or an article of clothing, seems in this light to involve a confusion about, or denial of, that inseparability. But if, on the other hand, mind and body are entirely discrete categories, then it is unclear why one kind of body should seem an especially appropriate structural model for creative subjectivity—that is, why Renaissance poets should want to imagine themselves as women at all.

At the crucial moment, Milton uses the conventions of the masque to obscure the issue further. The Lady insists that she has the power to bring Comus's castle down around his ears, and he—while granting that fact—moves forward to "force" her nonetheless. What is about to happen? Will the Lady's virginity, as a figure of the free mind, prove a source of magical power, or at least something unassailable from the outside? Will Comus turn out to be able to rape her after all, and if so, would he be committing merely an insignificant assault upon a "corporal rind," or would he be more seriously compromising a virginity that has been represented throughout the masque as a form of virtue?

Although the Lady is saved at the last moment, Milton does not depict the Lady as rescuing herself from rape, nor show the brothers as able to solve her dilemma. He wants to preserve virginity—the unpenetrated body—as the emblem of uncorruptible poetic creativity and the wellspring of virtue, but he is, realistically, aware that real bodies are indeed penetrable, suffering not only rape but disease, death, and decay. In *Lycidas,* written four years later, Milton is beset by a somewhat similar concern: the swollen and rotten bodies of the Church of England's communicants, forsaken by their pastors, have an unfortunate affinity with the presumably swollen and rotten body of the drowned Edward King, with whom the corrupt church members are supposed to be contrasted. In the elegy the solution is to deny the relevance of the material, accidental world to spiritual and moral truths: the material King may be sunk low but the "real" King is mounted high. In *Comus* the same option is available to Milton but he does not quite seize it. Perhaps the allegorical form of the masque forbids him to do so. Or perhaps Milton wants to insist simultaneously upon the proximity of *and* the distance between mind and body, inside and outside.

At any rate, the resolution of the Lady's dilemma represents a deflection in emphasis, a shifting of the terms in which the dilemma has been constructed. After Comus flees, the Lady is still fastened to Comus's chair, and requires the supernatural salvific agency of the nymph Sabrina. As the Attendant Spirit informs us, Sabrina was herself an innocent victim of intolerable persecution who was rescued by sympathetic powers, the water nymphs and their father Nereus, at the crisis of her fortunes. Sabrina's story, and her intervention in the Lady's case, addresses less the poem's tense mind-body problematic than what might seem the isolating consequences of the Lady's steely continence, and her insistence upon mental freedom in the face of physical peril. In order to assimilate that virtue into a Christian framework Milton must emphasize its ultimate dependence upon a charitable external power, a saving grace that simultaneously allows the Lady's reincorporation into her family and her social context.

As we have already seen, the extermination of the sinister hypocrite at the end of so many Renaissance plays follows upon the devastating revelation of his inability to dispense with the human and divine affinities he has attempted to repudiate. In *Comus,* where (as usual) the saint mirrors the machiavel, Milton must eventually domesticate the implications of the Lady's virtue, a virtue potentially alienated from and subversive of family ties. To perform this domestication he relies upon a principle of masque decorum, the convention that the dances that follow the masque, as Stephen Orgel writes, are "the moment when the masquer breaks through the limit of his stage, when the illusion moves out into the audience."[37] The audience at

Comus stands in for the witnesses, divine and human, in relation to which all human beings are imagined to achieve their subjectivity. In this respect, it functions just as the audience does in *Othello* or *Spanish Tragedy* or *Epicoene*. But whereas "the unmediated confrontation of actors and spectators was impossible in the playhouse,"[38] at Ludlow Castle the audience for the Lady's fictional trial is literally her own family. At the end of the masque, Milton does not so much resolve as simply terminate the skeptical dilemma. He brings the Lady home to her parents intact, subduing the threat of her inward unknowability and eliminating the distinction between observer and observed. Yet Comus and everything he represents remains at large, awaiting his victims in the dark and tangled wood the Lady has left behind.

37. Orgel, *The Jonsonian Masque* (Cambridge: Harvard University Press, 1965), p. 198.

38. Orgel, *The Jonsonian Masque*, p. 200.

𝕾 7 𝕰

CONCLUSION

FOR THE ENGLISH RENAISSANCE, it is a commonplace that spectacle depends upon, sometimes betrays, but never fully manifests a truth that remains shrouded, indiscernible, or ambiguous. The period's social and religious upheavals arguably provoke a keen, apparently nearly universal suspicion of "appearances." Whatever the origins of this distrust, it produces a distinctive way of thinking about human subjectivity that emphasizes the disparity between what a person is and what he or she seems to be to other people. On the Elizabethan and Jacobean stage, such chronic doubts about the adequacy of what can be seen tend to make theater an art of incompletion: a form of display that flaunts the limits of display.

In this book, I've considered several ways in which personal inwardness as it is represented in English Renaissance drama is connected with forms of inwardness elaborated simultaneously in cultural sites rarely associated with the stage. Religious polemicists and other "discoverers" of hidden iniquity people paranoid accounts with atheist hypocrites visible only to the god they deny: hypocrites who by relying upon their own inward resources become the uncanny, despised doubles of the resolute martyrs the polemicists admire. Not only the structure of "machiavellian" character but the metaphysical issues raised by that structure become, in different ways and for different reasons, central to *Richard III* and *The Spanish Tragedy.*

Marlowe likewise keeps returning to the implications of a personal inwardness withheld or withholdable from others. More than Kyd or Shakespeare, however, he concerns himself with the propriety of inquisitorial tactics designed to make a reluctant inwardness manifest. In play after play, Marlowe returns to the troubled, conceptually uncertain relationship between persuasive and coercive tactics of obtaining compliance with authority: strategies that have a particular pertinence in the strange ritual of the heresy trial. The heretic's inward freedom, challenging even while it succumbs to the power of the state and established church, offers Marlowe a model for the inwardness both of dramatic characters and of audience members, modifying the crude alternatives posed by contemporary defenders and enemies of the theater.

Inward truth, as it is conceived in the Renaissance, may be an intrinsically or originally theological concept, but not all of the settings in which it becomes important are explicitly religious ones. The heresy trial uneasily poses questions about the relation between divine omniscience and limited human vision, but so do the common-law legal proceedings for two secular "crimes of intention," treason and witchcraft, and so do some of the proceedings against sexual offenders conducted in the ecclesiastical courts. The jury's generally recognized difficulty of discerning inward truth "from the outside" in witchcraft and treason cases, and the difficulty accused persons experience proving their innocence of these crimes, corresponds closely to the epistemological problem-of-other-minds that Iago creates for Othello, and Shakespeare for the theater spectators.

The complexities of monitoring sexual conduct in an increasingly unmanageable urban environment become the subject of *Epicoene* and *Measure for Measure*. For Jonson the paradigm of unknowability is male potency or the lack of it, a lack that was only rarely a subject for judicial inquiry in England, but which Jonson nonetheless brings onstage again and again. The possibility of unknowable sexual truth becomes both the target of Jonsonian satire and a possible limit upon the effectiveness of satire, as well as upon any other means of social regulation. In *Measure for Measure* Shakespeare acknowledges the furtiveness and diversity of sexual conduct, and the apparently inextricable relationship between secrecy and arousal, all of which create difficulties for "legislating morality." At the same time, quite inconsistently, *Measure for Measure* insists upon a fundamental commensurability among human beings that ought to make such legislation possible. The play's denouement imposes a secular judicial solution upon sexual dilemmas even while suggesting the inevitable limitations of such solutions.

Inwardness as we have seen it elaborated in legal situations can be either a privilege or a burden. The guilty, the obstinate, and the unjustly persecuted can expediently conceal truths about themselves. The innocent can find their inward spotlessness frustratingly difficult to demonstrate. Authorities charged with the maintenance of public order can find the extent of resistance to, or evasion of, their mandates difficult to assess; besides, they are subject to charges that they have themselves concealed their true motives or tactics behind a facade of legitimacy. One equivocal recipient of this complex, sometimes covetous, sometimes paranoid attention to personal interiority is the female body, for women's bodies as Renaissance gynecology imagines them seem to provide a corporeal model for an "inward" subjective structure. Male poets, attracted by the limited but real privileges of the enclosed female body, appropriate it as an image for their own interior creativity. Milton's *Comus*, which arguably culminates this tradition, renders the male poet's identification with the female body into an extended contemplation of the relation between male and female, between mind and body, between freedom and constraint, between author and character, between individual and community.

In my introductory chapter, I warned against carelessly conflating the personal inwardness mentioned in so many Renaissance texts with related but nonetheless distinct matters: with a sense of personal uniqueness, with a notion of autonomy, with a conviction that the "self" is a unified or presocial entity, with a belief in a right to privacy, with an exaltation of the domestic sphere, with a commitment to competitive individualism. In my view, these matters are theoretically and historically separable; also, I shrink from unreflectively equating what personal inwardness might mean in the early modern period, and what its conceptual affiliations might have been, with what it might mean today.

At the same time, although I tried to avoid claiming too much at the outset of my study, I am less averse to making some suggestions at the end of my book about possible continuities between the sixteenth and the twentieth centuries. For the struggles of post-Reformation England over the nature and scope of personal inwardness, especially in religious and legal domains, contribute importantly to the eventual development of freedoms we enjoy today in Western democracies: the right to one's religious convictions, for instance; the right to refrain from self-incrimination; protection from "unreasonable" searches by agents of the state. None of these privileges are unqualified or automatic, of course, and it would be as foolish to overestimate their extent as to underestimate their importance. The particular institutional shapes such freedoms have taken in Anglo-American states owe much to historical circumstances, as the governments of Charles I, Oliver Cromwell, Charles II, and William and Mary successively struggle to come to terms with conflicts first ignited more than a century earlier.

In the late seventeenth and eighteenth century it begins to become common to describe matters pertaining to personal inwardness in terms of "rights." Most Americans in the late twentieth century seem thoroughly habituated to such language, even when they disagree violently over its consequences, as they do, for instance, on the issue of abortion. Such language would have seemed unfamiliar in sixteenth-century England—not the ancient concept of a "right," of course, but its application to problems of personal inwardness. The deployment of "rights language" in this new domain is a fascinating development, although one beyond the scope of my book. Perhaps even as increasingly resourceful technology and increasingly massive state power enable an ever easier invasion into the inwardness of persons, a more elaborate, abstractly ethical defense of that inwardness has seemed necessary in response. Or perhaps "rights language" replaces a religious formulation that no longer seems compelling.

So the Elizabethan and Jacobean models of personal inwardness that have concerned me in this book are not simply identical to currently available paradigms, but they are not wholly alien, either. Rather they have the affinity of an ancestor to a descendant. The religious framework in which early modern inwardness is articulated, in terms of a gap between a limited human onlooker and an unlimited divine one, is no longer common cultural currency. Perhaps for that reason, the dramatic representations that lean most heavily upon their theological underpinnings, like the stage machiavel, seem least plausible today. To my literate but unlearned undergraduates, the knowing, self-delighted villainy of a Richard III or a Volpone often seems psychologically "unrealistic": they find the nature of such characters' transgressive pleasure virtually incomprehensible. On the other hand, modern analogies to the issues that concern Marlowe or Jonson are ubiquitous, reflecting perhaps the extent to which the modern state has taken over some functions of the religious establishment, and the extent to which individuals define themselves in terms of sexual rather than religious authenticities.

When one spends a number of years writing a book, everything eventually seems refracted through the lens of one's own preoccupation. Life in the United States in the past decade has reminded me frequently of the residual power of the conceptual categories that I have discussed in this book. The awkward don't-ask-don't-tell compromise on the issue of gays in the military, with its predictably incoherent but at the same time carefully specified line between thought and behavior, vividly duplicates Elizabeth's 1559 statute on heresies, which allowed Catholics to retain a conviction imagined as residing inside their conscience provided it remained inoffensively invisible to the majority. Similarly, in recent years controversies have multiplied over definitions of hate speech, over the effects of pornography and televised violence, over the proper treatment of members of religious "cults," over the difference between seduction and harassment or rape: controversies that center upon the relationship between persuasion and coercion that so fascinated Marlowe.

It is especially easy to notice analogies between early modern court proceedings for sexual misconduct and some late twentieth-century media events. Paula Corbin Jones even threatens to provide the material proofs that courts then and now consider so desirable, offering to "identify 'the distinguishing characteristics in Clinton's genital area.'"[1] More typically, then and now, such proofs are unavailable. Thus the public event can consist only of a complainant and an alleged perpetrator mutually accusing one another of defamation, as in the confrontation between Anita Hill and Clarence Thomas. A flagrant contradiction between the complaint and the public comportment of the accused cannot absolve him: like Alexandro's detractors in *The Spanish Tragedy,* Thomas's could argue that "there's no credit in the countenance." At the same time, a more consistent or metonymic relationship between the public demeanor and the accusation of private vice, as in the Michael Jackson or Woody Allen cases, can prove just as titillating.

Interesting here, given my concern with the connection between legal inquiry and theater, is the close relationship between accusations of sexual misconduct and the celebrity industry (all the principals in these cases were featured on the cover of *People* magazine). Surely the lucrativeness of this industry rests upon its claim to represent a "private" and therefore more authentic life presumed to reside behind the glittering surface of the celebrity lifestyle. At the same time the account of celebrity inwardness is endlessly revisable, and thus remarketable, because few of the consumers of such truths have any way of verifying them. Anything might be the case, for instance,

1. "Jones vs. the President," cover story in *Time,* May 16, 1994, p. 44.

about Princess Di's eating disorders or her children's relationship to Prince Charles. The relationship of shameful secret to glamorous exterior is so predictably fixed that afternoon talk shows are full of apparently ordinary people who seem to want to induce the latter by admitting the former, as if sordid revelation will, all by itself, transform them into stars.

The particular cultural forms in which early modern England grapples with problems of personal inwardness—heresy inquisitions, treason trials, ecclesiastical court proceedings, five-act tragedies acted on open platforms—seem archaic in the late twentieth century. But we regard the issues which underlie those ancient forms as quaint at our peril, and only by forgetting the strangeness of the culture we ourselves inhabit.

ॐ INDEX ॐ